The
Essentials

The Essentials

HARVARD BUSINESS REVIEW PRESS
Boston, Massachusetts

Printed in the United States of America

14 13 12 11

Library of Congress Cataloging-in-Publication Data
HBR's 10 must reads : the essentials.
    p. cm.
    Includes index.
    ISBN 978-1-4221-3344-6 (pbk. : alk. paper) 1. Management. I. Harvard Business Review. II. Title: HBR's ten must reads. III. Title: Harvard Business Review's 10 must reads.
    HD31.H3948 2010
    658—dc22

                                            2010030742

The paper used in this publication meets the requirements of the American National Standard for Permanence of Paper for Publications and Documents in Libraries and Archives Z39.48-1992.

Contents

The
Essentials

Meeting the Challenge of Disruptive Change

by Clayton M. Christensen and Michael Overdorf

THESE ARE SCARY TIMES for managers in big companies. Even before the Internet and globalization, their track record for dealing with major, disruptive change was not good. Out of hundreds of department stores, for example, only one—Dayton Hudson—became a leader in discount retailing. Not one of the minicomputer companies succeeded in the personal computer business. Medical and business schools are struggling—and failing—to change their curricula fast enough to train the types of doctors and managers their markets need. The list could go on.

It's not that managers in big companies can't see disruptive changes coming. Usually they can. Nor do they lack resources to confront them. Most big companies have talented managers and specialists, strong product portfolios, first-rate technological know-how, and deep pockets. What managers lack is a habit of thinking about their organization's capabilities as carefully as they think about individual people's capabilities.

One of the hallmarks of a great manager is the ability to identify the right person for the right job and to train employees to succeed at the jobs they're given. But unfortunately, most managers assume that if each person working on a project is well matched to the job, then the organization in which they work will be, too. Often that is not the case. One could put two sets of identically capable people to work in different organizations, and what they accomplished would be significantly different. That's because organizations themselves—independent of the people and other resources in them—have capabilities. To succeed consistently, good managers need to be skilled not just in assessing people but also in assessing the abilities and disabilities of their organization as a whole.

This article offers managers a framework to help them understand what their organizations are capable of accomplishing. It will show them how their company's disabilities become more sharply defined even as its core capabilities grow. It will give them a way to recognize different kinds of change and make appropriate organizational responses to the opportunities that arise from each. And it will offer some bottom-line advice that runs counter to much that's assumed in our can-do business culture: if an organization faces major change—a disruptive innovation, perhaps—the worst possible approach may be to make drastic adjustments to the existing organization. In trying to transform an enterprise, managers can destroy the very capabilities that sustain it.

Before rushing into the breach, managers must understand precisely what types of change the existing organization is capable and incapable of handling. To help them do that, we'll first take a systematic look at how to recognize a company's core capabilities on an organizational level and then examine how those capabilities migrate as companies grow and mature.

Where Capabilities Reside

Our research suggests that three factors affect what an organization can and cannot do: its resources, its processes, and its values. When thinking about what sorts of innovations their organization will be able to embrace, managers need to assess how each of these factors might affect their organization's capacity to change.

Idea in Brief

Why do so few established companies innovate successfully? Of hundreds of department stores, for instance, only Dayton Hudson became a discount-retailing leader. And not one minicomputer company succeeded in the personal-computer business.

What's going on? After all, most established firms boast deep pockets and talented people. But when a new venture captures their imagination, they get their people working on it within organizational structures (such as functional teams) designed to surmount *old* challenges—not ones that the new venture is facing.

To avoid this mistake, ask:

- **"Does my organization have the right *resources* to support this innovation?"** Resources supporting business-as-usual—people, technologies, product designs, brands, customer and supplier relationships—rarely match those required for new ventures.

- **"Does my organization have the right *processes* to innovate?"** Processes supporting your established business—decision-making protocols, coordination patterns—may hamstring your new venture.

- **"Does my organization have the right *values* to innovate?"** Consider how you decide whether to commit to a new venture. For example, can you tolerate lower profit margins than your established enterprise demands?

- **"What team and structure will best support our innovation effort?"** Should you use a team dedicated to the project within your company? Create a separate spin-off organization?

By selecting the right team and organizational structure for your innovation—and infusing it with the right resources, processes, and values—you heighten your chances of innovating successfully.

Resources

When they ask the question, "What can this company do?" the place most managers look for the answer is in its resources—both the tangible ones like people, equipment, technologies, and cash, and the less tangible ones like product designs, information, brands, and relationships with suppliers, distributors, and customers. Without doubt, access to abundant, high-quality resources increases an organization's

Idea in Practice

Selecting the Right Structure for Your Innovation

If your innovation . . .	Select this type of team . . .	To operate . . .	Because . . .
Fits *well* with your existing values *and* processes	Functional teams who work sequentially on issues, or lightweight teams—ad hoc cross-functional teams who work simultaneously on multiple issues	Within your existing organization	Owing to the good fit with existing processes and values, no new capabilities or organizational structures are called for.
Fits *well* with existing values but *poorly* with existing processes	Heavyweight team dedicated exclusively to the innovation project, with complete responsibility for its success	Within your existing organization	The poor fit with existing processes requires new types of coordination among groups and individuals.
Fits *poorly* with existing values but *well* with existing processes	Heavyweight team dedicated exclusively to the innovation project, with complete responsibility for its success	Within your existing organization for development, followed by a spin-off for commercialization	In-house development capitalizes on existing processes. A spin-off for the commercialization phase facilitates new values—such as a different cost structure with lower profit margins.
Fits *poorly* with your existing processes *and* values	Heavyweight team dedicated exclusively to the innovation project, with complete responsibility for its success	In a separate spin-off or acquired organization	A spin-off enables the project to be governed by different values *and* ensures that new processes emerge.

chances of coping with change. But resource analysis doesn't come close to telling the whole story.

Processes

The second factor that affects what a company can and cannot do is its processes. By processes, we mean the patterns of interaction, co-ordination, communication, and decision making employees use to transform resources into products and services of greater worth. Such examples as the processes that govern product development, manufacturing, and budgeting come immediately to mind. Some processes are formal, in the sense that they are explicitly defined and documented. Others are informal: they are routines or ways of working that evolve over time. The former tend to be more visible, the latter less visible.

One of the dilemmas of management is that processes, by their very nature, are set up so that employees perform tasks in a consistent way, time after time. They are *meant* not to change or, if they must change, to change through tightly controlled procedures. When people use a process to do the task it was designed for, it is likely to perform efficiently. But when the same process is used to tackle a very different task, it is likely to perform sluggishly. Companies focused on developing and winning FDA approval for new drug compounds, for example, often prove inept at developing and winning approval for medical devices because the second task entails very different ways of working. In fact, a process that creates the capability to execute one task concurrently defines disabilities in executing other tasks.[1]

The most important capabilities and concurrent disabilities aren't necessarily embodied in the most visible processes, like logistics, development, manufacturing, or customer service. In fact, they are more likely to be in the less visible, background processes that support decisions about where to invest resources—those that define how market research is habitually done, how such analysis is translated into financial projections, how plans and budgets are negotiated internally, and so on. It is in those processes that many organizations' most serious disabilities in coping with change reside.

Values

The third factor that affects what an organization can and cannot do is its values. Sometimes the phrase "corporate values" carries an ethical connotation: one thinks of the principles that ensure patient well-being for Johnson & Johnson or that guide decisions about employee safety at Alcoa. But within our framework, "values" has a broader meaning. We define an organization's values as the standards by which employees set priorities that enable them to judge whether an order is attractive or unattractive, whether a customer is more important or less important, whether an idea for a new product is attractive or marginal, and so on. Prioritization decisions are made by employees at every level. Among salespeople, they consist of on-the-spot, day-to-day decisions about which products to push with customers and which to de-emphasize. At the executive tiers, they often take the form of decisions to invest, or not, in new products, services, and processes.

The larger and more complex a company becomes, the more important it is for senior managers to train employees throughout the organization to make independent decisions about priorities that are consistent with the strategic direction and the business model of the company. A key metric of good management, in fact, is whether such clear, consistent values have permeated the organization.

But consistent, broadly understood values also define what an organization cannot do. A company's values reflect its cost structure or its business model because those define the rules its employees must follow for the company to prosper. If, for example, a company's overhead costs require it to achieve gross profit margins of 40%, then a value or decision rule will have evolved that encourages middle managers to kill ideas that promise gross margins below 40%. Such an organization would be incapable of commercializing projects targeting low-margin markets—such as those in e-commerce—even though another organization's values, driven by a very different cost structure, might facilitate the success of the same project.

Different companies, of course, embody different values. But we want to focus on two sets of values in particular that tend to evolve in most companies in very predictable ways. The inexorable evolution of these two values is what makes companies progressively less capable of addressing disruptive change successfully.

As in the previous example, the first value dictates the way the company judges acceptable gross margins. As companies add features and functions to their products and services, trying to capture more attractive customers in premium tiers of their markets, they often add overhead cost. As a result, gross margins that were once attractive become unattractive. For instance, Toyota entered the North American market with the Corona model, which targeted the lower end of the market. As that segment became crowded with look-alike models from Honda, Mazda, and Nissan, competition drove down profit margins. To improve its margins, Toyota then developed more sophisticated cars targeted at higher tiers. The process of developing cars like the Camry and the Lexus added costs to Toyota's operation. It subsequently decided to exit the lower end of the market; the margins had become unacceptable because the company's cost structure, and consequently its values, had changed.

In a departure from that pattern, Toyota recently introduced the Echo model, hoping to rejoin the entry-level tier with a $10,000 car. It is one thing for Toyota's senior management to decide to launch this new model. It's another for the many people in the Toyota system—including its dealers—to agree that selling more cars at lower margins is a better way to boost profits and equity values than selling more Camrys, Avalons, and Lexuses. Only time will tell whether Toyota can manage this down-market move. To be successful with the Echo, Toyota's management will have to swim against a very strong current—the current of its own corporate values.

The second value relates to how big a business opportunity has to be before it can be interesting. Because a company's stock price represents the discounted present value of its projected earnings stream, most managers feel compelled not just to maintain growth but to maintain a constant rate of growth. For a $40 million company to grow 25%, for instance, it needs to find $10 million in new business the next year. But a $40 billion company needs to find $10 billion in new business the next year to grow at that same rate. It follows that an opportunity that excites a small company isn't big enough to be

7

interesting to a large company. One of the bittersweet results of success, in fact, is that as companies become large, they lose the ability to enter small, emerging markets. This disability is not caused by a change in the resources within the companies—their resources typically are vast. Rather, it's caused by an evolution in values.

The problem is magnified when companies suddenly become much bigger through mergers or acquisitions. Executives and Wall Street financiers who engineer megamergers between already-huge pharmaceutical companies, for example, need to take this effect into account. Although their merged research organizations might have more resources to throw at new product development, their commercial organizations will probably have lost their appetites for all but the biggest blockbuster drugs. This constitutes a very real disability in managing innovation. The same problem crops up in high-tech industries as well. In many ways, Hewlett-Packard's recent decision to split itself into two companies is rooted in its recognition of this problem.

The Migration of Capabilities

In the start-up stages of an organization, much of what gets done is attributable to resources—people, in particular. The addition or departure of a few key people can profoundly influence its success. Over time, however, the locus of the organization's capabilities shifts toward its processes and values. As people address recurrent tasks, processes become defined. And as the business model takes shape and it becomes clear which types of business need to be accorded highest priority, values coalesce. In fact, one reason that many soaring young companies flame out after an IPO based on a single hot product is that their initial success is grounded in resources—often the founding engineers—and they fail to develop processes that can create a sequence of hot products.

Avid Technology, a producer of digital-editing systems for television, is an apt case in point. Avid's well-received technology removed tedium from the video-editing process. On the back of its star product, Avid's stock rose from $16 a share at its 1993 IPO to $49 in mid-1995. However, the strains of being a one-trick pony soon emerged as Avid faced a saturated market, rising inventories and receivables, increased competition, and shareholder lawsuits. Customers loved the product, but Avid's lack of effective processes for consistently developing new products and for controlling quality, delivery, and service ultimately tripped the company and sent its stock back down.

By contrast, at highly successful firms such as McKinsey & Company, the processes and values have become so powerful that it almost doesn't matter which people get assigned to which project teams. Hundreds of MBAs join the firm every year, and almost as many leave. But the company is able to crank out high-quality work year after year because its core capabilities are rooted in its processes and values rather than in its resources.

When a company's processes and values are being formed in its early and middle years, the founder typically has a profound impact. The founder usually has strong opinions about how employees should do their work and what the organization's priorities need to be. If the founder's judgments are flawed, of course, the company will likely fail. But if they're sound, employees will experience for themselves the validity of the founder's problem-solving and decision-making methods. Thus processes become defined. Likewise, if the company becomes financially successful by allocating resources according to criteria that reflect the founder's priorities, the company's values coalesce around those criteria.

As successful companies mature, employees gradually come to assume that the processes and priorities they've used so successfully so often are the right way to do their work. Once that happens and employees begin to follow processes and decide priorities by assumption rather than by conscious choice, those processes and values come to constitute the organization's culture.[2] As companies grow from a few employees to hundreds and thousands of them, the challenge of getting all employees to agree on what needs to be done and how can be daunting for even the best managers. Culture is a powerful management tool in those situations. It enables employees to act autonomously but causes them to act consistently.

Digital's Dilemma

A LOT OF BUSINESS THINKERS have analyzed Digital Equipment Corporation's abrupt fall from grace. Most have concluded that Digital simply read the market very badly. But if we look at the company's fate through the lens of our framework, a different picture emerges.

Digital was a spectacularly successful maker of minicomputers from the 1960s through the 1980s. One might have been tempted to assert, when personal computers first appeared in the market around 1980, that Digital's core capability was in building computers. But if that were the case, why did the company stumble?

Clearly, Digital had the resources to succeed in personal computers. Its engineers routinely designed computers that were far more sophisticated than PCs. The company had plenty of cash, a great brand, good technology, and so on. But it did not have the processes to succeed in the personal computer business. Minicomputer companies designed most of the key components of their computers internally and then integrated those components into proprietary configurations. Designing a new product platform took two to three years. Digital manufactured most of its own components and assembled them in a batch mode. It sold directly to corporate engineering organizations. Those processes worked extremely well in the minicomputer business.

PC makers, by contrast, outsourced most components from the best suppliers around the globe. New computer designs, made up of modular components,

Hence, the factors that define an organization's capabilities and disabilities evolve over time—they start in resources; then move to visible, articulated processes and values; and migrate finally to culture. As long as the organization continues to face the same sorts of problems that its processes and values were designed to address, managing the organization can be straightforward. But because those factors also define what an organization cannot do, they constitute disabilities when the problems facing the company change fundamentally. When the organization's capabilities reside primarily in its people, changing capabilities to address the new problems is relatively simple. But when the capabilities have come to reside in processes and values, and especially when they have become embedded in culture, change can be extraordinarily difficult. (See the sidebar "Digital's Dilemma.")

had to be completed in six to 12 months. The computers were manufactured in high-volume assembly lines and sold through retailers to consumers and businesses. None of these processes existed within Digital. In other words, although the people working at the company had the ability to design, build, and sell personal computers profitably, they were working in an organization that was incapable of doing so because its processes had been designed and had evolved to do other tasks well.

Similarly, because of its overhead costs, Digital had to adopt a set of values that dictated, "If it generates 50% gross margins or more, it's good business. If it generates less than 40% margins, it's not worth doing." Management had to ensure that all employees gave priority to projects according to these criteria or the company couldn't make money. Because PCs generated lower margins, they did not fit with Digital's values. The company's criteria for setting priorities always placed higher-performance minicomputers ahead of personal computers in the resource-allocation process.

Digital could have created a different organization that would have honed the different processes and values required to succeed in PCs—as IBM did. But Digital's mainstream organization simply was incapable of succeeding at the job.

Sustaining Versus Disruptive Innovation

Successful companies, no matter what the source of their capabilities, are pretty good at responding to evolutionary changes in their markets—what in *The Innovator's Dilemma* (Harvard Business School, 1997), Clayton Christensen referred to as *sustaining innovation*. Where they run into trouble is in handling or initiating revolutionary changes in their markets, or dealing with *disruptive innovation*.

Sustaining technologies are innovations that make a product or service perform better in ways that customers in the mainstream market already value. Compaq's early adoption of Intel's 32-bit 386 microprocessor instead of the 16-bit 286 chip was a sustaining innovation. So was Merrill Lynch's introduction of its Cash Management Account, which allowed customers to write checks against their equity accounts. Those were breakthrough innovations that sustained the best customers of these companies by providing something better than had previously been available.

Disruptive innovations create an entirely new market through the introduction of a new kind of product or service, one that's actually worse, initially, as judged by the performance metrics that mainstream customers value. Charles Schwab's initial entry as a bare-bones discount broker was a disruptive innovation relative to the offerings of full-service brokers like Merrill Lynch. Merrill Lynch's best customers wanted more than Schwab-like services. Early personal computers were a disruptive innovation relative to mainframes and minicomputers. PCs were not powerful enough to run the computing applications that existed at the time they were introduced. These innovations were disruptive in that they didn't address the next-generation needs of leading customers in existing markets. They had other attributes, of course, that enabled new market applications to emerge—and the disruptive innovations improved so rapidly that they ultimately could address the needs of customers in the mainstream of the market as well.

Sustaining innovations are nearly always developed and introduced by established industry leaders. But those same companies never introduce—or cope well with—disruptive innovations. Why? Our resources-processes-values framework holds the answer. Industry leaders are organized to develop and introduce sustaining technologies. Month after month, year after year, they launch new and improved products to gain an edge over the competition. They do so by developing processes for evaluating the technological potential of sustaining innovations and for assessing their customers' needs for alternatives. Investment in sustaining technology also fits in with the values of leading companies in that they promise higher margins from better products sold to leading-edge customers.

Disruptive innovations occur so intermittently that no company has a routine process for handling them. Furthermore, because disruptive products nearly always promise lower profit margins per unit sold and are not attractive to the company's best customers, they're inconsistent with the established company's values. Merrill

Lynch had the resources—the people, money, and technology—required to succeed at the sustaining innovations (Cash Management Account) and the disruptive innovations (bare-bones discount brokering) that it has confronted in recent history. But its processes and values supported only the sustaining innovation: they became disabilities when the company needed to understand and confront the discount and on-line brokerage businesses.

The reason, therefore, that large companies often surrender emerging growth markets is that smaller, disruptive companies are actually more capable of pursuing them. Start-ups lack resources, but that doesn't matter. Their values can embrace small markets, and their cost structures can accommodate low margins. Their market research and resource allocation processes allow managers to proceed intuitively; every decision need not be backed by careful research and analysis. All these advantages add up to the ability to embrace and even initiate disruptive change. But how can a large company develop those capabilities?

Creating Capabilities to Cope with Change

Despite beliefs spawned by popular change-management and reengineering programs, processes are not nearly as flexible or adaptable as resources are—and values are even less so. So whether addressing sustaining or disruptive innovations, when an organization needs new processes and values—because it needs new capabilities—managers must create a new organizational space where those capabilities can be developed. There are three possible ways to do that. Managers can

- create new organizational structures within corporate boundaries in which new processes can be developed,

- spin out an independent organization from the existing organization and develop within it the new processes and values required to solve the new problem,

- acquire a different organization whose processes and values closely match the requirements of the new task.

Creating new capabilities internally

When a company's capabilities reside in its processes, and when new challenges require new processes—that is, when they require different people or groups in a company to interact differently and at a different pace than they habitually have done—managers need to pull the relevant people out of the existing organization and draw a new boundary around a new group. Often, organizational boundaries were first drawn to facilitate the operation of existing processes, and they impede the creation of new processes. New team boundaries facilitate new patterns of working together that ultimately can coalesce as new processes. In *Revolutionizing Product Development* (The Free Press, 1992), Steven Wheelwright and Kim Clark referred to these structures as "heavyweight teams."

These teams are entirely dedicated to the new challenge, team members are physically located together, and each member is charged with assuming personal responsibility for the success of the entire project. At Chrysler, for example, the boundaries of the groups within its product development organization historically had been defined by components—power train, electrical systems, and so on. But to accelerate auto development, Chrysler needed to focus not on components but on automobile platforms—the minivan, small car, Jeep, and truck, for example—so it created heavyweight teams. Although these organizational units aren't as good at focusing on component design, they facilitated the definition of new processes that were much faster and more efficient in integrating various subsystems into new car designs. Companies as diverse as Medtronic for its cardiac pacemakers, IBM for its disk drives, and Eli Lilly for its new blockbuster drug Zyprexa have used heavyweight teams as vehicles for creating new processes so they could develop better products faster.

Creating capabilities through a spinout organization

When the mainstream organization's values would render it incapable of allocating resources to an innovation project, the company should spin it out as a new venture. Large organizations cannot be expected to allocate the critical financial and human resources needed to build a strong position in small, emerging markets. And it is very difficult for a company whose cost structure is tailored to compete in high-end markets to be profitable in low-end markets as well. Spinouts are very much in vogue among managers in old-line companies struggling with the question of how to address the Internet. But that's not always appropriate. When a disruptive innovation requires a different cost structure in order to be profitable and competitive, or when the current size of the opportunity is insignificant relative to the growth needs of the mainstream organization, then—and only then—is a spinout organization required.

Hewlett-Packard's laser-printer division in Boise, Idaho, was hugely successful, enjoying high margins and a reputation for superior product quality. Unfortunately, its ink-jet project, which represented a disruptive innovation, languished inside the mainstream HP printer business. Although the processes for developing the two types of printers were basically the same, there was a difference in values. To thrive in the ink-jet market, HP needed to be comfortable with lower gross margins and a smaller market than its laser printers commanded, and it needed to be willing to embrace relatively lower performance standards. It was not until HP's managers decided to transfer the unit to a separate division in Vancouver, British Columbia, with the goal of competing head-to-head with its own laser business, that the ink-jet business finally became successful.

How separate does such an effort need to be? A new physical location isn't always necessary. The primary requirement is that the project not be forced to compete for resources with projects in the mainstream organization. As we have seen, projects that are inconsistent with a company's mainstream values will naturally be accorded lowest priority. Whether the independent organization is physically separate is less important than its independence from the normal decision-making criteria in the resource allocation process. The sidebar "Fitting the Tool to the Task" goes into more detail about what kind of innovation challenge is best met by which organizational structure.

Managers think that developing a new operation necessarily means abandoning the old one, and they're loathe to do that since it

Fitting the Tool to the Task

SUPPOSE THAT AN ORGANIZATION needs to react to or initiate an innovation. The matrix illustrated below can help managers understand what kind of team should work on the project and what organizational structure that team needs to work within. The vertical axis asks the manager to measure the extent to which the organization's existing processes are suited to getting the new job done effectively. The horizontal axis asks managers to assess whether the organization's values will permit the company to allocate the resources the new initiative needs.

In region A, the project is a good fit with the company's processes and values, so no new capabilities are called for. A functional or a lightweight team can tackle the project within the existing organizational structure. A functional team works on function-specific issues, then passes the project on to the next function. A lightweight team is cross-functional, but team members stay under the control of their respective functional managers.

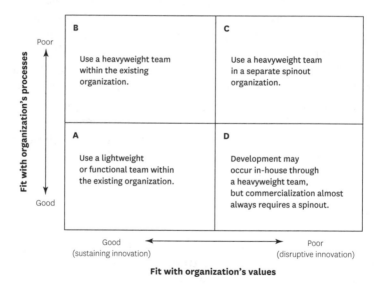

B

Use a heavyweight team within the existing organization.

C

Use a heavyweight team in a separate spinout organization.

A

Use a lightweight or functional team within the existing organization.

D

Development may occur in-house through a heavyweight team, but commercialization almost always requires a spinout.

Poor

Good

Fit with organization's processes

Good
(sustaining innovation)

Poor
(disruptive innovation)

Fit with organization's values

works perfectly well for what it was designed to do. But when disruptive change appears on the horizon, managers need to assemble the capabilities to confront that change before it affects the mainstream business. They actually need to run two businesses in tandem—one whose processes are tuned to the existing business model

In region B, the project is a good fit with the company's values but not with its processes. It presents the organization with new types of problems and therefore requires new types of interactions and coordination among groups and individuals. The team, like the team in region A, is working on a sustaining rather than a disruptive innovation. In this case, a heavyweight team is a good bet, but the project can be executed within the mainstream company. A heavyweight team—whose members work solely on the project and are expected to behave like general managers, shouldering responsibility for the project's success—is designed so that new processes and new ways of working together can emerge.

In region C, the manager faces a disruptive change that doesn't fit the organization's existing processes or values. To ensure success, the manager should create a spinout organization and commission a heavyweight development team to tackle the challenge. The spinout will allow the project to be governed by different values—a different cost structure, for example, with lower profit margins. The heavyweight team (as in region B) will ensure that new processes can emerge.

Similarly, in region D, when a manager faces a disruptive change that fits the organization's current processes but doesn't fit its values, the key to success almost always lies in commissioning a heavyweight development team to work in a spinout. Development may occasionally happen successfully in-house, but successful commercialization will require a spinout.

Unfortunately, most companies employ a one-size-fits-all organizing strategy, using lightweight or functional teams for programs of every size and character. But such teams are tools for exploiting established capabilities. And among those few companies that have accepted the heavyweight gospel, many have attempted to organize *all* of their development teams in a heavyweight fashion. Ideally, each company should tailor the team structure and organizational location to the process and values required by each project.

and another that is geared toward the new model. Merrill Lynch, for example, has accomplished an impressive global expansion of its institutional financial services through careful execution of its existing planning, acquisition, and partnership processes. Now, however, faced with the on-line world, the company is required to plan, acquire, and form partnerships more rapidly. Does that mean Merrill Lynch should change the processes that have worked so well in its traditional investment-banking business? Doing so would be disastrous, if we consider the question through the lens of our framework. Instead, Merrill should retain the old processes when working with the existing business (there are probably a few billion dollars still to be made under the old business model!) and create additional processes to deal with the new class of problems.

One word of warning: in our studies of this challenge, we have never seen a company succeed in addressing a change that disrupts its mainstream values without the personal, attentive oversight of the CEO—precisely because of the power of values in shaping the normal resource allocation process. Only the CEO can ensure that the new organization gets the required resources and is free to create processes and values that are appropriate to the new challenge. CEOs who view spinouts as a tool to get disruptive threats off their personal agendas are almost certain to meet with failure. We have seen no exceptions to this rule.

Creating capabilities through acquisitions

Just as innovating managers need to make separate assessments of the capabilities and disabilities that reside in their company's resources, processes, and values, so must they do the same with acquisitions when seeking to buy capabilities. Companies that successfully gain new capabilities through acquisitions are those that know where those capabilities reside in the acquisition and assimilate them accordingly. Acquiring managers begin by asking, "What created the value that I just paid so dearly for? Did I justify the price because of the acquisition's resources? Or was a substantial portion of its worth created by processes and values?"

If the capabilities being purchased are embedded in an acquired company's processes and values, then the last thing the acquiring manager should do is integrate the acquisition into the parent organization. Integration will vaporize the processes and values of the acquired firm. Once the acquisition's managers are forced to adopt the buyer's way of doing business, its capabilities will disappear.

A better strategy is to let the business stand alone and to infuse the parent's resources into the acquired company's processes and values. This approach truly constitutes the acquisition of new capabilities.

If, however, the acquired company's resources were the reason for its success and the primary rationale for the acquisition, then integrating it into the parent can make a lot of sense. Essentially, that means plugging the acquired people, products, technology, and customers into the parent's processes as a way of leveraging the parent's existing capabilities.

The perils of the ongoing DaimlerChrysler merger can be better understood in this light. Chrysler had few resources that could be considered unique. Its recent success in the market was rooted in its processes—particularly in its processes for designing products and integrating the efforts of its subsystem suppliers. What is the best way for Daimler to leverage Chrysler's capabilities? Wall Street is pressuring management to consolidate the two organizations to cut costs. But if the two companies are integrated, the very processes that made Chrysler such an attractive acquisition will likely be compromised.

The situation is reminiscent of IBM's 1984 acquisition of the telecommunications company Rolm. There wasn't anything in Rolm's pool of resources that IBM didn't already have. Rather, it was Rolm's processes for developing and finding new markets for PBX products that mattered. Initially, IBM recognized the value in preserving the informal and unconventional culture of the Rolm organization, which stood in stark contrast to IBM's methodical style. However, in 1987 IBM terminated Rolm's subsidiary status and decided to fully integrate the company into its own corporate structure. IBM's managers soon learned the folly of that decision. When they tried to push Rolm's resources—its products and its customers—through the processes that had been honed in the large-computer business, the Rolm business stumbled badly. And it was impossible for a computer company whose values had been whetted on profit margins of 18% to get excited about products with much lower profit margins. IBM's integration of Rolm destroyed the very source of the deal's original worth. Daimler-Chrysler, bowing to the investment community's drumbeat for efficiency savings, now stands on the edge of the same precipice. Often, it seems, financial analysts have a better intuition about the value of resources than they do about the value of processes.

By contrast, Cisco Systems' acquisitions process has worked well because, we would argue, it has kept resources, processes, and values in the right perspective. Between 1993 and 1997, it primarily acquired small companies that were less than two years old, early-stage organizations whose market value was built primarily upon their resources, particularly their engineers and products. Cisco plugged those resources into its own effective development, logistics, manufacturing, and marketing processes and threw away whatever nascent processes and values came with the acquisitions because those weren't what it had paid for. On a couple of occasions when the company acquired a larger, more mature organization—notably its 1996 acquisition of StrataCom—Cisco did not integrate. Rather, it let StrataCom stand alone and infused Cisco's substantial resources into StrataCom's organization to help it grow more rapidly.[3]

Managers whose organizations are confronting change must first determine whether they have the resources required to succeed. They then need to ask a separate question: Does the organization have the processes and values it needs to succeed in this new situation? Asking this second question is not as instinctive for most managers because the processes by which work is done and the values by which employees make their decisions have served them well in the past. What we hope this framework introduces into managers' thinking is the idea that the very capabilities that make their organizations effective also define their disabilities. In that regard, a little time spent soul-searching for honest answers to the following questions will pay off handsomely: Are the processes by which work habitually gets done in the organization appropriate for this new problem? And will the values of the organization cause this initiative to get high priority or to languish?

If the answers to those questions are no, it's okay. Understanding a problem is the most crucial step in solving it. Wishful thinking about these issues can set teams that need to innovate on a course fraught with roadblocks, second-guessing, and frustration. The reason that innovation often seems to be so difficult for established companies is that they employ highly capable people and then set them to work within organizational structures whose processes and values weren't designed for the task at hand. Ensuring that capable people are ensconced in capable organizations is a major responsibility of management in a transformational age such as ours.

Originally published in March 2000. Reprint R00202

Notes

1. See Dorothy Leonard-Barton, "Core Capabilities and Core Rigidities: A Paradox in Managing New Product Development," *Strategic Management Journal* (summer, 1992).

2. Our description of the development of an organization's culture draws heavily from Edgar Schein's research, as first laid out in his book *Organizational Culture and Leadership* (Jossey-Bass Publishers, 1985).

3. See Charles A. Holloway, Stephen C. Wheelwright, and Nicole Tempest, "Cisco Systems, Inc.: Post-Acquisition Manufacturing Integration," a case published jointly by the Stanford and Harvard business schools, 1998.

Competing on Analytics

by Thomas H. Davenport

WE ALL KNOW THE POWER of the killer app. Over the years, ground-breaking systems from companies such as American Airlines (electronic reservations), Otis Elevator (predictive maintenance), and American Hospital Supply (online ordering) have dramatically boosted their creators' revenues and reputations. These heralded—and coveted—applications amassed and applied data in ways that upended customer expectations and optimized operations to unprecedented degrees. They transformed technology from a supporting tool into a strategic weapon.

Companies questing for killer apps generally focus all their firepower on the one area that promises to create the greatest competitive advantage. But a new breed of company is upping the stakes. Organizations such as Amazon, Harrah's, Capital One, and the Boston Red Sox have dominated their fields by deploying industrial-strength analytics across a wide variety of activities. In essence, they are transforming their organizations into armies of killer apps and crunching their way to victory.

Organizations are competing on analytics not just because they can—business today is awash in data and data crunchers—but also because they should. At a time when firms in many industries offer similar products and use comparable technologies, business processes are among the last remaining points of differentiation. And analytics competitors wring every last drop of value from those processes. So, like other companies, they know what products their customers want, but they also know what prices those customers will pay, how many items each will buy in a lifetime, and what triggers will make people buy more. Like other companies, they know compensation costs and turnover rates, but they can also calculate how much personnel contribute to or detract from the bottom line and how salary levels relate to individuals' performance. Like other companies, they know when inventories are running low, but they can also predict problems with demand and supply chains, to achieve low rates of inventory and high rates of perfect orders.

And analytics competitors do all those things in a coordinated way, as part of an overarching strategy championed by top leadership and pushed down to decision makers at every level. Employees hired for their expertise with numbers or trained to recognize their importance are armed with the best evidence and the best quantitative tools. As a result, they make the best decisions: big and small, every day, over and over and over.

Although numerous organizations are embracing analytics, only a handful have achieved this level of proficiency. But analytics competitors are the leaders in their varied fields—consumer products, finance, retail, and travel and entertainment among them. Analytics has been instrumental to Capital One, which has exceeded 20% growth in earnings per share every year since it became a public company. It has allowed Amazon to dominate online retailing and turn a profit despite enormous investments in growth and infrastructure. In sports, the real secret weapon isn't steroids, but stats, as dramatic victories by the Boston Red Sox, the New England Patriots, and the Oakland A's attest.

At such organizations, virtuosity with data is often part of the brand. Progressive makes advertising hay from its detailed parsing of individual insurance rates. Amazon customers can watch the company learning about them as its service grows more targeted with frequent purchases. Thanks to Michael Lewis's best-selling book *Moneyball,* which demonstrated the power of statistics in

Idea in Brief

It's virtually impossible to differentiate yourself from competitors based on products alone. Your rivals sell offerings similar to yours. And thanks to cheap offshore labor, you're hard-pressed to beat overseas competitors on product cost.

How to pull ahead of the pack? Become an **analytics competitor:** Use sophisticated data-collection technology and analysis to wring every last drop of value from all your business processes. With analytics, you discern not only what your customers want but also how much they're willing to pay and what keeps them loyal. You look beyond compensation costs to calculate your workforce's exact contribution to your bottom line. And you don't just track existing inventories; you also predict and prevent future inventory problems.

Analytics competitors seize the lead in their fields. Capital One's analytics initiative, for example, has spurred at least 20% growth in earnings per share every year since the company went public.

Make analytics part of *your* overarching competitive strategy, and push it down to decision makers at every level. You'll arm your employees with the best evidence and quantitative tools for making the best decisions—big and small, every day.

professional baseball, the Oakland A's are almost as famous for their geeky number crunching as they are for their athletic prowess.

To identify characteristics shared by analytics competitors, I and two of my colleagues at Babson College's Working Knowledge Research Center studied 32 organizations that have made a commitment to quantitative, fact-based analysis. Eleven of those organizations we classified as full-bore analytics competitors, meaning top management had announced that analytics was key to their strategies; they had multiple initiatives under way involving complex data and statistical analysis, and they managed analytical activity at the enterprise (not departmental) level.

This article lays out the characteristics and practices of these statistical masters and describes some of the very substantial changes other companies must undergo in order to compete on quantitative turf. As one would expect, the transformation requires a significant investment in technology, the accumulation of massive stores of data, and the formulation of companywide strategies for managing

Idea in Practice

To become an analytics competitor:

Champion Analytics from the Top

Acknowledge and endorse the changes in culture, processes, and skills that analytics competition will mean for much of your workforce. And prepare yourself to lead an analytics-focused organization: You will have to understand the theory behind various quantitative methods so you can recognize their limitations. If you lack background in statistical methods, consult experts who understand your business and know how analytics can be applied to it.

Create a Single Analytics Initiative

Place all data-collection and analysis activities under a common leadership, with common technology

and tools. You'll facilitate data sharing and avoid the impediments of inconsistent reporting formats, data definitions, and standards.

Example: Procter & Gamble created a centrally managed "überanalytics" group of 100 analysts drawn from many different functions. It applies this critical mass of expertise to pressing cross-functional issues. For instance, sales and marketing analysts supply data on growth opportunities in existing markets to supply-chain analysts, who can then design more responsive supply networks.

Focus Your Analytics Effort

Channel your resources into analytics initiatives that most directly serve your overarching competitive strategy. Harrah's, for

---

the data. But at least as important, it requires executives' vocal, unswerving commitment and willingness to change the way employees think, work, and are treated. As Gary Loveman, CEO of analytics competitor Harrah's, frequently puts it, "Do we think this is true? Or do we know?"

Anatomy of an Analytics Competitor

One analytics competitor that's at the top of its game is Marriott International. Over the past 20 years, the corporation has honed to a science its system for establishing the optimal price for guest rooms (the key analytics process in hotels, known as revenue management).

instance, aims much of its analytical activity at improving customer loyalty, customer service, and related areas such as pricing and promotions.

Establish an Analytics Culture

Instill a companywide respect for measuring, testing, and evaluating quantitative evidence. Urge employees to base decisions on hard facts. Gauge and reward performance the same way—applying metrics to compensation and rewards.

Hire the Right People

Pursue and hire analysts who possess top-notch quantitative-analysis skills, can express complex ideas in simple terms, and can interact productively with decision makers. This combination may be difficult to find, so start recruiting well before you need to fill analyst positions.

Use the Right Technology

Prepare to spend significant resources on technology such as customer relationship management (CRM) or enterprise resource planning (ERP) systems. Present data in standard formats, integrate it, store it in a data warehouse, and make it easily accessible to everyone. And expect to spend years gathering enough data to conduct meaningful analyses.

Example: It took Dell Computer seven years to create a database that includes 1.5 million records of all its print, radio, broadcast TV, and cable ads. Dell couples the database with data on sales for each region in which the ads appeared (before and after their appearance). The information enables Dell to fine-tune its promotions for every medium—in every region.

Today, its ambitions are far grander. Through its Total Hotel Optimization program, Marriott has expanded its quantitative expertise to areas such as conference facilities and catering, and made related tools available over the Internet to property revenue managers and hotel owners. It has developed systems to optimize offerings to frequent customers and assess the likelihood of those customers' defecting to competitors. It has given local revenue managers the power to override the system's recommendations when certain local factors can't be predicted (like the large number of Hurricane Katrina evacuees arriving in Houston). The company has even created a revenue opportunity model, which computes actual revenues as a percentage of the optimal rates that could have been charged.

That figure has grown from 83% to 91% as Marriott's revenue-management analytics has taken root throughout the enterprise. The word is out among property owners and franchisees: If you want to squeeze the most revenue from your inventory, Marriott's approach is the ticket.

Clearly, organizations such as Marriott don't behave like traditional companies. Customers notice the difference in every interaction; employees and vendors live the difference every day. Our study found three key attributes among analytics competitors:

Widespread use of modeling and optimization

Any company can generate simple descriptive statistics about aspects of its business—average revenue per employee, for example, or average order size. But analytics competitors look well beyond basic statistics. These companies use predictive modeling to identify the most profitable customers—plus those with the greatest profit potential and the ones most likely to cancel their accounts. They pool data generated in-house and data acquired from outside sources (which they analyze more deeply than do their less statistically savvy competitors) for a comprehensive understanding of their customers. They optimize their supply chains and can thus determine the impact of an unexpected constraint, simulate alternatives, and route shipments around problems. They establish prices in real time to get the highest yield possible from each of their customer transactions. They create complex models of how their operational costs relate to their financial performance.

Leaders in analytics also use sophisticated experiments to measure the overall impact or "lift" of intervention strategies and then apply the results to continuously improve subsequent analyses. Capital One, for example, conducts more than 30,000 experiments a year, with different interest rates, incentives, direct-mail packaging, and other variables. Its goal is to maximize the likelihood both that potential customers will sign up for credit cards and that they will pay back Capital One.

Progressive employs similar experiments using widely available insurance industry data. The company defines narrow groups, or cells, of customers: for example, motorcycle riders ages 30 and above, with college educations, credit scores over a certain level, and no accidents. For each cell, the company performs a regression analysis to identify factors that most closely correlate with the losses that group engenders. It then sets prices for the cells, which should enable the company to earn a profit across a portfolio of customer groups, and uses simulation software to test the financial implications of those hypotheses. With this approach, Progressive can profitably insure customers in traditionally high-risk categories. Other insurers reject high-risk customers out of hand, without bothering to delve more deeply into the data (although even traditional competitors, such as Allstate, are starting to embrace analytics as a strategy).

An enterprise approach
Analytics competitors understand that most business functions— even those, like marketing, that have historically depended on art rather than science—can be improved with sophisticated quantitative techniques. These organizations don't gain advantage from one killer app, but rather from multiple applications supporting many parts of the business—and, in a few cases, being rolled out for use by customers and suppliers.

UPS embodies the evolution from targeted analytics user to comprehensive analytics competitor. Although the company is among the world's most rigorous practitioners of operations research and industrial engineering, its capabilities were, until fairly recently, narrowly focused. Today, UPS is wielding its statistical skill to track the movement of packages and to anticipate and influence the actions of people—assessing the likelihood of customer attrition and identifying sources of problems. The UPS Customer Intelligence Group, for example, is able to accurately predict customer defections by examining usage patterns and complaints. When the data point to a potential defector, a salesperson contacts that customer to review and resolve the problem, dramatically reducing the loss of accounts. UPS still lacks the breadth of initiatives of a full-bore analytics competitor, but it is heading in that direction.

Analytics competitors treat all such activities from all provenances as a single, coherent initiative, often massed under one rubric, such as "information-based strategy" at Capital One or "information-based customer management" at Barclays Bank. These programs operate not just under a common label but also under common leadership and with common technology and tools. In traditional companies, "business intelligence" (the term IT people use for analytics and reporting processes and software) is generally managed by departments; number-crunching functions select their own tools, control their own data warehouses, and train their own people. But that way, chaos lies. For one thing, the proliferation of user-developed spreadsheets and databases inevitably leads to multiple versions of key indicators within an organization. Furthermore, research has shown that between 20% and 40% of spreadsheets contain errors; the more spreadsheets floating around a company, therefore, the more fecund the breeding ground for mistakes. Analytics competitors, by contrast, field centralized groups to ensure that critical data and other resources are well managed and that different parts of the organization can share data easily, without the impediments of inconsistent formats, definitions, and standards.

Some analytics competitors apply the same enterprise approach to people as to technology. Procter & Gamble, for example, recently created a kind of überanalytics group consisting of more than 100 analysts from such functions as operations, supply chain, sales, consumer research, and marketing. Although most of the analysts are embedded in business operating units, the group is centrally managed. As a result of this consolidation, P&G can apply a critical mass of expertise to its most pressing issues. So, for example, sales and marketing analysts supply data on opportunities for growth in existing markets to analysts who design corporate supply networks. The supply chain analysts, in turn, apply their expertise in certain decision-analysis techniques to such new areas as competitive intelligence.

The group at P&G also raises the visibility of analytical and database-based decision making within the company. Previously, P&G's crack analysts had improved business processes and saved the firm money; but because they were squirreled away in dispersed domains, many executives didn't know what services they offered or how effective they could be. Now those executives are more likely to tap the company's deep pool of expertise for their projects. Meanwhile, masterful number crunching has become part of the story P&G tells to investors, the press, and the public.

Senior executive advocates

A companywide embrace of analytics impels changes in culture, processes, behavior, and skills for many employees. And so, like any major transition, it requires leadership from executives at the very top who have a passion for the quantitative approach. Ideally, the principal advocate is the CEO. Indeed, we found several chief executives who have driven the shift to analytics at their companies over the past few years, including Loveman of Harrah's, Jeff Bezos of Amazon, and Rich Fairbank of Capital One. Before he retired from the Sara Lee Bakery Group, former CEO Barry Beracha kept a sign on his desk that summed up his personal and organizational philosophy: "In God we trust. All others bring data." We did come across some companies in which a single functional or business unit leader was trying to push analytics throughout the organization, and a few were making some progress. But we found that these lower-level people lacked the clout, the perspective, and the cross-functional scope to change the culture in any meaningful way.

CEOs leading the analytics charge require both an appreciation of and a familiarity with the subject. A background in statistics isn't necessary, but those leaders must understand the theory behind various quantitative methods so that they recognize those methods' limitations—which factors are being weighed and which ones aren't. When the CEOs need help grasping quantitative techniques, they turn to experts who understand the business and how analytics can be applied to it. We interviewed several leaders who had retained such advisers, and these executives stressed the need to find someone who can explain things in plain language and be trusted not to spin the numbers. A few CEOs we spoke with had surrounded themselves with very analytical people—professors, consultants, MIT

Going to Bat for Stats

THE ANALYSIS-VERSUS-INSTINCT DEBATE, a favorite of political commentators during the last two U.S. presidential elections, is raging in professional sports, thanks to several popular books and high-profile victories. For now, analysis seems to hold the lead.

Most notably, statistics are a major part of the selection and deployment of players. *Moneyball*, by Michael Lewis, focuses on the use of analytics in player selection for the Oakland A's—a team that wins on a shoestring. The New England Patriots, a team that devotes an enormous amount of attention to statistics, won three of the last four Super Bowls, and their payroll is currently ranked 24th in the league. The Boston Red Sox have embraced "sabermetrics" (the application of analysis to baseball), even going so far as to hire Bill James, the famous baseball statistician who popularized that term. Analytic HR strategies are taking hold in European soccer as well. One leading team, Italy's A.C. Milan, uses predictive models from its Milan Lab research center to prevent injuries by analyzing physiological, orthopedic, and psychological data from a variety of sources. A fast-rising English soccer team, the Bolton Wanderers, is known for its manager's use of extensive data to evaluate players' performance.

Still, sports managers—like business leaders—are rarely fact-or-feeling purists. St. Louis Cardinals manager Tony La Russa, for example, brilliantly combines analytics with intuition to decide when to substitute a charged-up player in the batting lineup or whether to hire a spark-plug personality to improve morale. In his recent book, *Three Nights in August,* Buzz Bissinger describes that balance: "La Russa appreciated the information generated by computers. He studied the rows and the columns. But he also knew they could take you only so far in baseball, maybe even confuse you with a fog of overanalysis. As far as he knew, there was no way to quantify desire. And those numbers told him exactly what he needed to know when added to twenty-four years of managing experience."

That final sentence is the key. Whether scrutinizing someone's performance record or observing the expression flitting across an employee's face, leaders consult their own experience to understand the "evidence" in all its forms.

---

graduates, and the like. But that was a personal preference rather than a necessary practice.

Of course, not all decisions should be grounded in analytics— at least not wholly so. Personnel matters, in particular, are often well and appropriately informed by instinct and anecdote. More organizations are subjecting recruiting and hiring decisions to statistical analysis (see the sidebar "Going to Bat for Stats"). But research shows that human beings can make quick, surprisingly accurate assessments of personality and character based on simple observations. For analytics-minded leaders, then, the challenge boils down to knowing when to run with the numbers and when to run with their guts.

Their Sources of Strength

Analytics competitors are more than simple number-crunching factories. Certainly, they apply technology—with a mixture of brute force and finesse—to multiple business problems. But they also direct their energies toward finding the right focus, building the right culture, and hiring the right people to make optimal use of the data they constantly churn. In the end, people and strategy, as much as information technology, give such organizations strength.

The right focus

Although analytics competitors encourage universal fact-based decisions, they must choose where to direct resource-intensive efforts. Generally, they pick several functions or initiatives that together serve an overarching strategy. Harrah's, for example, has aimed much of its analytical activity at increasing customer loyalty, customer service, and related areas like pricing and promotions. UPS has broadened its focus from logistics to customers, in the interest of providing superior service. While such multipronged strategies define analytics competitors, executives we interviewed warned companies against becoming too diffuse in their initiatives or losing clear sight of the business purpose behind each.

Another consideration when allocating resources is how amenable certain functions are to deep analysis. There are at least seven common targets for analytical activity, and specific industries may present their own (see "Things You Can Count On"). Statistical models and algorithms that dangle the possibility of performance

Things you can count on

Analytics competitors make expert use of statistics and modeling to improve a wide variety of functions. Here are some common applications:

Function	Description	Exemplars
Supply chain	Simulate and optimize supply chain flows; reduce inventory and stock-outs.	Dell, Wal-Mart, Amazon
Customer selection, loyalty, and service	Identify customers with the greatest profit potential; increase likelihood that they will want the product or service offering; retain their loyalty.	Harrah's, Capital One, Barclays
Pricing	Identify the price that will maximize yield, or profit.	Progressive, Marriott
Human capital	Select the best employees for particular tasks or jobs, at particular compensation levels.	New England Patriots, Oakland A's, Boston Red Sox
Product and service quality	Detect quality problems early and minimize them.	Honda, Intel
Financial performance	Better understand the drivers of financial performance and the effects of nonfinancial factors.	MCI, Verizon
Research and development	Improve quality, efficacy, and, where applicable, safety of products and services.	Novartis, Amazon, Yahoo

breakthroughs make some prospects especially tempting. Marketing, for example, has always been tough to quantify because it is rooted in psychology. But now consumer products companies can hone their market research using multiattribute utility theory—a tool for understanding and predicting consumer behaviors and decisions. Similarly, the advertising industry is adopting econometrics—statistical techniques for measuring the lift provided by different ads and promotions over time.

The most proficient analytics practitioners don't just measure their own navels—they also help customers and vendors measure theirs. Wal-Mart, for example, insists that suppliers use its Retail

Link system to monitor product movement by store, to plan promotions and layouts within stores, and to reduce stock-outs. E.&J. Gallo provides distributors with data and analysis on retailers' costs and pricing so they can calculate the per-bottle profitability for each of Gallo's 95 wines. The distributors, in turn, use that information to help retailers optimize their mixes while persuading them to add shelf space for Gallo products. Procter & Gamble offers data and analysis to its retail customers, as part of a program called Joint Value Creation, and to its suppliers to help improve responsiveness and reduce costs. Hospital supplier Owens & Minor furnishes similar services, enabling customers and suppliers to access and analyze their buying and selling data, track ordering patterns in search of consolidation opportunities, and move off-contract purchases to group contracts that include products distributed by Owens & Minor and its competitors. For example, Owens & Minor might show a hospital chain's executives how much money they could save by consolidating purchases across multiple locations or help them see the trade-offs between increasing delivery frequency and carrying inventory.

The right culture

Culture is a soft concept; analytics is a hard discipline. Nonetheless, analytics competitors must instill a companywide respect for measuring, testing, and evaluating quantitative evidence. Employees are urged to base decisions on hard facts. And they know that their performance is gauged the same way. Human resource organizations within analytics competitors are rigorous about applying metrics to compensation and rewards. Harrah's, for example, has made a dramatic change from a rewards culture based on paternalism and tenure to one based on such meticulously collected performance measurements as financial and customer service results. Senior executives also set a consistent example with their own behavior, exhibiting a hunger for and confidence in fact and analysis. One exemplar of such leadership was Beracha of the Sara Lee Bakery Group, known to his employees as a "data dog" because he hounded them for data to support any assertion or hypothesis.

Not surprisingly, in an analytics culture, there's sometimes tension between innovative or entrepreneurial impulses and the requirement for evidence. Some companies place less emphasis on blue-sky development, in which designers or engineers chase after a gleam in someone's eye. In these organizations, R&D, like other functions, is rigorously metric-driven. At Yahoo, Progressive, and Capital One, process and product changes are tested on a small scale and implemented as they are validated. That approach, well established within various academic and business disciplines (including engineering, quality management, and psychology), can be applied to most corporate processes—even to not-so-obvious candidates, like human resources and customer service. HR, for example, might create profiles of managers' personality traits and leadership styles and then test those managers in different situations. It could then compare data on individuals' performance with data about personalities to determine what traits are most important to managing a project that is behind schedule, say, or helping a new group to assimilate.

There are, however, instances when a decision to change something or try something new must be made too quickly for extensive analysis, or when it's not possible to gather data beforehand. For example, even though Amazon's Jeff Bezos greatly prefers to rigorously quantify users' reactions before rolling out new features, he couldn't test the company's search-inside-the-book offering without applying it to a critical mass of books (120,000, to begin with). It was also expensive to develop, and that increased the risk. In this case, Bezos trusted his instincts and took a flier. And the feature did prove popular when introduced.

The right people
Analytical firms hire analytical people—and like all companies that compete on talent, they pursue the best. When Amazon needed a new head for its global supply chain, for example, it recruited Gang Yu, a professor of management science and software entrepreneur who is one of the world's leading authorities on optimization analytics. Amazon's business model requires the company to manage a constant flow of new products, suppliers, customers, and promotions, as well

as deliver orders by promised dates. Since his arrival, Yu and his team have been designing and building sophisticated supply chain systems to optimize those processes. And while he tosses around phrases like "nonstationary stochastic processes," he's also good at explaining the new approaches to Amazon's executives in clear business terms.

Established analytics competitors such as Capital One employ squadrons of analysts to conduct quantitative experiments and, with the results in hand, design credit card and other financial offers. These efforts call for a specialized skill set, as you can see from this job description (typical for a Capital One analyst):

High conceptual problem-solving and quantitative analytical aptitudes . . . Engineering, financial, consulting, and/or other analytical quantitative educational/work background. Ability to quickly learn how to use software applications. Experience with Excel models. Some graduate work preferred but not required (e.g., MBA). Some experience with project management methodology, process improvement tools (Lean, Six Sigma), or statistics preferred.

Other firms hire similar kinds of people, but analytics competitors have them in much greater numbers. Capital One is currently seeking three times as many analysts as operations people—hardly the common practice for a bank. "We are really a company of analysts," one executive there noted. "It's the primary job in this place."

Good analysts must also have the ability to express complex ideas in simple terms and have the relationship skills to interact well with decision makers. One consumer products company with a 30-person analytics group looks for what it calls "PhDs with personality"—people with expertise in math, statistics, and data analysis who can also speak the language of business and help market their work internally and sometimes externally. The head of a customer analytics group at Wachovia Bank describes the rapport with others his group seeks: "We are trying to build our people as part of the business team," he explains. "We want them sitting at the business table, participating in a discussion of what the key issues are, determining what information needs the businesspeople have, and recommending actions to the business partners. We want this [analytics group] to be not just a general utility, but rather an active and critical part of the business unit's success."

Of course, a combination of analytical, business, and relationship skills may be difficult to find. When the software company SAS (a sponsor of this research, along with Intel) knows it will need an expert in state-of-the-art business applications such as predictive modeling or recursive partitioning (a form of decision tree analysis applied to very complex data sets), it begins recruiting up to 18 months before it expects to fill the position.

In fact, analytical talent may be to the early 2000s what programming talent was to the late 1990s. Unfortunately, the U.S. and European labor markets aren't exactly teeming with analytically sophisticated job candidates. Some organizations cope by contracting work to countries such as India, home to many statistical experts. That strategy may succeed when offshore analysts work on stand-alone problems. But if an iterative discussion with business decision makers is required, the distance can become a major barrier.

The right technology

Competing on analytics means competing on technology. And while the most serious competitors investigate the latest statistical algorithms and decision science approaches, they also constantly monitor and push the IT frontier. The analytics group at one consumer products company went so far as to build its own supercomputer because it felt that commercially available models were inadequate for its demands. Such heroic feats usually aren't necessary, but serious analytics does require the following:

A data strategy. Companies have invested many millions of dollars in systems that snatch data from every conceivable source. Enterprise resource planning, customer relationship management, point-of-sale, and other systems ensure that no transaction or other significant exchange occurs without leaving a mark. But to compete on that information, companies must present it in standard formats, integrate it, store it in a data warehouse, and make it easily accessible to anyone and everyone. And they will need *a lot* of it. For example, a company may spend several years accumulating data on different marketing approaches before it has gathered enough to reliably analyze the effectiveness of an advertising campaign. Dell employed DDB Matrix, a unit of the advertising agency DDB Worldwide, to create (over a period of seven years) a database that includes 1.5 million records on all the computer maker's print, radio, network TV, and cable ads, coupled with data on Dell sales for each region in which the ads appeared (before and after their appearance). That information allows Dell to fine-tune its promotions for every medium in every region.

Business intelligence software. The term "business intelligence," which first popped up in the late 1980s, encompasses a wide array of processes and software used to collect, analyze, and disseminate data, all in the interests of better decision making. Business intelligence tools allow employees to extract, transform, and load (or ETL, as people in the industry would say) data for analysis and then make those analyses available in reports, alerts, and scorecards. The popularity of analytics competition is partly a response to the emergence of integrated packages of these tools.

Computing hardware. The volumes of data required for analytics applications may strain the capacity of low-end computers and servers. Many analytics competitors are converting their hardware to 64-bit processors that churn large amounts of data quickly.

The Long Road Ahead

Most companies in most industries have excellent reasons to pursue strategies shaped by analytics. Virtually all the organizations we identified as aggressive analytics competitors are clear leaders in their fields, and they attribute much of their success to the masterful exploitation of data. Rising global competition intensifies the need for this sort of proficiency. Western companies unable to beat their

You Know You Compete on Analytics When . . .

1. You apply sophisticated information systems and rigorous analysis not only to your core capability but also to a range of functions as varied as marketing and human resources.

2. Your senior executive team not only recognizes the importance of analytics capabilities but also makes their development and maintenance a primary focus.

3. You treat fact-based decision making not only as a best practice but also as a part of the culture that's constantly emphasized and communicated by senior executives.

4. You hire not only people with analytical skills but a lot of people with *the very best* analytical skills—and consider them a key to your success.

5. You not only employ analytics in almost every function and department but also consider it so strategically important that you manage it at the enterprise level.

6. You not only are expert at number crunching but also invent proprietary metrics for use in key business processes.

7. You not only use copious data and in-house analysis but also share them with customers and suppliers.

8. You not only avidly consume data but also seize every opportunity to generate information, creating a "test and learn" culture based on numerous small experiments.

9. You not only have committed to competing on analytics but also have been building your capabilities for several years.

10. You not only emphasize the importance of analytics internally but also make quantitative capabilities part of your company's story, to be shared in the annual report and in discussions with financial analysts.

Indian or Chinese competitors on product cost, for example, can seek the upper hand through optimized business processes.

Companies just now embracing such strategies, however, will find that they take several years to come to fruition. The organizations in our study described a long, sometimes arduous journey. The

UK Consumer Cards and Loans business within Barclays Bank, for example, spent five years executing its plan to apply analytics to the marketing of credit cards and other financial products. The company had to make process changes in virtually every aspect of its consumer business: underwriting risk, setting credit limits, servicing accounts, controlling fraud, cross selling, and so on. On the technical side, it had to integrate data on 10 million Barclaycard customers, improve the quality of the data, and build systems to step up data collection and analysis. In addition, the company embarked on a long series of small tests to begin learning how to attract and retain the best customers at the lowest price. And it had to hire new people with top-drawer quantitative skills.

Much of the time—and corresponding expense—that any company takes to become an analytics competitor will be devoted to technological tasks: refining the systems that produce transaction data, making data available in warehouses, selecting and implementing analytic software, and assembling the hardware and communications environment. And because those who don't record history are doomed not to learn from it, companies that have collected little information—or the wrong kind—will need to amass a sufficient body of data to support reliable forecasting. "We've been collecting data for six or seven years, but it's only become usable in the last two or three, because we needed time and experience to validate conclusions based on the data," remarked a manager of customer data analytics at UPS.

And, of course, new analytics competitors will have to stock their personnel larders with fresh people. (When Gary Loveman became COO, and then CEO, of Harrah's, he brought in a group of statistical experts who could design and implement quantitatively based marketing campaigns and loyalty programs.) Existing employees, meanwhile, will require extensive training. They need to know what data are available and all the ways the information can be analyzed; and they must learn to recognize such peculiarities and shortcomings as missing data, duplication, and quality problems. An analytics-minded executive at Procter & Gamble suggested to me that firms should begin to keep managers in their jobs for longer periods because of the time required to master quantitative approaches to their businesses.

The German pathologist Rudolph Virchow famously called the task of science "to stake out the limits of the knowable." Analytics competitors pursue a similar goal, although the universe they seek to know is a more circumscribed one of customer behavior, product movement, employee performance, and financial reactions. Every day, advances in technology and techniques give companies a better and better handle on the critical minutiae of their operations.

The Oakland A's aren't the only ones playing moneyball. Companies of every stripe want to be part of the game.

Originally published in January 2006. Reprint R0601H

Managing Oneself

by Peter F. Drucker

HISTORY'S GREAT ACHIEVERS—a Napoléon, a da Vinci, a Mozart— have always managed themselves. That, in large measure, is what makes them great achievers. But they are rare exceptions, so unusual both in their talents and their accomplishments as to be considered outside the boundaries of ordinary human existence. Now, most of us, even those of us with modest endowments, will have to learn to manage ourselves. We will have to learn to develop ourselves. We will have to place ourselves where we can make the greatest contribution. And we will have to stay mentally alert and engaged during a 50-year working life, which means knowing how and when to change the work we do.

What Are My Strengths?

Most people think they know what they are good at. They are usually wrong. More often, people know what they are not good at—and even then more people are wrong than right. And yet, a person can perform only from strength. One cannot build performance on weaknesses, let alone on something one cannot do at all.

Throughout history, people had little need to know their strengths. A person was born into a position and a line of work: The peasant's son would also be a peasant; the artisan's daughter, an artisan's wife; and so on. But now people have choices. We need to know our strengths in order to know where we belong.

The only way to discover your strengths is through feedback analysis. Whenever you make a key decision or take a key action, write down what you expect will happen. Nine or 12 months later, compare the actual results with your expectations. I have been practicing this method for 15 to 20 years now, and every time I do it, I am surprised. The feedback analysis showed me, for instance—and to my great surprise—that I have an intuitive understanding of technical people, whether they are engineers or accountants or market researchers. It also showed me that I don't really resonate with generalists.

Feedback analysis is by no means new. It was invented sometime in the fourteenth century by an otherwise totally obscure German theologian and picked up quite independently, some 150 years later, by John Calvin and Ignatius of Loyola, each of whom incorporated it into the practice of his followers. In fact, the steadfast focus on performance and results that this habit produces explains why the institutions these two men founded, the Calvinist church and the Jesuit order, came to dominate Europe within 30 years.

Practiced consistently, this simple method will show you within a fairly short period of time, maybe two or three years, where your strengths lie—and this is the most important thing to know. The method will show you what you are doing or failing to do that deprives you of the full benefits of your strengths. It will show you where you are not particularly competent. And finally, it will show you where you have no strengths and cannot perform.

Several implications for action follow from feedback analysis. First and foremost, concentrate on your strengths. Put yourself where your strengths can produce results.

Second, work on improving your strengths. Analysis will rapidly show where you need to improve skills or acquire new ones. It will also show the gaps in your knowledge—and those can usually be filled. Mathematicians are born, but everyone can learn trigonometry.

Third, discover where your intellectual arrogance is causing disabling ignorance and overcome it. Far too many people—especially

Idea in Brief

We live in an age of unprecedented opportunity: If you've got ambition, drive, and smarts, you can rise to the top of your chosen profession—regardless of where you started out. But with opportunity comes responsibility. Companies today aren't managing their knowledge workers' careers. Rather, we must each be our own chief executive officer.

Simply put, it's up to you to carve out your place in the work world and know when to change course. And it's up to you to keep yourself engaged and productive during a work life that may span some 50 years.

To do all of these things well, you'll need to cultivate a deep understanding of yourself. What are your most valuable strengths and most dangerous weaknesses? Equally important, how do you learn and work with others? What are your most deeply held values? And in what type of work environment can you make the greatest contribution?

The implication is clear: Only when you operate from a combination of your strengths and self-knowledge can you achieve true—and lasting—excellence.

---

people with great expertise in one area—are contemptuous of knowledge in other areas or believe that being bright is a substitute for knowledge. First-rate engineers, for instance, tend to take pride in not knowing anything about people. Human beings, they believe, are much too disorderly for the good engineering mind. Human resources professionals, by contrast, often pride themselves on their ignorance of elementary accounting or of quantitative methods altogether. But taking pride in such ignorance is self-defeating. Go to work on acquiring the skills and knowledge you need to fully realize your strengths.

It is equally essential to remedy your bad habits—the things you do or fail to do that inhibit your effectiveness and performance. Such habits will quickly show up in the feedback. For example, a planner may find that his beautiful plans fail because he does not follow through on them. Like so many brilliant people, he believes that ideas move mountains. But bulldozers move mountains; ideas show where the bulldozers should go to work. This planner will have to learn that the work does not stop when the plan is completed. He

Idea in Practice

To build a life of excellence, begin by asking yourself these questions:

"What are my strengths?"

To accurately identify your strengths, use **feedback analysis**. Every time you make a key decision, write down the outcome you expect. Several months later, compare the actual results with your expected results. Look for patterns in what you're seeing: What results are you skilled at generating? What abilities do you need to enhance in order to get the results you want? What unproductive habits are preventing you from creating the outcomes you desire? In identifying opportunities for improvement, don't waste time cultivating skill areas where you have little competence. Instead, concentrate on—and build on— your strengths.

"How do I work?"

In what ways do you work best? Do you process information most effectively by reading it, or by hearing others discuss it? Do you accomplish the most by working with other people, or by working alone? Do you perform best while making decisions, or while advising others on key matters? Are you in top form when things get stressful, or do you function optimally in a highly predictable environment?

"What are my values?"

What are your ethics? What do you see as your most important responsibilities for living a worthy, ethical life? Do your organization's ethics resonate with your own values? If not, your career will likely be marked by frustration and poor performance.

"Where do I belong?"

Consider your strengths, preferred work style, and values. Based on these qualities, in what kind of work environment would you fit in best? Find the perfect fit, and you'll transform yourself from a merely acceptable employee into a star performer.

"What can I contribute?"

In earlier eras, companies told businesspeople what their contribution should be. Today, you have choices. To decide how you can best enhance your organization's performance, first ask what the situation requires. Based on your strengths, work style, and values, how might you make the greatest contribution to your organization's efforts?

must find people to carry out the plan and explain it to them. He must adapt and change it as he puts it into action. And finally, he must decide when to stop pushing the plan.

At the same time, feedback will also reveal when the problem is a lack of manners. Manners are the lubricating oil of an organization. It is a law of nature that two moving bodies in contact with each other create friction. This is as true for human beings as it is for inanimate objects. Manners—simple things like saying "please" and "thank you" and knowing a person's name or asking after her family—enable two people to work together whether they like each other or not. Bright people, especially bright young people, often do not understand this. If analysis shows that someone's brilliant work fails again and again as soon as cooperation from others is required, it probably indicates a lack of courtesy—that is, a lack of manners.

Comparing your expectations with your results also indicates what not to do. We all have a vast number of areas in which we have no talent or skill and little chance of becoming even mediocre. In those areas a person—and especially a knowledge worker—should not take on work, jobs, and assignments. One should waste as little effort as possible on improving areas of low competence. It takes far more energy and work to improve from incompetence to mediocrity than it takes to improve from first-rate performance to excellence. And yet most people—especially most teachers and most organizations—concentrate on making incompetent performers into mediocre ones. Energy, resources, and time should go instead to making a competent person into a star performer.

How Do I Perform?

Amazingly few people know how they get things done. Indeed, most of us do not even know that different people work and perform differently. Too many people work in ways that are not their ways, and that almost guarantees nonperformance. For knowledge workers, How do I perform? may be an even more important question than What are my strengths?

Like one's strengths, how one performs is unique. It is a matter of personality. Whether personality be a matter of nature or nurture, it surely is formed long before a person goes to work. And *how* a person performs is a given, just as *what* a person is good at or not good at is a given. A person's way of performing can be slightly modified, but it is unlikely to be completely changed—and certainly not easily. Just as people achieve results by doing what they are good at, they also achieve results by working in ways that they best perform. A few common personality traits usually determine how a person performs.

Am I a reader or a listener?

The first thing to know is whether you are a reader or a listener. Far too few people even know that there are readers and listeners and that people are rarely both. Even fewer know which of the two they themselves are. But some examples will show how damaging such ignorance can be.

When Dwight Eisenhower was Supreme Commander of the Allied forces in Europe, he was the darling of the press. His press conferences were famous for their style—General Eisenhower showed total command of whatever question he was asked, and he was able to describe a situation and explain a policy in two or three beautifully polished and elegant sentences. Ten years later, the same journalists who had been his admirers held President Eisenhower in open contempt. He never addressed the questions, they complained, but rambled on endlessly about something else. And they constantly ridiculed him for butchering the King's English in incoherent and ungrammatical answers.

Eisenhower apparently did not know that he was a reader, not a listener. When he was Supreme Commander in Europe, his aides made sure that every question from the press was presented in writing at least half an hour before a conference was to begin. And then Eisenhower was in total command. When he became president, he succeeded two listeners, Franklin D. Roosevelt and Harry Truman. Both men knew themselves to be listeners and both enjoyed free-for-all press conferences. Eisenhower may have felt that he had to do what his two predecessors had done. As a result, he never even heard the questions journalists asked. And Eisenhower is not even an extreme case of a nonlistener.

A few years later, Lyndon Johnson destroyed his presidency, in large measure, by not knowing that he was a listener. His predecessor, John Kennedy, was a reader who had assembled a brilliant group of writers as his assistants, making sure that they wrote to him before discussing their memos in person. Johnson kept these people on his staff—and they kept on writing. He never, apparently, understood one word of what they wrote. Yet as a senator, Johnson had been superb; for parliamentarians have to be, above all, listeners.

Few listeners can be made, or can make themselves, into competent readers—and vice versa. The listener who tries to be a reader will, therefore, suffer the fate of Lyndon Johnson, whereas the reader who tries to be a listener will suffer the fate of Dwight Eisenhower. They will not perform or achieve.

How do I learn?
The second thing to know about how one performs is to know how one learns. Many first-class writers—Winston Churchill is but one example—do poorly in school. They tend to remember their schooling as pure torture. Yet few of their classmates remember it the same way. They may not have enjoyed the school very much, but the worst they suffered was boredom. The explanation is that writers do not, as a rule, learn by listening and reading. They learn by writing. Because schools do not allow them to learn this way, they get poor grades.

Schools everywhere are organized on the assumption that there is only one right way to learn and that it is the same way for everybody. But to be forced to learn the way a school teaches is sheer hell for students who learn differently. Indeed, there are probably half a dozen different ways to learn.

There are people, like Churchill, who learn by writing. Some people learn by taking copious notes. Beethoven, for example, left behind an enormous number of sketchbooks, yet he said he never actually looked at them when he composed. Asked why he kept them, he is reported to have replied, "If I don't write it down immediately, I forget it right away. If I put it into a sketchbook, I never forget it and I never have to look it up again." Some people learn by doing. Others learn by hearing themselves talk.

A chief executive I know who converted a small and mediocre family business into the leading company in its industry was one of those people who learn by talking. He was in the habit of calling his entire senior staff into his office once a week and then talking at them for two or three hours. He would raise policy issues and argue three different positions on each one. He rarely asked his associates for comments or questions; he simply needed an audience to hear himself talk. That's how he learned. And although he is a fairly extreme case, learning through talking is by no means an unusual method. Successful trial lawyers learn the same way, as do many medical diagnosticians (and so do I).

Of all the important pieces of self-knowledge, understanding how you learn is the easiest to acquire. When I ask people, "How do you learn?" most of them know the answer. But when I ask, "Do you act on this knowledge?" few answer yes. And yet, acting on this knowledge is the key to performance; or rather, *not* acting on this knowledge condemns one to nonperformance.

Am I a reader or a listener? and How do I learn? are the first questions to ask. But they are by no means the only ones. To manage yourself effectively, you also have to ask, Do I work well with people, or am I a loner? And if you do work well with people, you then must ask, In what relationship?

Some people work best as subordinates. General George Patton, the great American military hero of World War II, is a prime example. Patton was America's top troop commander. Yet when he was proposed for an independent command, General George Marshall, the U.S. chief of staff—and probably the most successful picker of men in U.S. history—said, "Patton is the best subordinate the American army has ever produced, but he would be the worst commander."

Some people work best as team members. Others work best alone. Some are exceptionally talented as coaches and mentors; others are simply incompetent as mentors.

Another crucial question is, Do I produce results as a decision maker or as an adviser? A great many people perform best as advisers but cannot take the burden and pressure of making the decision. A good many other people, by contrast, need an adviser to force themselves to think; then they can make decisions and act on them with speed, self-confidence, and courage.

This is a reason, by the way, that the number two person in an organization often fails when promoted to the number one position. The top spot requires a decision maker. Strong decision makers often put somebody they trust into the number two spot as their adviser—and in that position the person is outstanding. But in the number one spot, the same person fails. He or she knows what the decision should be but cannot accept the responsibility of actually making it.

Other important questions to ask include, Do I perform well under stress, or do I need a highly structured and predictable environment? Do I work best in a big organization or a small one? Few people work well in all kinds of environments. Again and again, I have seen people who were very successful in large organizations flounder miserably when they moved into smaller ones. And the reverse is equally true.

The conclusion bears repeating: Do not try to change yourself—you are unlikely to succeed. But work hard to improve the way you perform. And try not to take on work you cannot perform or will only perform poorly.

What Are My Values?

To be able to manage yourself, you finally have to ask, What are my values? This is not a question of ethics. With respect to ethics, the rules are the same for everybody, and the test is a simple one. I call it the "mirror test."

In the early years of this century, the most highly respected diplomat of all the great powers was the German ambassador in London. He was clearly destined for great things—to become his country's foreign minister, at least, if not its federal chancellor. Yet in 1906 he abruptly resigned rather than preside over a dinner given by the diplomatic corps for Edward VII. The king was a notorious womanizer and made it clear what kind of dinner he wanted. The ambassador is reported to have said, "I refuse to see a pimp in the mirror in the morning when I shave."

That is the mirror test. Ethics requires that you ask yourself, What kind of person do I want to see in the mirror in the morning? What is ethical behavior in one kind of organization or situation is ethical behavior in another. But ethics is only part of a value system—especially of an organization's value system.

To work in an organization whose value system is unacceptable or incompatible with one's own condemns a person both to frustration and to nonperformance.

Consider the experience of a highly successful human resources executive whose company was acquired by a bigger organization. After the acquisition, she was promoted to do the kind of work she did best, which included selecting people for important positions. The executive deeply believed that a company should hire people for such positions from the outside only after exhausting all the inside possibilities. But her new company believed in first looking outside "to bring in fresh blood." There is something to be said for both approaches—in my experience, the proper one is to do some of both. They are, however, fundamentally incompatible—not as policies but as values. They bespeak different views of the relationship between organizations and people; different views of the responsibility of an organization to its people and their development; and different views of a person's most important contribution to an enterprise. After several years of frustration, the executive quit—at considerable financial loss. Her values and the values of the organization simply were not compatible.

Similarly, whether a pharmaceutical company tries to obtain results by making constant, small improvements or by achieving occasional, highly expensive, and risky "breakthroughs" is not primarily an economic question. The results of either strategy may be pretty much the same. At bottom, there is a conflict between a value system that sees the company's contribution in terms of helping physicians do better what they already do and a value system that is oriented toward making scientific discoveries.

Whether a business should be run for short-term results or with a focus on the long term is likewise a question of values. Financial analysts believe that businesses can be run for both simultaneously. Successful businesspeople know better. To be sure, every company has to produce short-term results. But in any conflict between short-term results and long-term growth, each company will determine its own priority. This is not primarily a disagreement about economics. It is fundamentally a value conflict regarding the function of a business and the responsibility of management.

Value conflicts are not limited to business organizations. One of the fastest-growing pastoral churches in the United States measures success by the number of new parishioners. Its leadership believes that what matters is how many newcomers join the congregation. The Good Lord will then minister to their spiritual needs or at least to the needs of a sufficient percentage. Another pastoral, evangelical church believes that what matters is people's spiritual growth. The church eases out newcomers who join but do not enter into its spiritual life.

Again, this is not a matter of numbers. At first glance, it appears that the second church grows more slowly. But it retains a far larger proportion of newcomers than the first one does. Its growth, in other words, is more solid. This is also not a theological problem, or only secondarily so. It is a problem about values. In a public debate, one pastor argued, "Unless you first come to church, you will never find the gate to the Kingdom of Heaven."

"No," answered the other. "Until you first look for the gate to the Kingdom of Heaven, you don't belong in church."

Organizations, like people, have values. To be effective in an organization, a person's values must be compatible with the organization's values. They do not need to be the same, but they must be close enough to coexist. Otherwise, the person will not only be frustrated but also will not produce results.

A person's strengths and the way that person performs rarely conflict; the two are complementary. But there is sometimes a conflict between a person's values and his or her strengths. What one does well—even very well and successfully—may not fit with one's value system. In that case, the work may not appear to be worth devoting one's life to (or even a substantial portion thereof).

If I may, allow me to interject a personal note. Many years ago, I too had to decide between my values and what I was doing success- fully. I was doing very well as a young investment banker in London in the mid-1930s, and the work clearly fit my strengths. Yet I did not see myself making a contribution as an asset manager. People, I real- ized, were what I valued, and I saw no point in being the richest man in the cemetery. I had no money and no other job prospects. Despite the continuing Depression, I quit—and it was the right thing to do. Values, in other words, are and should be the ultimate test.

Where Do I Belong?

A small number of people know very early where they belong. Math- ematicians, musicians, and cooks, for instance, are usually mathe- maticians, musicians, and cooks by the time they are four or five years old. Physicians usually decide on their careers in their teens, if not earlier. But most people, especially highly gifted people, do not really know where they belong until they are well past their mid-twenties. By that time, however, they should know the answers to the three questions: What are my strengths? How do I perform? and, What are my values? And then they can and should decide where they belong.

Or rather, they should be able to decide where they do *not* belong. The person who has learned that he or she does not perform well in a big organization should have learned to say no to a position in one. The person who has learned that he or she is not a decision maker should have learned to say no to a decision-making assignment. A General Patton (who probably never learned this himself) should have learned to say no to an independent command.

Equally important, knowing the answer to these questions en- ables a person to say to an opportunity, an offer, or an assignment, "Yes, I will do that. But this is the way I should be doing it. This is the way it should be structured. This is the way the relationships should be. These are the kind of results you should expect from me, and in this time frame, because this is who I am."

Successful careers are not planned. They develop when people are prepared for opportunities because they know their strengths, their method of work, and their values. Knowing where one belongs can transform an ordinary person—hardworking and competent but otherwise mediocre—into an outstanding performer.

What Should I Contribute?

Throughout history, the great majority of people never had to ask the question, What should I contribute? They were told what to contribute, and their tasks were dictated either by the work itself—as it was for the peasant or artisan—or by a master or a mistress—as it was for domestic servants. And until very recently, it was taken for granted that most people were subordinates who did as they were told. Even in the 1950s and 1960s, the new knowledge workers (the so-called organization men) looked to their company's personnel department to plan their careers.

Then in the late 1960s, no one wanted to be told what to do any longer. Young men and women began to ask, What do *I* want to do? And what they heard was that the way to contribute was to "do your own thing." But this solution was as wrong as the organization men's had been. Very few of the people who believed that doing one's own thing would lead to contribution, self-fulfillment, and success achieved any of the three.

But still, there is no return to the old answer of doing what you are told or assigned to do. Knowledge workers in particular have to learn to ask a question that has not been asked before: What *should* my contribution be? To answer it, they must address three distinct elements: What does the situation require? Given my strengths, my way of performing, and my values, how can I make the greatest contribution to what needs to be done? And finally, What results have to be achieved to make a difference?

Consider the experience of a newly appointed hospital administrator. The hospital was big and prestigious, but it had been coasting on its reputation for 30 years. The new administrator decided that his contribution should be to establish a standard of excellence in one important area within two years. He chose to focus on the emergency room, which was big, visible, and sloppy. He decided that every patient who came into the ER had to be seen by a qualified nurse within 60 seconds. Within 12 months, the hospital's emergency room had become a model for all hospitals in the United States, and within another two years, the whole hospital had been transformed.

As this example suggests, it is rarely possible—or even particularly fruitful—to look too far ahead. A plan can usually cover no more than 18 months and still be reasonably clear and specific. So the question in most cases should be, Where and how can I achieve results that will make a difference within the next year and a half? The answer must balance several things. First, the results should be hard to achieve—they should require "stretching," to use the current buzzword. But also, they should be within reach. To aim at results that cannot be achieved—or that can be only under the most unlikely circumstances—is not being ambitious; it is being foolish. Second, the results should be meaningful. They should make a difference. Finally, results should be visible and, if at all possible, measurable. From this will come a course of action: what to do, where and how to start, and what goals and deadlines to set.

Responsibility for Relationships

Very few people work by themselves and achieve results by themselves—a few great artists, a few great scientists, a few great athletes. Most people work with others and are effective with other people. That is true whether they are members of an organization or independently employed. Managing yourself requires taking responsibility for relationships. This has two parts.

The first is to accept the fact that other people are as much individuals as you yourself are. They perversely insist on behaving like human beings. This means that they too have their strengths; they too have their ways of getting things done; they too have their values. To be effective, therefore, you have to know the strengths, the performance modes, and the values of your coworkers.

That sounds obvious, but few people pay attention to it. Typical is the person who was trained to write reports in his or her first assignment because that boss was a reader. Even if the next boss is a listener, the person goes on writing reports that, invariably, produce no results. Invariably the boss will think the employee is stupid, incompetent, and lazy, and he or she will fail. But that could have been avoided if the employee had only looked at the new boss and analyzed how *this* boss performs.

Bosses are neither a title on the organization chart nor a "function." They are individuals and are entitled to do their work in the way they do it best. It is incumbent on the people who work with them to observe them, to find out how they work, and to adapt themselves to what makes their bosses most effective. This, in fact, is the secret of "managing" the boss.

The same holds true for all your coworkers. Each works his or her way, not your way. And each is entitled to work in his or her way. What matters is whether they perform and what their values are. As for how they perform—each is likely to do it differently. The first secret of effectiveness is to understand the people you work with and depend on so that you can make use of their strengths, their ways of working, and their values. Working relationships are as much based on the people as they are on the work.

The second part of relationship responsibility is taking responsibility for communication. Whenever I, or any other consultant, start to work with an organization, the first thing I hear about are all the personality conflicts. Most of these arise from the fact that people do not know what other people are doing and how they do their work, or what contribution the other people are concentrating on and what results they expect. And the reason they do not know is that they have not asked and therefore have not been told.

This failure to ask reflects human stupidity less than it reflects human history. Until recently, it was unnecessary to tell any of these things to anybody. In the medieval city, everyone in a district plied the same trade. In the countryside, everyone in a valley planted the same crop as soon as the frost was out of the ground. Even those few people who did things that were not "common" worked alone, so they did not have to tell anyone what they were doing.

Today the great majority of people work with others who have different tasks and responsibilities. The marketing vice president may have come out of sales and know everything about sales, but she knows nothing about the things she has never done—pricing, advertising, packaging, and the like. So the people who do these things must make sure that the marketing vice president understands what they are trying to do, why they are trying to do it, how they are going to do it, and what results to expect.

If the marketing vice president does not understand what these high-grade knowledge specialists are doing, it is primarily their fault, not hers. They have not educated her. Conversely, it is the marketing vice president's responsibility to make sure that all of her coworkers understand how she looks at marketing: what her goals are, how she works, and what she expects of herself and of each one of them.

Even people who understand the importance of taking responsibility for relationships often do not communicate sufficiently with their associates. They are afraid of being thought presumptuous or inquisitive or stupid. They are wrong. Whenever someone goes to his or her associates and says, "This is what I am good at. This is how I work. These are my values. This is the contribution I plan to concentrate on and the results I should be expected to deliver," the response is always, "This is most helpful. But why didn't you tell me earlier?"

And one gets the same reaction—without exception, in my experience—if one continues by asking, "And what do I need to know about your strengths, how you perform, your values, and your proposed contribution?" In fact, knowledge workers should request this of everyone with whom they work, whether as subordinate, superior, colleague, or team member. And again, whenever this is done, the reaction is always, "Thanks for asking me. But why didn't you ask me earlier?"

Organizations are no longer built on force but on trust. The existence of trust between people does not necessarily mean that they like one another. It means that they understand one another. Taking responsibility for relationships is therefore an absolute necessity. It is a duty. Whether one is a member of the organization, a consultant to it, a supplier, or a distributor, one owes that responsibility to all one's coworkers: those whose work one depends on as well as those who depend on one's own work.

The Second Half of Your Life

When work for most people meant manual labor, there was no need to worry about the second half of your life. You simply kept on doing what you had always done. And if you were lucky enough to survive 40 years of hard work in the mill or on the railroad, you were quite happy to spend the rest of your life doing nothing. Today, however, most work is knowledge work, and knowledge workers are not "finished" after 40 years on the job, they are merely bored.

We hear a great deal of talk about the midlife crisis of the executive. It is mostly boredom. At 45, most executives have reached the peak of their business careers, and they know it. After 20 years of doing very much the same kind of work, they are very good at their jobs. But they are not learning or contributing or deriving challenge and satisfaction from the job. And yet they are still likely to face another 20 if not 25 years of work. That is why managing oneself increasingly leads one to begin a second career.

There are three ways to develop a second career. The first is actually to start one. Often this takes nothing more than moving from one kind of organization to another: the divisional controller in a large corporation, for instance, becomes the controller of a medium-sized hospital. But there are also growing numbers of people who move into different lines of work altogether: the business executive or government official who enters the ministry at 45, for instance; or the midlevel manager who leaves corporate life after 20 years to attend law school and become a small-town attorney.

We will see many more second careers undertaken by people who have achieved modest success in their first jobs. Such people have substantial skills, and they know how to work. They need a community—the house is empty with the children gone—and they need income as well. But above all, they need challenge.

The second way to prepare for the second half of your life is to develop a parallel career. Many people who are very successful in their first careers stay in the work they have been doing, either on a full-time or part-time or consulting basis. But in addition, they create a parallel job, usually in a nonprofit organization, that takes another ten hours of work a week. They might take over the administration of their church, for instance, or the presidency of the local Girl Scouts council. They might run the battered women's shelter, work as a children's librarian for the local public library, sit on the school board, and so on.

Finally, there are the social entrepreneurs. These are usually people who have been very successful in their first careers. They love their work, but it no longer challenges them. In many cases they keep on doing what they have been doing all along but spend less and less of their time on it. They also start another activity, usually a nonprofit. My friend Bob Buford, for example, built a very successful television company that he still runs. But he has also founded and built a successful nonprofit organization that works with Protestant churches, and he is building another to teach social entrepreneurs how to manage their own nonprofit ventures while still running their original businesses.

People who manage the second half of their lives may always be a minority. The majority may "retire on the job" and count the years until their actual retirement. But it is this minority, the men and women who see a long working-life expectancy as an opportunity both for themselves and for society, who will become leaders and models.

There is one prerequisite for managing the second half of your life: You must begin long before you enter it. When it first became clear 30 years ago that working-life expectancies were lengthening very fast, many observers (including myself) believed that retired people would increasingly become volunteers for nonprofit institutions. That has not happened. If one does not begin to volunteer before one is 40 or so, one will not volunteer once past 60.

Similarly, all the social entrepreneurs I know began to work in their chosen second enterprise long before they reached their peak in their original business. Consider the example of a successful lawyer, the legal counsel to a large corporation, who has started a venture to establish model schools in his state. He began to do volunteer legal work for the schools when he was around 35. He was elected to the school board at age 40. At age 50, when he had amassed a fortune, he started his own enterprise to build and to run model schools. He is, however, still working nearly full-time as the lead counsel in the company he helped found as a young lawyer.

There is another reason to develop a second major interest, and to develop it early. No one can expect to live very long without experiencing a serious setback in his or her life or work. There is the competent engineer who is passed over for promotion at age 45. There is the competent college professor who realizes at age 42 that she will never get a professorship at a big university, even though she may be fully qualified for it. There are tragedies in one's family life: the breakup of one's marriage or the loss of a child. At such times, a second major interest—not just a hobby—may make all the difference. The engineer, for example, now knows that he has not been very successful in his job. But in his outside activity—as church treasurer, for example—he is a success. One's family may break up, but in that outside activity there is still a community.

In a society in which success has become so terribly important, having options will become increasingly vital. Historically, there was no such thing as "success." The overwhelming majority of people did not expect anything but to stay in their "proper station," as an old English prayer has it. The only mobility was downward mobility.

In a knowledge society, however, we expect everyone to be a success. This is clearly an impossibility. For a great many people, there is at best an absence of failure. Wherever there is success, there has to be failure. And then it is vitally important for the individual, and equally for the individual's family, to have an area in which he or she can contribute, make a difference, and be *somebody*. That means finding a second area—whether in a second career, a parallel career, or a social venture—that offers an opportunity for being a leader, for being respected, for being a success.

The challenges of managing oneself may seem obvious, if not elementary. And the answers may seem self-evident to the point of appearing naïve. But managing oneself requires new and unprecedented things from the individual, and especially from the knowledge worker. In effect, managing oneself demands that each knowledge worker think and behave like a chief executive officer. Further, the shift from manual workers who do as they are told to knowledge workers who have to manage themselves profoundly challenges social structure. Every existing society, even the most individualistic one, takes two things for granted, if only subconsciously: that organizations outlive workers, and that most people stay put.

But today the opposite is true. Knowledge workers outlive organizations, and they are mobile. The need to manage oneself is therefore creating a revolution in human affairs.

Originally published in January 1999. Reprint R0501K

What Makes a Leader?

by Daniel Goleman

EVERY BUSINESSPERSON KNOWS a story about a highly intelligent, highly skilled executive who was promoted into a leadership position only to fail at the job. And they also know a story about someone with solid—but not extraordinary—intellectual abilities and technical skills who was promoted into a similar position and then soared.

Such anecdotes support the widespread belief that identifying individuals with the "right stuff" to be leaders is more art than science. After all, the personal styles of superb leaders vary: Some leaders are subdued and analytical; others shout their manifestos from the mountaintops. And just as important, different situations call for different types of leadership. Most mergers need a sensitive negotiator at the helm, whereas many turnarounds require a more forceful authority.

I have found, however, that the most effective leaders are alike in one crucial way: They all have a high degree of what has come to be known as *emotional intelligence*. It's not that IQ and technical skills are irrelevant. They do matter, but mainly as "threshold capabilities"; that is, they are the entry-level requirements for executive positions. But my research, along with other recent studies, clearly shows that emotional intelligence is the sine qua non of leadership. Without it, a person can have the best training in the world, an incisive, analytical mind, and an endless supply of smart ideas, but he still won't make a great leader.

In the course of the past year, my colleagues and I have focused on how emotional intelligence operates at work. We have examined the relationship between emotional intelligence and effective performance, especially in leaders. And we have observed how emotional intelligence shows itself on the job. How can you tell if someone has high emotional intelligence, for example, and how can you recognize it in yourself? In the following pages, we'll explore these questions, taking each of the components of emotional intelligence—self-awareness, self-regulation, motivation, empathy, and social skill—in turn.

Evaluating Emotional Intelligence

Most large companies today have employed trained psychologists to develop what are known as "competency models" to aid them in identifying, training, and promoting likely stars in the leadership firmament. The psychologists have also developed such models for lower-level positions. And in recent years, I have analyzed competency models from 188 companies, most of which were large and global and included the likes of Lucent Technologies, British Airways, and Credit Suisse.

In carrying out this work, my objective was to determine which personal capabilities drove outstanding performance within these organizations, and to what degree they did so. I grouped capabilities into three categories: purely technical skills like accounting and business planning; cognitive abilities like analytical reasoning; and competencies demonstrating emotional intelligence, such as the ability to work with others and effectiveness in leading change.

To create some of the competency models, psychologists asked senior managers at the companies to identify the capabilities that typified the organization's most outstanding leaders. To create other models, the psychologists used objective criteria, such as a division's profitability, to differentiate the star performers at senior levels within their organizations from the average ones. Those

Idea in Brief

What distinguishes great leaders from merely good ones? It isn't IQ or technical skills, says Daniel Goleman. It's **emotional intelligence**: a group of five skills that enable the best leaders to maximize their own *and* their followers' performance. When senior managers at one company had a critical mass of EI capabilities, their divisions outperformed yearly earnings goals by 20%.

The EI skills are:

- *Self-awareness*—knowing one's strengths, weaknesses, drives, values, and impact on others

- *Self-regulation*—controlling or redirecting disruptive impulses and moods

- *Motivation*—relishing achievement for its own sake

- *Empathy*—understanding other people's emotional makeup

- *Social skill*—building rapport with others to move them in desired directions

We're each born with certain levels of EI skills. But we can strengthen these abilities through persistence, practice, and feedback from colleagues or coaches.

individuals were then extensively interviewed and tested, and their capabilities were compared. This process resulted in the creation of lists of ingredients for highly effective leaders. The lists ranged in length from seven to 15 items and included such ingredients as initiative and strategic vision.

When I analyzed all this data, I found dramatic results. To be sure, intellect was a driver of outstanding performance. Cognitive skills such as big-picture thinking and long-term vision were particularly important. But when I calculated the ratio of technical skills, IQ, and emotional intelligence as ingredients of excellent performance, emotional intelligence proved to be twice as important as the others for jobs at all levels.

Moreover, my analysis showed that emotional intelligence played an increasingly important role at the highest levels of the company, where differences in technical skills are of negligible importance. In other words, the higher the rank of a person considered to be a star performer, the more emotional intelligence capabilities showed up as the reason for his or her effectiveness. When I compared star performers with average ones in senior leadership positions, nearly

Idea in Practice

Understanding EI'S Components

EI Component	Definition	Hallmarks	Example
Self-awareness	Knowing one's emotions, strengths, weaknesses, drives, values, and goals—and their impact on others	• Self-confidence • Realistic self-assessment • Self-deprecating sense of humor • Thirst for constructive criticism	A manager knows tight deadlines bring out the worst in him. So he plans his time to get work done well in advance.
Self-regulation	Controlling or redirecting disruptive emotions and impulses	• Trustworthiness • Integrity • Comfort with ambiguity and change	When a team botches a presentation, its leader resists the urge to scream. Instead, she considers possible reasons for the failure, explains the consequences to her team, and explores solutions with them.
Motivation	Being driven to achieve for the sake of achievement	• A passion for the work itself and for new challenges • Unflagging energy to improve • Optimism in the face of failure	A portfolio manager at an investment company sees his fund tumble for three consecutive quarters. Major clients defect. Instead of blaming external circumstances, she decides to learn from the experience—and engineers a turnaround.

Empathy	Considering others' feelings, especially when making decisions	• Expertise in attracting and retaining talent • Ability to develop others • Sensitivity to cross-cultural differences	An American consultant and her team pitch a project to a potential client in Japan. Her team interprets the client's silence as disapproval, and prepares to leave. The consultant reads the client's body language and senses interest. She continues the meeting, and her team gets the job.
Social Skill	Managing relationships to move people in desired directions	• Effectiveness in leading change • Persuasiveness • Extensive networking • Expertise in building and leading teams	A manager wants his company to adopt a better Internet strategy. He finds kindred spirits and assembles a de facto team to create a prototype Web site. He persuades allies in other divisions to fund the company's participation in a relevant convention. His company forms an Internet division—and puts him in charge of it.

Strengthening Your EI

Use practice and feedback from others to strengthen specific EI skills.

Example: An executive learned from others that she lacked empathy, especially the ability to listen. She wanted to fix the problem, so she asked a coach to tell her when she exhibited poor listening skills. She then role-played incidents to practice giving better responses; for example, not interrupting. She also began observing executives skilled at listening—and imitated their behavior.

The five components of emotional intelligence at work

	Definition	Hallmarks
Self-awareness	The ability to recognize and understand your moods, emotions, and drives, as well as their effect on others	Self-confidence Realistic self-assessment Self-deprecating sense of humor
Self-Regulation	The ability to control or redirect disruptive impulses and moods The propensity to suspend judgment—to think before acting	Trustworthiness and integrity Comfort with ambiguity Openness to change
Motivation	A passion to work for reasons that go beyond money or status A propensity to pursue goals with energy and persistence	Strong drive to achieve Optimism, even in the face of failure Organizational commitment
Empathy	The ability to understand the emotional makeup of other people Skill in treating people according to their emotional reactions	Expertise in building and retaining talent Cross-cultural sensitivity Service to clients and customers
Social Skill	Proficiency in managing relationships and building networks An ability to find common ground and build rapport	Effectiveness in leading change Persuasiveness Expertise in building and leading teams

90% of the difference in their profiles was attributable to emotional intelligence factors rather than cognitive abilities.

Other researchers have confirmed that emotional intelligence not only distinguishes outstanding leaders but can also be linked to strong performance. The findings of the late David McClelland, the renowned researcher in human and organizational behavior, are a good example. In a 1996 study of a global food and beverage company, McClelland found that when senior managers had a critical mass of emotional intelligence capabilities, their divisions outperformed yearly earnings goals by 20%. Meanwhile, division leaders without that critical mass underperformed by almost the same amount. McClelland's findings, interestingly, held as true in the company's U.S. divisions as in its divisions in Asia and Europe.

In short, the numbers are beginning to tell us a persuasive story about the link between a company's success and the emotional intelligence of its leaders. And just as important, research is also demonstrating that people can, if they take the right approach, develop their emotional intelligence. (See the sidebar "Can Emotional Intelligence Be Learned?")

Self-Awareness

Self-awareness is the first component of emotional intelligence— which makes sense when one considers that the Delphic oracle gave the advice to "know thyself" thousands of years ago. Self-awareness means having a deep understanding of one's emotions, strengths, weaknesses, needs, and drives. People with strong self-awareness are neither overly critical nor unrealistically hopeful. Rather, they are honest—with themselves and with others.

People who have a high degree of self-awareness recognize how their feelings affect them, other people, and their job performance. Thus, a self-aware person who knows that tight deadlines bring out the worst in him plans his time carefully and gets his work done well in advance. Another person with high self-awareness will be able to work with a demanding client. She will understand the client's impact on her moods and the deeper reasons for her frustration. "Their

Can Emotional Intelligence Be Learned?

FOR AGES, PEOPLE HAVE DEBATED if leaders are born or made. So too goes the debate about emotional intelligence. Are people born with certain levels of empathy, for example, or do they acquire empathy as a result of life's experiences? The answer is both. Scientific inquiry strongly suggests that there is a genetic component to emotional intelligence. Psychological and developmental research indicates that nurture plays a role as well. How much of each perhaps will never be known, but research and practice clearly demonstrate that emotional intelligence can be learned.

One thing is certain: Emotional intelligence increases with age. There is an old-fashioned word for the phenomenon: maturity. Yet even with maturity, some people still need training to enhance their emotional intelligence. Unfortunately, far too many training programs that intend to build leadership skills—including emotional intelligence—are a waste of time and money. The problem is simple: They focus on the wrong part of the brain.

Emotional intelligence is born largely in the neurotransmitters of the brain's limbic system, which governs feelings, impulses, and drives. Research indicates that the limbic system learns best through motivation, extended practice, and feedback. Compare this with the kind of learning that goes on in the neocortex, which governs analytical and technical ability. The neocortex grasps concepts and logic. It is the part of the brain that figures out how to use a computer or make a sales call by reading a book. Not surprisingly—but mistakenly—it is also the part of the brain targeted by most training programs aimed at enhancing emotional intelligence. When such programs take, in effect, a neocortical approach, my research with the Consortium for Research on Emotional Intelligence in Organizations has shown they can even have a *negative* impact on people's job performance.

To enhance emotional intelligence, organizations must refocus their training to include the limbic system. They must help people break old behavioral habits and establish new ones. That not only takes much more time than conventional training programs, it also requires an individualized approach.

Imagine an executive who is thought to be low on empathy by her colleagues. Part of that deficit shows itself as an inability to listen; she interrupts people and doesn't pay close attention to what they're saying. To fix the problem, the executive needs to be motivated to change, and then she needs practice and feedback from others in the company. A colleague or coach could be tapped to let the executive know when she has been observed failing to listen. She would then have to replay the incident and give a better response; that is, demonstrate her ability to absorb what others are saying. And the executive could be directed to observe certain executives who listen well and to mimic their behavior.

With persistence and practice, such a process can lead to lasting results. I know one Wall Street executive who sought to improve his empathy—specifically his ability to read people's reactions and see their perspectives. Before beginning his quest, the executive's subordinates were terrified of working with him. People even went so far as to hide bad news from him. Naturally, he was shocked when finally confronted with these facts. He went home and told his family—but they only confirmed what he had heard at work. When their opinions on any given subject did not mesh with his, they, too, were frightened of him.

Enlisting the help of a coach, the executive went to work to heighten his empathy through practice and feedback. His first step was to take a vacation to a foreign country where he did not speak the language. While there, he monitored his reactions to the unfamiliar and his openness to people who were different from him. When he returned home, humbled by his week abroad, the executive asked his coach to shadow him for parts of the day, several times a week, to critique how he treated people with new or different perspectives. At the same time, he consciously used on-the-job interactions as opportunities to practice "hearing" ideas that differed from his. Finally, the executive had himself videotaped in meetings and asked those who worked for and with him to critique his ability to acknowledge and understand the feelings of others. It took several months, but the executive's emotional intelligence did ultimately rise, and the improvement was reflected in his overall performance on the job.

It's important to emphasize that building one's emotional intelligence cannot—will not—happen without sincere desire and concerted effort. A brief seminar won't help; nor can one buy a how-to manual. It is much harder to learn to empathize—to internalize empathy as a natural response to people—than it is to become adept at regression analysis. But it can be done. "Nothing great was ever achieved without enthusiasm," wrote Ralph Waldo Emerson. If your goal is to become a real leader, these words can serve as a guidepost in your efforts to develop high emotional intelligence.

trivial demands take us away from the real work that needs to be done," she might explain. And she will go one step further and turn her anger into something constructive.

Self-awareness extends to a person's understanding of his or her values and goals. Someone who is highly self-aware knows where he is headed and why; so, for example, he will be able to be firm in turning down a job offer that is tempting financially but does not fit with his principles or long-term goals. A person who lacks self-awareness is apt to make decisions that bring on inner turmoil by treading on buried values. "The money looked good so I signed on," someone might say two years into a job, "but the work means so little to me that I'm constantly bored." The decisions of self-aware people mesh with their values; consequently, they often find work to be energizing.

How can one recognize self-awareness? First and foremost, it shows itself as candor and an ability to assess oneself realistically. People with high self-awareness are able to speak accurately and openly—although not necessarily effusively or confessionally—about their emotions and the impact they have on their work. For instance, one manager I know of was skeptical about a new personal-shopper service that her company, a major department-store chain, was about to introduce. Without prompting from her team or her boss, she offered them an explanation: "It's hard for me to get behind the rollout of this service," she admitted, "because I really wanted to run the project, but I wasn't selected. Bear with me while I deal with that." The manager did indeed examine her feelings; a week later, she was supporting the project fully.

Such self-knowledge often shows itself in the hiring process. Ask a candidate to describe a time he got carried away by his feelings and did something he later regretted. Self-aware candidates will be frank in admitting to failure—and will often tell their tales with a smile. One of the hallmarks of self-awareness is a self-deprecating sense of humor.

Self-awareness can also be identified during performance reviews. Self-aware people know—and are comfortable talking about—their limitations and strengths, and they often demonstrate a thirst for constructive criticism. By contrast, people with low self-awareness interpret the message that they need to improve as a threat or a sign of failure.

Self-aware people can also be recognized by their self-confidence. They have a firm grasp of their capabilities and are less likely to set themselves up to fail by, for example, overstretching on assignments. They know, too, when to ask for help. And the risks they take on the job are calculated. They won't ask for a challenge that they know they can't handle alone. They'll play to their strengths.

Consider the actions of a midlevel employee who was invited to sit in on a strategy meeting with her company's top executives. Although she was the most junior person in the room, she did not sit there quietly, listening in awestruck or fearful silence. She knew she had a head for clear logic and the skill to present ideas persuasively, and she offered cogent suggestions about the company's strategy. At the same time, her self-awareness stopped her from wandering into territory where she knew she was weak.

Despite the value of having self-aware people in the workplace, my research indicates that senior executives don't often give self-awareness the credit it deserves when they look for potential leaders. Many executives mistake candor about feelings for "wimpiness" and fail to give due respect to employees who openly acknowledge their shortcomings. Such people are too readily dismissed as "not tough enough" to lead others.

In fact, the opposite is true. In the first place, people generally admire and respect candor. Furthermore, leaders are constantly required to make judgment calls that require a candid assessment of capabilities—their own and those of others. Do we have the management expertise to acquire a competitor? Can we launch a new product within six months? People who assess themselves honestly—that is, self-aware people—are well suited to do the same for the organizations they run.

Self-Regulation

Biological impulses drive our emotions. We cannot do away with them—but we can do much to manage them. Self-regulation, which is like an ongoing inner conversation, is the component of emotional intelligence that frees us from being prisoners of our feelings. People

73

engaged in such a conversation feel bad moods and emotional impulses just as everyone else does, but they find ways to control them and even to channel them in useful ways.

Imagine an executive who has just watched a team of his employees present a botched analysis to the company's board of directors. In the gloom that follows, the executive might find himself tempted to pound on the table in anger or kick over a chair. He could leap up and scream at the group. Or he might maintain a grim silence, glaring at everyone before stalking off.

But if he had a gift for self-regulation, he would choose a different approach. He would pick his words carefully, acknowledging the team's poor performance without rushing to any hasty judgment. He would then step back to consider the reasons for the failure. Are they personal—a lack of effort? Are there any mitigating factors? What was his role in the debacle? After considering these questions, he would call the team together, lay out the incident's consequences, and offer his feelings about it. He would then present his analysis of the problem and a well-considered solution.

Why does self-regulation matter so much for leaders? First of all, people who are in control of their feelings and impulses—that is, people who are reasonable—are able to create an environment of trust and fairness. In such an environment, politics and infighting are sharply reduced and productivity is high. Talented people flock to the organization and aren't tempted to leave. And self-regulation has a trickle-down effect. No one wants to be known as a hothead when the boss is known for her calm approach. Fewer bad moods at the top mean fewer throughout the organization.

Second, self-regulation is important for competitive reasons. Everyone knows that business today is rife with ambiguity and change. Companies merge and break apart regularly. Technology transforms work at a dizzying pace. People who have mastered their emotions are able to roll with the changes. When a new program is announced, they don't panic; instead, they are able to suspend judgment, seek out information, and listen to the executives as they explain the new program. As the initiative moves forward, these people are able to move with it.

Sometimes they even lead the way. Consider the case of a manager at a large manufacturing company. Like her colleagues, she had used a certain software program for five years. The program drove how she collected and reported data and how she thought about the company's strategy. One day, senior executives announced that a new program was to be installed that would radically change how information was gathered and assessed within the organization. While many people in the company complained bitterly about how disruptive the change would be, the manager mulled over the reasons for the new program and was convinced of its potential to improve performance. She eagerly attended training sessions—some of her colleagues refused to do so—and was eventually promoted to run several divisions, in part because she used the new technology so effectively.

I want to push the importance of self-regulation to leadership even further and make the case that it enhances integrity, which is not only a personal virtue but also an organizational strength. Many of the bad things that happen in companies are a function of impulsive behavior. People rarely plan to exaggerate profits, pad expense accounts, dip into the till, or abuse power for selfish ends. Instead, an opportunity presents itself, and people with low impulse control just say yes.

By contrast, consider the behavior of the senior executive at a large food company. The executive was scrupulously honest in his negotiations with local distributors. He would routinely lay out his cost structure in detail, thereby giving the distributors a realistic understanding of the company's pricing. This approach meant the executive couldn't always drive a hard bargain. Now, on occasion, he felt the urge to increase profits by withholding information about the company's costs. But he challenged that impulse—he saw that it made more sense in the long run to counteract it. His emotional self-regulation paid off in strong, lasting relationships with distributors that benefited the company more than any short-term financial gains would have.

The signs of emotional self-regulation, therefore, are easy to see: a propensity for reflection and thoughtfulness; comfort with ambiguity and change; and integrity—an ability to say no to impulsive urges.

Like self-awareness, self-regulation often does not get its due. People who can master their emotions are sometimes seen as cold fish—their considered responses are taken as a lack of passion. People with fiery temperaments are frequently thought of as "classic" leaders—their outbursts are considered hallmarks of charisma and power. But when such people make it to the top, their impulsiveness often works against them. In my research, extreme displays of negative emotion have never emerged as a driver of good leadership.

Motivation

If there is one trait that virtually all effective leaders have, it is motivation. They are driven to achieve beyond expectations—their own and everyone else's. The key word here is *achieve*. Plenty of people are motivated by external factors, such as a big salary or the status that comes from having an impressive title or being part of a prestigious company. By contrast, those with leadership potential are motivated by a deeply embedded desire to achieve for the sake of achievement.

If you are looking for leaders, how can you identify people who are motivated by the drive to achieve rather than by external rewards? The first sign is a passion for the work itself—such people seek out creative challenges, love to learn, and take great pride in a job well done. They also display an unflagging energy to do things better. People with such energy often seem restless with the status quo. They are persistent with their questions about why things are done one way rather than another; they are eager to explore new approaches to their work.

A cosmetics company manager, for example, was frustrated that he had to wait two weeks to get sales results from people in the field. He finally tracked down an automated phone system that would beep each of his salespeople at 5 pm every day. An automated message then prompted them to punch in their numbers—how many calls and sales they had made that day. The system shortened the feedback time on sales results from weeks to hours.

That story illustrates two other common traits of people who are driven to achieve. They are forever raising the performance bar, and they like to keep score. Take the performance bar first. During performance reviews, people with high levels of motivation might ask to be "stretched" by their superiors. Of course, an employee who combines self-awareness with internal motivation will recognize her limits—but she won't settle for objectives that seem too easy to fulfill.

And it follows naturally that people who are driven to do better also want a way of tracking progress—their own, their team's, and their company's. Whereas people with low achievement motivation are often fuzzy about results, those with high achievement motivation often keep score by tracking such hard measures as profitability or market share. I know of a money manager who starts and ends his day on the Internet, gauging the performance of his stock fund against four industry-set benchmarks.

Interestingly, people with high motivation remain optimistic even when the score is against them. In such cases, self-regulation combines with achievement motivation to overcome the frustration and depression that come after a setback or failure. Take the case of an another portfolio manager at a large investment company. After several successful years, her fund tumbled for three consecutive quarters, leading three large institutional clients to shift their business elsewhere.

Some executives would have blamed the nosedive on circumstances outside their control; others might have seen the setback as evidence of personal failure. This portfolio manager, however, saw an opportunity to prove she could lead a turnaround. Two years later, when she was promoted to a very senior level in the company, she described the experience as "the best thing that ever happened to me; I learned so much from it."

Executives trying to recognize high levels of achievement motivation in their people can look for one last piece of evidence: commitment to the organization. When people love their jobs for the work itself, they often feel committed to the organizations that make that work possible. Committed employees are likely to stay with an organization even when they are pursued by headhunters waving money.

It's not difficult to understand how and why a motivation to achieve translates into strong leadership. If you set the performance bar high for yourself, you will do the same for the organization when you are in a position to do so. Likewise, a drive to surpass goals and an interest in keeping score can be contagious. Leaders with these traits can often build a team of managers around them with the same traits. And of course, optimism and organizational commitment are fundamental to leadership—just try to imagine running a company without them.

Empathy

Of all the dimensions of emotional intelligence, empathy is the most easily recognized. We have all felt the empathy of a sensitive teacher or friend; we have all been struck by its absence in an unfeeling coach or boss. But when it comes to business, we rarely hear people praised, let alone rewarded, for their empathy. The very word seems unbusinesslike, out of place amid the tough realities of the marketplace.

But empathy doesn't mean a kind of "I'm OK, you're OK" mushiness. For a leader, that is, it doesn't mean adopting other people's emotions as one's own and trying to please everybody. That would be a nightmare—it would make action impossible. Rather, empathy means thoughtfully considering employees' feelings—along with other factors—in the process of making intelligent decisions.

For an example of empathy in action, consider what happened when two giant brokerage companies merged, creating redundant jobs in all their divisions. One division manager called his people together and gave a gloomy speech that emphasized the number of people who would soon be fired. The manager of another division gave his people a different kind of speech. He was up-front about his own worry and confusion, and he promised to keep people informed and to treat everyone fairly.

The difference between these two managers was empathy. The first manager was too worried about his own fate to consider the feelings of his anxiety-stricken colleagues. The second knew intuitively what his people were feeling, and he acknowledged their fears with his words. Is it any surprise that the first manager saw his division sink as many demoralized people, especially the most talented, departed? By contrast, the second manager continued to be a strong leader, his best people stayed, and his division remained as productive as ever.

Empathy is particularly important today as a component of leadership for at least three reasons: the increasing use of teams; the rapid pace of globalization; and the growing need to retain talent.

Consider the challenge of leading a team. As anyone who has ever been a part of one can attest, teams are cauldrons of bubbling emotions. They are often charged with reaching a consensus—which is hard enough with two people and much more difficult as the numbers increase. Even in groups with as few as four or five members, alliances form and clashing agendas get set. A team's leader must be able to sense and understand the viewpoints of everyone around the table.

That's exactly what a marketing manager at a large information technology company was able to do when she was appointed to lead a troubled team. The group was in turmoil, overloaded by work and missing deadlines. Tensions were high among the members. Tinkering with procedures was not enough to bring the group together and make it an effective part of the company.

So the manager took several steps. In a series of one-on-one sessions, she took the time to listen to everyone in the group—what was frustrating them, how they rated their colleagues, whether they felt they had been ignored. And then she directed the team in a way that brought it together: She encouraged people to speak more openly about their frustrations, and she helped people raise constructive complaints during meetings. In short, her empathy allowed her to understand her team's emotional makeup. The result was not just heightened collaboration among members but also added business, as the team was called on for help by a wider range of internal clients.

Globalization is another reason for the rising importance of empathy for business leaders. Cross-cultural dialogue can easily lead to miscues and misunderstandings. Empathy is an antidote. People who have it are attuned to subtleties in body language; they can hear the message beneath the words being spoken. Beyond that, they have a deep understanding of both the existence and the importance of cultural and ethnic differences.

Consider the case of an American consultant whose team had just pitched a project to a potential Japanese client. In its dealings with Americans, the team was accustomed to being bombarded with questions after such a proposal, but this time it was greeted with a long silence. Other members of the team, taking the silence as disapproval, were ready to pack and leave. The lead consultant gestured them to stop. Although he was not particularly familiar with Japanese culture, he read the client's face and posture and sensed not rejection but interest—even deep consideration. He was right: When the client finally spoke, it was to give the consulting firm the job.

Finally, empathy plays a key role in the retention of talent, particularly in today's information economy. Leaders have always needed empathy to develop and keep good people, but today the stakes are higher. When good people leave, they take the company's knowledge with them.

That's where coaching and mentoring come in. It has repeatedly been shown that coaching and mentoring pay off not just in better performance but also in increased job satisfaction and decreased turnover. But what makes coaching and mentoring work best is the nature of the relationship. Outstanding coaches and mentors get inside the heads of the people they are helping. They sense how to give effective feedback. They know when to push for better performance and when to hold back. In the way they motivate their protégés, they demonstrate empathy in action.

In what is probably sounding like a refrain, let me repeat that empathy doesn't get much respect in business. People wonder how leaders can make hard decisions if they are "feeling" for all the people who will be affected. But leaders with empathy do more than sympathize with people around them: They use their knowledge to improve their companies in subtle but important ways.

Social Skill

The first three components of emotional intelligence are self-management skills. The last two, empathy and social skill, concern a person's ability to manage relationships with others. As a component of emotional intelligence, social skill is not as simple as it sounds. It's not just a matter of friendliness, although people with high levels of social skill are rarely mean-spirited. Social skill, rather, is friendliness with a purpose: moving people in the direction you desire, whether that's agreement on a new marketing strategy or enthusiasm about a new product.

Socially skilled people tend to have a wide circle of acquaintances, and they have a knack for finding common ground with people of all kinds—a knack for building rapport. That doesn't mean they socialize continually; it means they work according to the assumption that nothing important gets done alone. Such people have a network in place when the time for action comes.

Social skill is the culmination of the other dimensions of emotional intelligence. People tend to be very effective at managing relationships when they can understand and control their own emotions and can empathize with the feelings of others. Even motivation contributes to social skill. Remember that people who are driven to achieve tend to be optimistic, even in the face of setbacks or failure. When people are upbeat, their "glow" is cast upon conversations and other social encounters. They are popular, and for good reason.

Because it is the outcome of the other dimensions of emotional intelligence, social skill is recognizable on the job in many ways that will by now sound familiar. Socially skilled people, for instance, are adept at managing teams—that's their empathy at work. Likewise, they are expert persuaders—a manifestation of self-awareness, self-regulation, and empathy combined. Given those skills, good persuaders know when to make an emotional plea, for instance, and when an appeal to reason will work better. And motivation, when publicly visible, makes such people excellent collaborators; their passion for the work spreads to others, and they are driven to find solutions.

But sometimes social skill shows itself in ways the other emotional intelligence components do not. For instance, socially skilled people may at times appear not to be working while at work. They seem to be idly schmoozing—chatting in the hallways with colleagues or joking around with people who are not even connected to their "real" jobs. Socially skilled people, however, don't think it makes sense to arbitrarily limit the scope of their relationships. They build bonds widely because they know that in these fluid times, they may need help someday from people they are just getting to know today.

For example, consider the case of an executive in the strategy department of a global computer manufacturer. By 1993, he was convinced that the company's future lay with the Internet. Over the course of the next year, he found kindred spirits and used his social skill to stitch together a virtual community that cut across levels, divisions, and nations. He then used this de facto team to put up a corporate Web site, among the first by a major company. And, on his own initiative, with no budget or formal status, he signed up the company to participate in an annual Internet industry convention. Calling on his allies and persuading various divisions to donate funds, he recruited more than 50 people from a dozen different units to represent the company at the convention.

Management took notice: Within a year of the conference, the executive's team formed the basis for the company's first Internet division, and he was formally put in charge of it. To get there, the executive had ignored conventional boundaries, forging and maintaining connections with people in every corner of the organization.

Is social skill considered a key leadership capability in most companies? The answer is yes, especially when compared with the other components of emotional intelligence. People seem to know intuitively that leaders need to manage relationships effectively; no leader is an island. After all, the leader's task is to get work done through other people, and social skill makes that possible. A leader who cannot express her empathy may as well not have it at all. And a leader's motivation will be useless if he cannot communicate his passion to the organization. Social skill allows leaders to put their emotional intelligence to work.

It would be foolish to assert that good-old-fashioned IQ and technical ability are not important ingredients in strong leadership. But the recipe would not be complete without emotional intelligence. It was once thought that the components of emotional intelligence were "nice to have" in business leaders. But now we know that, for the sake of performance, these are ingredients that leaders "need to have."

It is fortunate, then, that emotional intelligence can be learned. The process is not easy. It takes time and, most of all, commitment. But the benefits that come from having a well-developed emotional intelligence, both for the individual and for the organization, make it worth the effort.

Originally published in June 1996. Reprint R0401H

Putting the Balanced Scorecard to Work

by Robert S. Kaplan and David P. Norton

TODAY'S MANAGERS RECOGNIZE the impact that measures have on performance. But they rarely think of measurement as an essential part of their strategy. For example, executives may introduce new strategies and innovative operating processes intended to achieve breakthrough performance, then continue to use the same short-term financial indicators they have used for decades, measures like return-on-investment, sales growth, and operating income. These managers fail not only to introduce new measures to monitor new goals and processes but also to question whether or not their old measures are relevant to the new initiatives.

Effective measurement, however, must be an integral part of the management process. The balanced scorecard, first proposed in the January–February 1992 issue of HBR ("The Balanced Scorecard—Measures that Drive Performance"), provides executives with a comprehensive framework that translates a company's strategic objectives into a coherent set of performance measures. Much more than a measurement exercise, the balanced scorecard is a management system that can motivate breakthrough improvements in such critical areas as product, process, customer, and market development.

The scorecard presents managers with four different perspectives from which to choose measures. It complements traditional financial indicators with measures of performance for customers, internal processes, and innovation and improvement activities. These measures differ from those traditionally used by companies in a few important ways:

Clearly, many companies already have myriad operational and physical measures for local activities. But these local measures are bottom-up and derived from ad hoc processes. The scorecard's measures, on the other hand, are grounded in an organization's strategic objectives and competitive demands. And, by requiring managers to select a limited number of critical indicators within each of the four perspectives, the scorecard helps focus this strategic vision.

In addition, while traditional financial measures report on what happened last period without indicating how managers can improve performance in the next, the scorecard functions as the cornerstone of a company's current *and* future success.

Moreover, unlike conventional metrics, the information from the four perspectives provides balance between external measures like operating income and internal measures like new product development. This balanced set of measures both reveals the trade-offs that managers have already made among performance measures and encourages them to achieve their goals in the future without making trade-offs among key success factors.

Finally, many companies that are now attempting to implement local improvement programs such as process reengineering, total quality, and employee empowerment lack a sense of integration. The balanced scorecard can serve as the focal point for the organization's efforts, defining and communicating priorities to managers, employees, investors, even customers. As a senior executive at one major company said, "Previously, the one-year budget was our primary management planning device. The balanced scorecard is now used as the language, the benchmark against which all new projects and businesses are evaluated."

The balanced scorecard is not a template that can be applied to businesses in general or even industrywide. Different market situations, product strategies, and competitive environments require different scorecards. Business units devise customized scorecards to fit

Idea in Brief

What makes a balanced scorecard special? Four characteristics stand out:

1. **It is a top-down reflection of the company's mission and strategy.** By contrast, the measures most companies track are bottom-up: deriving from local activities or ad hoc processes, they are often irrelevant to the overall strategy.

2. **It is forward-looking.** It addresses current and future success. Traditional financial measures describe how the company performed during the last reporting period—without indicating how managers can improve performance during the next

3. **It integrates external and internal measures.** This helps managers see where they have made trade-offs between performance measures in the past and helps ensure that future success on one measure does not come at the expense of another.

4. **It helps you focus.** Many companies track more measures than they can possibly use. But a balanced scorecard requires managers to reach agreement on only those measures that are most critical to the success of the company's strategy. Fifteen to twenty distinct measures are usually enough, each measure custom-designed for the unit to which it applies.

their mission, strategy, technology, and culture. In fact, a critical test of a scorecard's success is its transparency: from the 15 to 20 scorecard measures, an observer should be able to see through to the business unit's competitive strategy. A few examples will illustrate how the scorecard uniquely combines management and measurement in different companies.

Rockwater: Responding to a Changing Industry

Rockwater, a wholly owned subsidiary of Brown & Root/Halliburton, a global engineering and construction company, is a worldwide leader in underwater engineering and construction. Norman

Idea in Practice

Linking measurements to strategy is the heart of a successful scorecard development process. The three key questions to ask here:

1. If we succeed with our vision and strategy, how will we look different

   - to our shareholders and customers?

   - in terms of our internal processes?

   - in terms of our ability to innovate and grow?

2. What are the critical success factors in each of the four scorecard perspectives?

3. What are the key measurements that will tell us whether we're addressing those success factors as planned?

The balanced scorecard also brings an organizational focus to the variety of local change programs under way in a company at any given time. As the benchmark against which all new projects are evaluated, the scorecard functions as more than just a measurement system. In the words of FMC Corp. executive Larry Brady, it becomes "the cornerstone of the way you run the business," that is, "the core of the management system" itself.

Example: Rockwater, an underwater engineering and construction firm, crafted a five-pronged

strategy: to provide services that surpassed customers' expectations and needs; to achieve high levels of customer satisfaction; to make continuous improvements in safety, equipment reliability, responsiveness, and cost effectiveness; to recruit and retain high-quality employees; and to realize shareholder expectations. Using the balanced scorecard, Rockwater's senior management translated this strategy into tangible goals and actions.

- The financial measures they chose included return-on-capital employed and cash flow, because shareholders had indicated a preference for short-term results.

- Customer measures focused on those clients most interested in a high value-added relationship.

- The company introduced new benchmarks that emphasized the integration of key internal processes. It also added a safety index as a means of controlling indirect costs associated with accidents.

- Learning and growth targets emphasized the percentage of revenue coming from new services and the rate of improvement of safety and rework measures.

Chambers, hired as CEO in late 1989, knew that the industry's competitive world had changed dramatically. "In the 1970s, we were a bunch of guys in wet suits diving off barges into the North Sea with burning torches," Chambers said. But competition in the subsea contracting business had become keener in the 1980s, and many smaller companies left the industry. In addition, the focus of competition had shifted. Several leading oil companies wanted to develop long-term partnerships with their suppliers rather than choose suppliers based on low-price competition.

With his senior management team, Chambers developed a vision: "As our customers' preferred provider, we shall be the industry leader in providing the highest standards of safety and quality to our clients." He also developed a strategy to implement the vision. The five elements of that strategy were: services that surpass customers' expectations and needs; high levels of customer satisfaction; continuous improvement of safety, equipment reliability, responsiveness, and cost effectiveness; high-quality employees; and realization of shareholder expectations. Those elements were in turn developed into strategic objectives (see the chart "Rockwater's Strategic Objectives"). If, however, the strategic objectives were to create value for the company, they had to be translated into tangible goals and actions.

Rockwater's senior management team transformed its vision and strategy into the balanced scorecard's four sets of performance measures (see the chart "Rockwater's Balanced Scorecard").

Financial measures
The financial perspective included three measures of importance to the shareholder. Return-on-capital-employed and cash flow reflected preferences for short-term results, while forecast reliability signaled the corporate parent's desire to reduce the historical uncertainty caused by unexpected variations in performance. Rockwater management added two financial measures. Project profitability provided focus on the project as the basic unit for planning and control, and sales backlog helped reduce uncertainty of performance.

Rockwater's strategic objectives

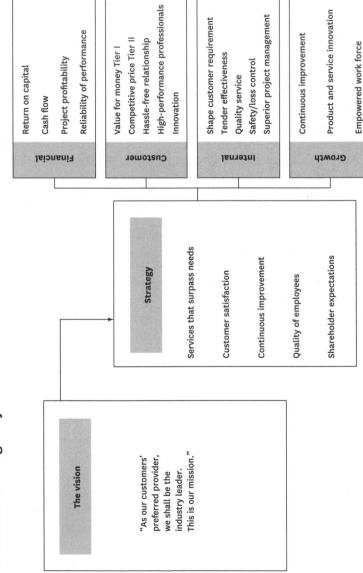

The vision

"As our customers' preferred provider, we shall be the industry leader. This is our mission."

Strategy

Services that surpass needs

Customer satisfaction

Continuous improvement

Quality of employees

Shareholder expectations

Financial

Return on capital

Cash flow

Project profitability

Reliability of performance

Customer

Value for money Tier I

Competitive price Tier II

Hassle-free relationship

High-performance professionals

Innovation

Internal

Shape customer requirement

Tender effectiveness

Quality service

Safety/loss control

Superior project management

Growth

Continuous improvement

Product and service innovation

Empowered work force

Rockwater's balanced scorecard

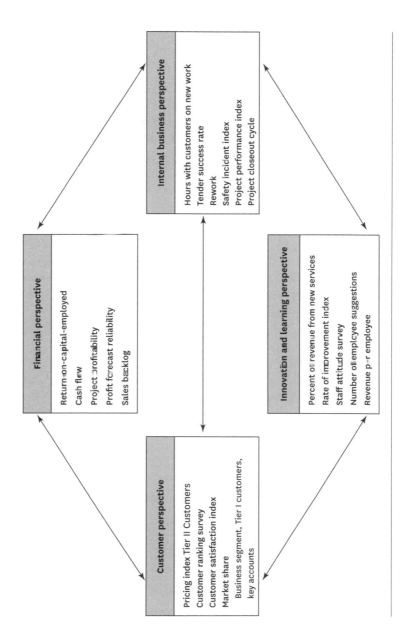

Financial perspective

Return-on-capital-employed
Cash flow
Project profitability
Profit forecast reliability
Sales backlog

Internal business perspective

Hours with customers on new work
Tender success rate
Rework
Safety incident index
Project performance index
Project closeout cycle

Customer perspective

Pricing index Tier II Customers
Customer ranking survey
Customer satisfaction index
Market share
Business segment, Tier I customers,
key accounts

Innovation and learning perspective

Percent of revenue from new services
Rate of improvement index
Staff attitude survey
Number of employee suggestions
Revenue per employee

Customer satisfaction

Rockwater wanted to recognize the distinction between its two types of customers: Tier I customers, oil companies that wanted a high value-added relationship, and Tier II customers, those that chose suppliers solely on the basis of price. A price index, incorporating the best available intelligence on competitive position, was included to ensure that Rockwater could still retain Tier II customers' business when required by competitive conditions.

The company's strategy, however, was to emphasize value-based business. An independent organization conducted an annual survey to rank customers' perceptions of Rockwater's services compared to those of its competitors. In addition, Tier I customers were asked to supply monthly satisfaction and performance ratings. Rockwater executives felt that implementing these ratings gave them a direct tie to their customers and a level of market feedback unsurpassed in most industries. Finally, market share by key accounts provided objective evidence that improvements in customer satisfaction were being translated into tangible benefits.

Internal Processes

To develop measures of internal processes, Rockwater executives defined the life cycle of a project from launch (when a customer need was recognized) to completion (when the customer need had been satisfied). Measures were formulated for each of the five business-process phases in this project cycle (see the chart "How Rockwater Fulfills Customer Needs"):

- *Identify:* number of hours spent with prospects discussing new work;

- *Win:* tender success rate;

- *Prepare and Deliver:* project performance effectiveness index, safety/loss control, rework;

- *Closeout*: length of project closeout cycle.

The internal business measures emphasized a major shift in Rockwater's thinking. Formerly, the company stressed performance for each functional department. The new focus emphasized measures that integrated key business processes. The development of a comprehensive and timely index of project performance effectiveness was viewed as a key core competency for the company. Rockwater felt that safety was also a major competitive factor. Internal studies had revealed that the indirect costs from an accident could be 5 to 50 times the direct costs. The scorecard included a safety index, derived from a comprehensive safety measurement system, that could identify and classify all undesired events with the potential for harm to people, property, or process.

The Rockwater team deliberated about the choice of metric for the identification stage. It recognized that hours spent with key prospects discussing new work was an input or process measure rather than an output measure. The management team wanted a metric that would clearly communicate to all members of the organization the importance of building relationships with and satisfying customers. The team believed that spending quality time with key customers was a prerequisite for influencing results. This input measure was deliberately chosen to educate employees about the importance of working closely to identify and satisfy customer needs.

How Rockwater fulfills customer needs

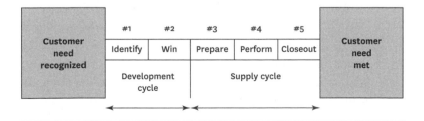

Innovation and improvement

The innovation and learning objectives are intended to drive improvement in financial, customer, and internal process performance. At Rockwater, such improvements came from product and service innovation that would create new sources of revenue and market expansion, as well as from continuous improvement in internal work processes. The first objective was measured by percent revenue from new services and the second objective by a continuous improvement index that represented the rate of improvement of several key operational measures, such as safety and rework. But in order to drive both product/service innovation and operational improvements, a supportive climate of empowered, motivated employees was believed necessary. A staff attitude survey and a metric for the number of employee suggestions measured whether or not such a climate was being created. Finally, revenue per employee measured the outcomes of employee commitment and training programs.

The balanced scorecard has helped Rockwater's management emphasize a process view of operations, motivate its employees, and incorporate client feedback into its operations. It developed a consensus on the necessity of creating partnerships with key customers, the importance of order-of-magnitude reductions in safety-related incidents, and the need for improved management at every phase of multiyear projects. Chambers sees the scorecard as an invaluable tool to help his company ultimately achieve its mission: to be number one in the industry.

Apple Computer: Adjusting Long-Term Performance

Apple Computer developed a balanced scorecard to focus senior management on a strategy that would expand discussions beyond gross margin, return on equity, and market share. A small steering committee, intimately familiar with the deliberations and strategic thinking of Apple's Executive Management Team, chose to concentrate on measurement categories within each of the four perspectives and to select multiple measurements within each category. For the financial perspective, Apple emphasized shareholder value; for the customer perspective, market share and customer satisfaction; for the internal process perspective, core competencies; and, finally, for the innovation and improvement perspective, employee attitudes. Apple's management stressed these categories in the following order.

Customer satisfaction

Historically, Apple had been a technology- and product-focused company that competed by designing better computers. Customer satisfaction metrics are just being introduced to orient employees toward becoming a customer-driven company. J.D. Power & Associates, a customer-survey company, now works for the computer industry. However, because it recognized that its customer base was not homogeneous, Apple felt that it had to go beyond J.D. Power & Associates and develop its own independent surveys in order to track its key market segments around the world.

Core competencies

Company executives wanted employees to be highly focused on a few key competencies: for example, user-friendly interfaces, powerful software architectures, and effective distribution systems. However, senior executives recognized that measuring performance along these competency dimensions could be difficult. As a result, the company is currently experimenting with obtaining quantitative measures of these hard-to-measure competencies.

Employee commitment and alignment

Apple conducts a comprehensive employee survey in each of its organizations every two years; surveys of randomly selected employees are performed more frequently. The survey questions are concerned with how well employees understand the company's strategy as well as whether or not they are asked to deliver results that are consistent with that strategy. The results of the survey are displayed in terms of both the actual level of employee responses and the overall trend of responses.

Market share

Achieving a critical threshold of market share was important to senior management not only for the obvious sales growth benefits but also to attract and retain software developers to Apple platforms.

Shareholder value

Shareholder value is included as a performance indicator, even though this measure is a result—not a driver—of performance. The measure is included to offset the previous emphasis on gross margin and sales growth, measures that ignored the investments required today to generate growth for tomorrow. In contrast, the shareholder value metric quantifies the impact of proposed investments for business creation and development. The majority of Apple's business is organized on a functional basis—sales, product design, and worldwide manufacturing and operations—so shareholder value can be calculated only for the entire company instead of at a decentralized level. The measure, however, helps senior managers in each major organizational unit assess the impact of their activities on the entire company's valuation and evaluate new business ventures.

While these five performance indicators have only recently been developed, they have helped Apple's senior managers focus their strategy in a number of ways. First of all, the balanced scorecard at Apple serves primarily as a planning device, instead of as a control device. To put it another way, Apple uses the measures to adjust the "long wave" of corporate performance, not to drive operating changes. Moreover, the metrics at Apple, with the exception of shareholder value, can be driven both horizontally and vertically into each functional organization. Considered vertically, each individual measure can be broken down into its component parts in order to evaluate how each part contributes to the functioning of the whole. Thought of horizontally, the measures can identify how, for example, design and manufacturing contribute to an area such as customer satisfaction. In addition, Apple has found that its balanced scorecard has helped develop a language of measurable outputs for how to launch and leverage programs.

The five performance indicators at Apple are benchmarked against best-in-class organizations. Today they are used to build business plans and are incorporated into senior executives' compensation plans.

Advanced Micro Devices: Consolidating Strategic Information

Advanced Micro Devices (AMD), a semiconductor company, executed a quick and easy transition to a balanced scorecard. It already had a clearly defined mission, strategy statement, and shared understanding among senior executives about its competitive niche. It also had many performance measures from many different sources and information systems. The balanced scorecard consolidated and focused these diverse measures into a quarterly briefing book that contained seven sections: financial measures; customer-based measures, such as on-time delivery, lead time, and performance-to-schedule; measures of critical business processes in wafer fabrication, assembly and test, new product development, process technology development (e.g., submicron etching precision); and, finally, measures for corporate quality. In addition, organizational learning was measured by imposing targeted rates of improvements for key operating parameters, such as cycle time and yields by process.

At present, AMD sees its scorecard as a systematic repository for strategic information that facilitates long-term trend analysis for planning and performance evaluation.

Driving the Process of Change

The experiences of these companies and others reveal that the balanced scorecard is most successful when it is used to drive the process of change. Rockwater, for instance, came into existence after the merger of two different organizations. Employees came from different cultures, spoke different languages, and had different operating experiences and backgrounds. The balanced scorecard

Building a balanced scorecard

Each organization is unique and so follows its own path for building a balanced scorecard. At Apple and AMD, for instance, a senior finance or business development executive, intimately familiar with the strategic thinking of the top management group, constructed the initial scorecard without extensive deliberations. At Rockwater, however, senior management had yet to define sharply the organization's strategy, much less the key performance levers that drive and measure the strategy's success.

Companies like Rockwater can follow a systematic development plan to create the balanced scorecard and encourage commitment to the scorecard among senior and mid-level managers. What follows is a typical project profile:

1. Preparation

The organization must first define the business unit for which a top-level scorecard is appropriate. In general, a scorecard is appropriate for a business unit that has its own customers, distribution channels, production facilities, and financial performance measures.

2. Interviews: First Round

Each senior manager in the business unit—typically between 6 and 12 executives—receives background material on the balanced scorecard as well as internal documents that describe the company's vision, mission, and strategy.

The balanced scorecard facilitator (either an outside consultant or the company executive who organizes the effort) conducts interviews of approximately 90 minutes each with the senior managers to obtain their input on the company's strategic objectives and tentative proposals for balanced scorecard measures. The facilitator may also interview some principal shareholders to learn about their expectations for the business unit's financial performance, as well as some key customers to learn about their performance expectations for top-ranked suppliers.

3. Executive Workshop: First Round

The top management team is brought together with the facilitator to undergo the process of developing the scorecard (see the chart "Begin by Linking Measurements to Strategy"). During the workshop, the group debates the proposed mission and strategy statements until a consensus is reached. The group then moves from the mission and strategy statement to answer the question, "If I succeed with my vision and strategy, how will my performance differ for shareholders; for customers; for internal business processes; for my ability to innovate, grow, and improve?"

Videotapes of interviews with shareholder and customer representatives can be shown to provide an external perspective to the deliberations. After defining the key success factors, the group formulates a preliminary balanced scorecard containing operational measures for the strategic objectives. Frequently, the group proposes far more than four or five measures for each perspective. At this time, narrowing the choices is not critical, though straw votes can be taken to see whether or not some of the proposed measures are viewed as low priority by the group.

4. Interviews: Second Round

The facilitator reviews, consolidates, and documents the output from the executive workshop and interviews each senior executive about the tentative balanced scorecard. The facilitator also seeks opinions about issues involved in implementing the scorecard.

5. Executive Workshop: Second Round

A second workshop, involving the senior management team, their direct subordinates, and a larger number of middle managers, debates the organization's vision, strategy statements, and the tentative scorecard. The participants, working in groups, comment on the proposed measures, link the various change programs under way to the measures, and start to develop an implementation plan. At the end of the workshop, participants are asked to formulate stretch objectives for each of the proposed measures, including targeted rates of improvement.

6. Executive Workshop: Third Round

The senior executive team meets to come to a final consensus on the vision, objectives, and measurements developed in the first two workshops; to develop stretch targets for each measure on the scorecard; and to identify preliminary action programs to achieve the targets. The team must agree on an implementation program, including communicating the scorecard to employees, integrating the scorecard into a management philosophy, and developing an information system to support the scorecard.

7. Implementation

A newly formed team develops an implementation plan for the scorecard, including linking the measures to databases and information systems, communicating the balanced scorecard throughout the organization, and

(continued)

encouraging and facilitating the development of second-level metrics for decentralized units. As a result of this process, for instance, an entirely new executive information system that links top-level business unit metrics down through shop floor and site-specific operational measures could be developed.

8. Periodic Reviews

Each quarter or month, a blue book of information on the balanced scorecard measures is prepared for both top management review and discussion with managers of decentralized divisions and departments. The balanced scorecard metrics are revisited annually as part of the strategic planning, goal setting, and resource allocation processes.

Begin by linking measurements to strategy

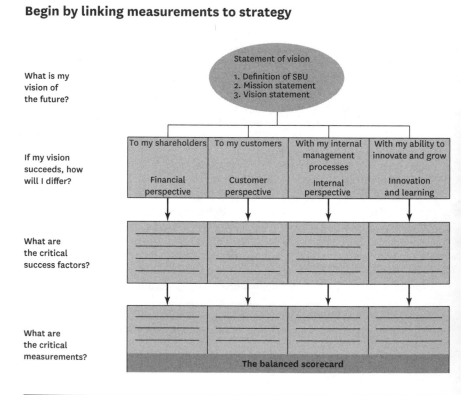

helped the company focus on what it had to do well in order to become the industry leader.

Similarly, Joseph De Feo, chief executive of Service Businesses, one of the three operating divisions of Barclays Bank, had to transform what had been a captive, internal supplier of services into a global competitor. The scorecard highlighted areas where, despite apparent consensus on strategy, there still was considerable disagreement about how to make the strategy operational. With the help of the scorecard, the division eventually achieved consensus concerning the highest priority areas for achievement and improvement and identified additional areas that needed attention, such as quality and productivity. De Feo assessed the impact of the scorecard, saying, "It helped us to drive major change, to become more market oriented, throughout our organization. It provided a shared understanding of our goals and what it took to achieve them."

Analog Devices, a semiconductor company, served as the prototype for the balanced scorecard and now uses it each year to update the targets and goals for division managers. Jerry Fishman, president of Analog, said, "At the beginning, the scorecard drove significant and considerable change. It still does when we focus attention on particular areas, such as the gross margins on new products. But its main impact today is to help sustain programs that our people have been working on for years." Recently, the company has been attempting to integrate the scorecard metrics with *hoshin* planning, a procedure that concentrates an entire company on achieving one or two key objectives each year. Analog's hoshin objectives have included customer service and new product development, for which measures already exist on the company's scorecard.

But the scorecard isn't always the impetus for such dramatic change. For example, AMD's scorecard has yet to have a significant impact because company management didn't use it to drive the change process. Before turning to the scorecard, senior managers had already formulated and gained consensus for the company's mission, strategy, and key performance measures. AMD competes in a single industry segment. The top 12 managers are intimately familiar with the markets, engineering, technology, and other key

The Scorecard's Impact on External Reporting

SEVERAL MANAGERS HAVE ASKED whether or not the balanced scorecard is applicable to external reporting. If the scorecard is indeed a driver of long-term performance, shouldn't this information be relevant to the investment community?

In fact, the scorecard does not translate easily to the investment community. A scorecard makes sense primarily for business units and divisions with a well-defined strategy. Most companies have several divisions, each with its own mission and strategy, whose scorecards cannot be aggregated into an overall corporate scorecard. And if the scorecard does indeed provide a transparent vision into a unit's strategy, then the information, even the measures being used, might be highly sensitive data that could reveal much of value to competitors. But most important, as a relatively recent innovation, the scorecard would benefit from several years of experimentation within companies before it becomes a systematic part of reporting to external constituencies.

Even if the scorecard itself were better suited to external reporting, at present the financial community itself shows little interest in making the change from financial to strategic reporting. One company president has found the outside financial community leery of the principles that ground the scorecard: "We use the scorecard more with our customers than with our investors. The financial community is skeptical about long-term indicators and occasionally tells us about some empirical evidence of a negative correlation between stock prices and attention to total quality and internal processes."

However, the investment community has begun to focus on some key metrics of new product performance. Could this be an early sign of a shift to strategic thinking?

---

levers in this segment. The summary and aggregate information in the scorecard were neither new nor surprising to them. And managers of decentralized production units also already had a significant amount of information about their own operations. The scorecard did enable them to see the breadth and totality of company operations, enhancing their ability to become better managers for the entire company. But, on balance, the scorecard could only encapsulate knowledge that managers in general had already learned.

AMD's limited success with the balanced scorecard demonstrates that the scorecard has its greatest impact when used to drive a change process. Some companies link compensation of senior executives to achieving stretch targets for the scorecard measures. Most are attempting to translate the scorecard into operational measures that become the focus for improvement activities in local units. The scorecard is not just a measurement system; it is a management system to motivate breakthrough competitive performance.

Implementing the Balanced Scorecard at FMC Corporation: An Interview with Larry D. Brady

FMC Corporation is one of the most diversified companies in the United States, producing more than 300 product lines in 21 divisions organized into 5 business segments: industrial chemicals, performance chemicals, precious metals, defense systems, and machinery and equipment. Based in Chicago, FMC has worldwide revenues in excess of $4 billion.

Since 1984, the company has realized annual returns-on-investment of greater than 15%. Coupled with a major recapitalization in 1986, these returns resulted in an increasing shareholder value that significantly exceeded industrial averages. In 1992, the company completed a strategic review to determine the best future course to maximize shareholder value. As a result of that review, FMC adopted a growth strategy to complement its strong operating performance. This strategy required a greater external focus and appreciation of operating trade-offs.

To help make the shift, the company decided to use the balanced scorecard. In this interview conducted by Robert S. Kaplan, Larry D. Brady, executive vice president of FMC, talks about the company's experience implementing the scorecard.

Robert S. Kaplan: *What's the status of the balanced scorecard at FMC?*

Larry D. Brady: Although we are just completing the pilot phase of implementation, I think that the balanced scorecard is likely to become the cornerstone of the management system at FMC. It enables us to translate business unit strategies into a measurement system that meshes with our entire system of management.

For instance, one manager reported that while his division had measured many operating variables in the past, now, because of the scorecard, it had chosen 12 parameters as the key to its strategy implementation. Seven of these strategic variables were entirely new measurements for the division. The manager interpreted this finding as verifying what many other managers were reporting: the scorecard improved the understanding and consistency of strategy implementation. Another manager reported that, unlike monthly financial statements or even his strategic plan, if a rival were to see his scorecard, he would lose his competitive edge.

It's rare to get that much enthusiasm among divisional managers for a corporate initiative. What led you and them to the balanced scorecard?

FMC had a clearly defined mission: to become our customers' most valued supplier. We had initiated many of the popular improvement programs: total quality, managing by objectives, organizational effectiveness, building a high-performance organization. But these efforts had not been effective. Every time we promoted a new program, people in each division would sit back and ask, "How is that supposed to fit in with the six other things we're supposed to be doing?"

Corporate staff groups were perceived by operating managers as pushing their pet programs on divisions. The diversity of initiatives, each with its own slogan, created confusion and mixed signals about where to concentrate and how the various programs interrelated. At the end of the day, with all these new initiatives, we were still asking division managers to deliver consistent short-term financial performance.

What kinds of measures were you using?

The FMC corporate executive team, like most corporate offices, reviews the financial performance of each operating division monthly. As a highly diversified company that redeploys assets from mature cash generators to divisions with significant growth opportunities, the return-on-capital-employed (ROCE) measure was especially important for us. We were one of the few companies to in-flation-adjust our internal financial measures so that we could get a more accurate picture of a division's economic profitability.

At year-end, we rewarded division managers who delivered pre-dictable financial performance. We had run the company tightly for the past 20 years and had been successful. But it was becoming less clear where future growth would come from and where the com-pany should look for breakthroughs into new areas. We had become a high return-on-investment company but had less potential for fur-ther growth. It was also not at all clear from our financial reports what progress we were making in implementing long-term initia-tives. Questions from the corporate office about spending versus budget also reinforced a focus on the short-term and on internal operations.

But the problem went even deeper than that. Think about it. What is the value added of a corporate office that concentrates on making division managers accountable for financial results that can be added up across divisions? We combine a business that's doing well with a business that's doing poorly and have a total business that performs at an average level. Why not split the company up into independent companies and let the market reallocate capital? If we were going to create value by managing a group of diversified com-panies, we had to understand and provide strategic focus to their op-erations. We had to be sure that each division had a strategy that would give it sustainable competitive advantage. In addition, we had to be able to assess, through measurement of their operations, whether or not the divisions were meeting their strategic objectives.

If you're going to ask a division or the corporation to change its strategy, you had better change the system of measurement to be consistent with the new strategy.

How did the balanced scorecard emerge as the remedy to the limitations of measuring only short-term financial results?

In early 1992, we assembled a task force to integrate our various corporate initiatives. We wanted to understand what had to be done differently to achieve dramatic improvements in overall organizational effectiveness. We acknowledged that the company may have become too short-term and too internally focused in its business measures. Defining what should replace the financial focus was more difficult. We wanted managers to sustain their search for continuous improvement, but we also wanted them to identify the opportunities for breakthrough performance.

When divisions missed financial targets, the reasons were generally not internal. Typically, division management had inaccurately estimated market demands or had failed to forecast competitive reactions. A new measurement system was needed to lead operating managers beyond achieving internal goals to searching for competitive breakthroughs in the global marketplace. The system would have to focus on measures of customer service, market position, and new products that could generate long-term value for the business. We used the scorecard as the focal point for the discussion. It forced division managers to answer these questions: How do we become our customers' most valued supplier? How do we become more externally focused? What is my division's competitive advantage? What is its competitive vulnerability?

How did you launch the scorecard effort at FMC?

We decided to try a pilot program. We selected six division managers to develop prototype scorecards for their operations. Each division had to perform a strategic analysis to identify its sources of competitive advantage. The 15 to 20 measures in the balanced scorecard had to be organization-specific and had to communicate clearly what short-term measures of operating performance were consistent with a long-term trajectory of strategic success.

Were the six division managers free to develop their own scorecard?

We definitely wanted the division managers to perform their own strategic analysis and to develop their own measures. That was an essential part of creating a consensus between senior and divisional management on operating objectives. Senior management did, however, place some conditions on the outcomes.

First of all, we wanted the measures to be objective and quantifiable. Division managers were to be just as accountable for improving scorecard measures as they had been for using monthly financial reviews. Second, we wanted output measures not process-oriented measures. Many of the improvement programs under way were emphasizing time, quality, and cost measurements. Focusing on T-Q-C measurements, however, encourages managers to seek narrow process improvements instead of breakthrough output targets. Focusing on achieving outputs forces division managers to understand their industry and strategy and help them to quantify strategic success through specific output targets.

Could you illustrate the distinction between process measures and output measures?

You have to understand your industry well to develop the connection between process improvements and outputs achieved. Take three divisional examples of cycle-time measurement, a common process measure.

For much of our defense business, no premium is earned for early delivery. And the contracts allow for reimbursement of inventory holding costs. Therefore, attempts to reduce inventory or cycle times in this business produce no benefit for which the customer is willing to pay. The only benefits from cycle time or inventory reduction occur when reduction in factory-floor complexity leads to real reductions in product cost. The output performance targets must be real cash savings, not reduced inventory levels or cycle times.

In contrast, significant lead-time reductions could be achieved for our packaging machinery business. This improvement led to lower inventory and an option to access an additional 35% of the market. In this case, the cycle-time improvements could be tied to specific targets for increased sales and market share. It wasn't linear, but output seemed to improve each time we improved throughput times.

And in one of our agricultural machinery businesses, orders come within a narrow time window each year. The current build cycle is longer than the ordering window, so all units must be built to the sales forecast. This process of building to forecast leads to high inventory—more than twice the levels of our other businesses—and frequent overstocking and obsolescence of equipment. Incremental reductions in lead time do little to change the economics of this operation. But if the build cycle time could be reduced to less than the six-week ordering time window for part or all of the build schedule, then a breakthrough occurs. The division can shift to a build-to-order schedule and eliminate the excess inventory caused by building to forecasts. In this case, the benefit from cycle-time reductions is a step-function that comes only when the cycle time drops below a critical level.

So here we have three businesses, three different processes, all of which could have elaborate systems for measuring quality, cost, and time but would feel the impact of improvements in radically different ways. With all the diversity in our business units, senior management really can't have a detailed understanding of the relative impact of time and quality improvements on each unit. All of our senior managers, however, understand output targets, particularly when they are displayed with historical trends and future targets.

Benchmarking has become popular with a lot of companies. Does it tie in to the balanced scorecard measurements?

Unfortunately, benchmarking is one of those initially good ideas that has turned into a fad. About 95% of those companies that have tried benchmarking have spent a lot of money and have gotten very little in return. And the difference between benchmarking and the scorecard helps reinforce the difference between process measures and output measures. It's a lot easier to benchmark a process than to benchmark an output. With the scorecard, we ask each division manager to go outside their organization and determine the approaches that will allow achievement of their long-term output targets. Each of our output measures has an associated long-term target. We have been deliberately vague on specifying when the target is to be accomplished. We want to stimulate a thought process about how to do things differently to achieve the target rather than how to do existing things better. The activity of searching externally for how others have accomplished these breakthrough achievements is called target verification not benchmarking.

Were the division managers able to develop such output-oriented measures?

Well, the division managers did encounter some obstacles. Because of the emphasis on output measures and the previous focus on operations and financial measures, the customer and innovation perspectives proved the most difficult. These were also the two areas where the balanced scorecard process was most helpful in refining and understanding our existing strategies.

But the initial problem was that the management teams ran afoul of both conditions: the measures they proposed tended to be non-quantifiable and input- rather than output-oriented. Several divisions wanted to conduct customer surveys and provide an index of the results. We judged a single index to be of little value and opted instead for harder measures such as price premiums over competitors.

We did conclude, however, that the full customer survey was an excellent vehicle for promoting external focus and, therefore, decided to use survey results to kick-off discussion at our annual operating reviews.

Did you encounter any problems as you launched the six pilot projects?

At first, several divisional managers were less than enthusiastic about the additional freedom they were being given from headquarters. They knew that the heightened visibility and transparency of the scorecard took away the internal trade-offs they had gained experience in making. They initially interpreted the increase in visibility of divisional performance as just the latest attempt by corporate staff to meddle in their internal business processes.

To offset this concern, we designed targets around long-term objectives. We still closely examine the monthly and quarterly statistics, but these statistics now relate to progress in achieving long-term objectives and justify the proper balance between short-term and long-term performance.

We also wanted to transfer quickly the focus from a measurement system to achieving performance results. A measurement orientation reinforces concerns about control and a short-term focus. By emphasizing targets rather than measurements, we could demonstrate our purpose to achieve breakthrough performance.

But the process was not easy. One division manager described his own three-stage implementation process after receiving our directive to build a balanced scorecard: denial—hope it goes away; medicinal—it won't go away, so let's do it quickly and get it over with; ownership—let's do it for ourselves.

In the end, we were successful. We now have six converts who are helping us to spread the message throughout the organization.

I understand that you have started to apply the scorecard not just to operating units but to staff groups as well.

Applying the scorecard approach to staff groups has been even more eye-opening than our initial work with the six operating divisions. We have done very little to define our strategy for corporate staff utilization. I doubt that many companies can respond crisply to the question, "How does staff provide competitive advantage?" Yet we ask that question every day about our line operations. We have just started to ask our staff departments to explain to us whether they are offering low-cost or differentiated services. If they are offering neither, we should probably outsource the function. This area is loaded with real potential for organizational development and improved strategic capability.

My conversations with financial people in organizations reveal some concern about the expanded responsibilities implied by developing and maintaining a balanced scorecard. How does the role of the controller change as a company shifts its primary measurement system from a purely financial one to the balanced scorecard?

Historically, we have had two corporate departments involved in overseeing business unit performance. Corporate development was in charge of strategy, and the controller's office kept the historical records and budgeted and measured short-term performance.

Strategists came up with five- and ten-year plans, controllers one-year budgets and near-term forecasts. Little interplay occurred between the two groups. But the scorecard now bridges the two. The financial perspective builds on the traditional function performed by controllers. The other three perspectives make the division's long-term strategic objectives measurable.

In our old environment, division managers tried to balance short-term profits with long-term growth, while they were receiving different signals depending on whether or not they were reviewing strategic plans or budgets. This structure did not make the balancing of short-term profits and long-term growth an easy trade-off, and, frankly, it let senior management off the hook when it came to sharing responsibility for making the trade-offs.

Perhaps the corporate controller should take responsibility for all measurement and goal setting, including the systems required to implement these processes. The new corporate controller could be an outstanding system administrator, knowledgeable about the various trade-offs and balances, and skillful in reporting and presenting them. This role does not eliminate the need for strategic planning. It just makes the two systems more compatible. The scorecard can serve to motivate and evaluate performance. But I see its primary value as its ability to join together what had been strong but separated capabilities in strategy development and financial control. It's the operating performance bridge that corporations have never had.

How often do you envision reviewing a division's balanced scorecard?

I think we will ask group managers to review a monthly submission from each of their divisions, but the senior corporate team will probably review scorecards quarterly on a rotating basis so that we can review up to seven or eight division scorecards each month.

Isn't it inconsistent to assess a division's strategy on a monthly or quarterly basis? Doesn't such a review emphasize short-term performance?

I see the scorecard as a strategic measurement system, not a measure of our strategy. And I think that's an important distinction.

The monthly or quarterly scorecard measures operations that have been configured to be consistent with our long-term strategy.

Here's an example of the interaction between the short and the long term. We have pushed division managers to choose measures that will require them to create change, for example, penetration of key markets in which we are not currently represented. We can measure that penetration monthly and get valuable short-term information about the ultimate success of our long-term strategy. Of course, some measures, such as annual market share and innovation metrics, don't lend themselves to monthly updates. For the most part, however, the measures are calculated monthly.

Any final thoughts on the scorecard?

I think that it's important for companies not to approach the scorecard as the latest fad. I sense that a number of companies are turning to scorecards in the same way they turned to total quality management, high-performance organization, and so on. You hear about a good idea, several people on corporate staff work on it, probably with some expensive outside consultants, and you put in a system that's a bit different from what existed before. Such systems are only incremental, and you don't gain much additional value from them.

It gets worse if you think of the scorecard as a new measurement system that eventually requires hundreds and thousands of measurements and a big, expensive executive information system. These companies lose sight of the essence of the scorecard: its focus, its simplicity, and its vision. The real benefit comes from making the scorecard the cornerstone of the way you run the business. It should be the core of the management system, not the measurement system. Senior managers alone will determine whether the scorecard becomes a mere record-keeping exercise or the lever to streamline and focus strategy that can lead to breakthrough performance.

Originally published in September 1993. Reprint 93505

Innovation

The Classic Traps. *by Rosabeth Moss Kanter*

INNOVATION IS BACK AT the top of the corporate agenda. Never a fad, but always in or out of fashion, innovation gets rediscovered as a growth enabler every half-dozen years (about the length of a managerial generation). Too often, however, grand declarations about innovation are followed by mediocre execution that produces anemic results, and innovation groups are quietly disbanded in cost-cutting drives. Each generation embarks on the same enthusiastic quest for the next new thing and faces the same challenge of overcoming innovation stiflers. Over the past 25 years, I have conducted research and advised companies during at least four major waves of competitive challenges that led to widespread enthusiasm for innovation.

The first was the dawn of the global information age in the late 1970s and early 1980s, an era that introduced new industries and threatened to topple old ones. Entrepreneurs and foreign competitors imperiled established companies on their own turf. Information technology was beginning to evolve from the clunky mainframe to a consumer and desktop product, and companies such as Apple Computer made Silicon Valley garages the new base for product innovation in the United States. IBM emulated Apple's model by developing its PC in dingy surroundings in Boca Raton, Florida, freed from many corporate constraints. High-quality Japanese products, such as the Sony Walkman and Toyota cars, reflected not just good product design but also innovations in manufacturing processes that forced

American giants to create their own programs to generate new ideas faster. "Total quality management" became a passion.

The second wave was the pressure to restructure during the takeover scare of the late 1980s. Buyout groups were attacking traditional companies, seeking to unlock the value of underutilized assets; "shareholder value" became a rallying cry. In Europe, restructuring was associated with the privatization of state-owned enterprises now exposed to the pressures of capital markets. Software was emerging as a major force behind innovation, and the strategic value of IT was touted, with American Airlines' Sabre reservations system widely cited as an example of a process innovation that succeeded as a separate business. Companies created new-venture departments to make sure they captured the value of their own ideas and inventions, rather than allowing a behemoth like Microsoft to arise outside the firm. Financial innovations were the rage: leveraged and management buyouts, derivatives and other forms of financial engineering, or financial supermarkets combining banks and nearly everything else. The restructuring era also favored products that could be instantly global: After defeating a hostile takeover bid in the late 1980s, Gillette boldly and successfully launched Sensor Excel shaving systems in the early 1990s, in identical form worldwide, with a single advertising message.

Third was the digital mania of the 1990s. The promise (and threat) of the World Wide Web drove many established companies to seek radical new business models. Brick-and-mortar companies were at risk for extinction; many rushed to create stand-alone Web ventures, often unconnected to the core business and sometimes in conflict with it. Eyes were on the capital markets rather than on customers, and companies got rich without profits or revenues. AOL bought Time Warner, put its name first, and proceeded to destroy value rather than create innovation.

The current wave of innovation began in a more sober mood, following the dot-com crash and belt-tightening of the global recession. Having recognized the limits of acquisitions and become skeptical about technology hype, companies refocused on organic growth. Surviving giants such as General Electric and IBM have

Idea in Brief

Most companies fuel growth by creating new products and services. Yet too many firms repeat the same growth-sapping mistakes in their efforts to innovate.

For example, some companies adopt the wrong strategy: investing only in ideas they think will become blockbusters. Result? Small ideas that could have generated big profits get rejected. For years, Time, Inc. didn't develop new publications: managers wanted any start-up to succeed on the same scale as the enormously popular *People* magazine. Only after Time decided to gamble on a large number of new publications did revenues rise.

Other companies err on the side of process-strangling innovations by subjecting them to the strict performance criteria their existing businesses must follow. At AlliedSignal, new Internet-based products and services had to satisfy the same financial metrics as established businesses. Budgets contained no funds for investment—so managers working on innovations had to find their own funding. The consequences? Retrofitted versions of old ideas.

To avoid such traps, Kanter advocates applying lessons from past failures to your innovation efforts. For instance, augment potential "big bets" with promising midrange ideas and incremental innovations. And add flexibility to your innovation planning, budgeting, and reviews.

Your reward? Better odds that the new ideas percolating in your company today will score profitable successes in the market tomorrow.

adopted innovation as a corporate theme. GE, for instance, is committed to double-digit growth from within. For its part, IBM is seeking innovation by tackling difficult social problems that require—and showcase—its technology solutions. A good example is World Community Grid, a nonprofit IBM created that aggregates unused computer power from numerous partners to give AIDS researchers and other scientists the ability to work with unusually large data sets. This wave's central focus is on new products designed to offer users new features and functionality to meet emerging needs. Customers and consumer markets have returned to center stage, after having been temporarily crowded out by other obsessions. Companies are seeking new categories to enrich their existing businesses rather than grand new ventures that will take them into totally different

Idea in Practice

To innovate successfully, replace common mistakes with potent remedies:

Strategy Mistakes

- Rejecting opportunities that at first glance appear too small.

- Assuming that only new products count—not new services or improved processes.

- Launching too many minor product extensions that confuse customers and increase internal complexity.

Remedy: Widen your search and broaden your scope. Support a few big bets at the top that represent clear directions for the future and receive the lion's share of investment. Also create a portfolio of promising midrange ideas. And fund a broad base of early stage ideas or incremental innovations.

Process Mistakes

- Strangling innovation with the same tight planning, budgeting, and reviews applied to existing businesses.

- Rewarding managers for doing only what they committed to do—and discouraging them from making changes as circumstances warrant.

Remedy: Add flexibility to planning and control systems. For instance, reserve special funds for unexpected opportunities.

Example: After executives at the struggling UK television network BBC set aside funds in a corporate account to support innovation proposals, a new recruit used money originally allocated for a new BBC training film to make a pilot for *The Office.* The show became the BBC's biggest hit comedy in decades.

Structure Mistakes

- Isolating fledgling and established enterprises in separate silos.

realms. Signature innovations in this era include Apple's iPod and Procter & Gamble's Swiffer.

Each wave brought new concepts. For example, the rise of biotechnology, characterized by complicated licensing arrangements, helped legitimize the idea that established firms could outsource R&D and learn from entrepreneurial partners or that consumer products companies could turn to external idea shops, as well as their own labs, to invent new products. Approaches to

- Creating two classes of corporate citizens—those who have all the fun (innovators) and those who must make the money (mainstream business managers).

Remedy: Tighten the human connections between innovators and others throughout your organization. Convene frequent conversations between innovators and mainstream business managers to promote mutual learning and integration of new businesses into the organization. Create overlapping relationships—by having representatives from mainstream businesses rotate through innovation groups or innovation advisory boards. Identify people who lead informal networks that span innovation and mainstream groups, and encourage them to strengthen those connections.

Skills Mistakes

- Allowing innovators to rotate out of teams so quickly that team chemistry can't gel.

- Assuming that innovation teams should be led by the best technical people.

Remedy: Select innovation leaders with strong interpersonal skills. They'll keep the innovation team intact, help innovation teams embrace collective goals, leverage one another's different strengths, and share hard-to-document knowledge while innovations are under development.

Example: When Williams-Sonoma launched its ultimately successful e-commerce group, it put a manager in charge who wasn't a technology expert but who could assemble the right team. He chose a mixture of employees from other units who could be ambassadors to their former groups and new hires that brought diverse skills.

innovation also reflected changing economic conditions and geopolitical events. And, of course, innovation has covered a wide spectrum, including technologies, products, processes, and complete business ventures, each with its own requirements.

Still, despite changes to the environment and differences among types of innovation, each wave of enthusiasm has encountered similar dilemmas. Most of these stem from the tensions between protecting revenue streams from existing businesses critical to

The Lessons of Innovation

INNOVATION GOES IN OR OUT of fashion as a strategic driver of corporate growth, but with every wave of enthusiasm, executives make the same mistakes. Most of the time, they stumble in their R&D efforts because they are engaged in a difficult balancing act: They need to protect existing revenue streams while coaxing along new ones. But "corporate entrepreneurship" doesn't have to be an oxymoron. Innovation can flourish if executives heed business lessons from the past.

Strategy Lessons

- Not every innovation idea has to be a blockbuster. Sufficient numbers of small or incremental innovations can lead to big profits.

- Don't just focus on new product development: Transformative ideas can come from any function—for instance, marketing, production, finance, or distribution.

- Successful innovators use an "innovation pyramid," with several big bets at the top that get most of the investment; a portfolio of promising midrange ideas in test stage; and a broad base of early stage ideas or incremental innovations. Ideas and influence can flow up or down the pyramid.

Process Lessons

- Tight controls strangle innovation. The planning, budgeting, and reviews applied to existing businesses will squeeze the life out of an innovation effort.

---

current success and supporting new concepts that may be crucial to future success. These tensions are exacerbated by the long-known phenomenon that important innovations often arise from outside an industry and beyond the established players, creating extra pressure for companies to find the next big concept quickly. Consequently, a large body of knowledge about innovation dilemmas has arisen.

Books such as Tom Peters and Bob Waterman's *In Search of Excellence,* my own *The Change Masters,* and Gifford Pinchot's *Intrapreneuring* supported the 1980s innovation wave by pointing to the importance of relieving potential innovators of bureaucratic constraints so they could run with their ideas. This was followed by

- Companies should expect deviations from plan: If employees are rewarded simply for doing what they committed to do, rather than acting as circumstances would suggest, their employers will stifle and drive out innovation.

Structure Lessons

- While loosening formal controls, companies should tighten interpersonal connections between innovation efforts and the rest of the business.

- Game-changing innovations often cut across established channels or combine elements of existing capacity in new ways.

- If companies create two classes of corporate citizens—supplying the innovators with more perks, privileges, and prestige—those in the existing business will make every effort to crush the innovation.

Skills Lessons

- Even the most technical of innovations requires strong leaders with great relationship and communication skills.

- Members of successful innovation teams stick together through the development of an idea, even if the company's approach to career timing requires faster job rotation.

- Because innovations need connectors—people who know how to find partners in the mainstream business or outside world—they flourish in cultures that encourage collaboration.

a body of work documenting the difficulty of exploring the new while exploiting the old, reflected in Michael Tushman and Charles O'Reilly's call for more ambidextrous organizations in *Winning Through Innovation;* my work on managing the tensions between the powerful organizational mainstream and fragile new streams produced by innovation groups in *When Giants Learn to Dance;* and Clayton Christensen's more recent finding, in *The Innovator's Dilemma,* that listening to current customers can inhibit breakthrough innovation.

Yet despite all the research and literature, I still observe executives exhibiting the same lack of courage or knowledge that undercut previous waves of innovation. They declare that they want more innovation but then ask, "Who else is doing it?" They claim to seek new ideas but shoot down every one brought to them. And, repeatedly, companies make the same mistakes as their predecessors. For example, a 1983 HBR article by Harvard Business School professor Malcolm Salter, et al., "When Corporate Venture Capital Doesn't Work," provided warnings that companies failed to heed about exactly the same dilemmas they face today: With a few notable exceptions, such as Intel and Reuters, companies' venture-capital departments rarely create significant value for the core business.

It's inevitable that historical memory will fade—but not inevitable that we lose the lessons. Here's a chance to collect some of what is known about innovation traps and how to avoid them.

Strategy Mistakes: Hurdles Too High, Scope Too Narrow

The potential for premium prices and high margins lures executives to seek blockbuster innovations—the next iPod, Viagra, or Toyota Production System. Along the way, they expend enormous resources, though big hits are rare and unpredictable. Meanwhile, in seeking the killer app, managers may reject opportunities that at first glance appear too small, and people who aren't involved in the big projects may feel marginalized.

For years, large consumer products companies typically screened out ideas that couldn't result in revenues of several hundred million dollars within two years. This screen discouraged investments in ideas that couldn't be tested and measured using conventional market research, or that weren't grounded in experience, in favor of ideas that were close to current practice and hardly innovative. In the 1980s and 1990s, Pillsbury, Quaker Oats, and even Procter & Gamble (an innovation powerhouse today) were vulnerable to smaller companies that could quickly roll out new products, thus eroding the giants' market share. P&G, for example, lamented not having introduced a new toilet bowl cleaner before a competitor did, despite P&G labs' having developed similar technology. The rival, of course, gained dominant market share by being a first mover.

Likewise, Pillsbury and Quaker lagged the competition in bringing new concepts to market and, as underperformers, were eventually acquired.

Time Incorporated, the magazine wing of Time Warner, for a long time was slow to develop new publications because managers wanted any start-up to have the potential to grow into another *People* or *Sports Illustrated,* two of the company's legendary successes. During the period before Don Logan took the helm in 1992, almost no new magazines were launched. After Logan brought a different innovation strategy to the magazine group, Time developed (or bought) about 100 magazines, which dramatically increased the company's revenues, cash flow, and profits. Not every offering was a blockbuster, but Time had learned what successful innovators know: To get more successes, you have to be willing to risk more failures.

A related mistake is to act as if only products count, even though transformative new ideas can come from a range of functions, such as production and marketing. For instance, a fabric company that made complicated woven materials had a long-standing problem: yarn breakage during production, which was reflected in the cost of the company's products and represented a competitive disadvantage. But the top team at the fabric maker continued to talk about the company's search for really big product innovations, such as totally new materials. A new executive, who believed in opening the search for innovation to all employees, joined the company. After a meeting discussing the need for change, a veteran factory worker, who had joined as a young immigrant and still spoke with a heavy accent, tentatively approached the new executive with an idea for ending the breakage. The company tried it, and it worked. When asked how long he had had that idea, the worker replied, "Thirty-two years."

Similarly, because managers at Quaker Oats in the 1990s were too busy tweaking product formulas in minor ways, the company missed numerous opportunities in other arenas, such as distribution—for instance, taking advantage of the smaller, health-oriented outlets used by its Snapple beverage acquisition. And in a packaging coup,

Ocean Spray, the cranberry juice company, stole a march on America's largest juice purveyors (then including P&G and Coca-Cola) by getting an 18-month exclusive license for the introduction of Tetra Pak's paper bottles to the U.S. market. Ocean Spray boasted a more eclectic innovation strategy than that of its rivals, including idea forums to explore innovations in any domain and open to any employee. Paper bottles were an instant hit with children (and parents packing their lunches), and Ocean Spray's market share shot way up.

Early in its history, the U.S. auto industry gained a breakthrough innovation from its financial function: Consumer financing opened mass markets for products that previously only the affluent could afford. One Intel breakthrough was in marketing: It treated computer chips like potato chips. As a technology company, Intel could have left innovation to its R&D folks. But by marketing a component directly to consumers, Intel gained enormous power with computer manufacturers, which had little choice but to put an Intel Inside label on every machine.

Similarly, Cemex, the global cement company based in Mexico, has used widespread brainstorming to generate innovations that create other sources of value for a product that could easily become a commodity. Those innovations include branded, bagged cement and technology-enabled delivery methods to get cement to customers as fast as if it were a pizza. And while P&G is getting attention for its product innovations, such as the Swiffer and Crest Whitestrips, its innovations in new media, such as interactive Web sites for the soap operas it sponsors, may prove even more valuable for the company's future.

When a company is both too product centric and too revenue impatient, an additional problem can arise. The organization's innovation energy can dissipate across a raft of tiny me-too projects chasing immediate revenue. Perversely, such projects may raise costs in the long run. While a failure to encourage small wins can mean missed opportunities, too many trivial projects are like seeds sown on stony ground—they might sprout, but they do not take root and grow into anything useful. If new ideas take the form not of distinctive innovations but of modest product variations, the resulting proliferation can dilute the brand, confuse customers, and increase internal complexity—such as offering a dozen sizes and flavors of crackers rather than a new and different snack food, a problem Kraft currently faces.

Process Mistakes: Controls Too Tight

A second set of classic mistakes lies in process; specifically, the impulse to strangle innovation with tight controls—the same planning, budgeting, and reviews applied to existing businesses. The inherent uncertainty of the innovation process makes sidetracks or unexpected turns inevitable. The reason upstart Ocean Spray could grab the paper-bottle opportunity from large U.S. juice makers is that the big companies' funds had already been allocated for the year, and they wanted committees to study the packaging option before making commitments that would deviate from their plans.

AlliedSignal (now Honeywell) in 2000 sought new Internet-based products and services using established strategic-planning and budgeting processes through existing business units. The CEO asked the divisions to bring their best ideas for Internet-related innovations to the quarterly budget reviews. Although designated as a priority, these innovation projects were subjected to the same financial metrics the established businesses were. Budgets contained no additional funds for investment; managers working on innovations had to find their own sources of funding through savings or internal transfers. What emerged were often retrofitted versions of ideas that had been in the pipeline anyway.

Performance reviews, and their associated metrics, are another danger zone for innovations. Established companies don't just want plans; they want managers to stick to those plans. They often reward people for doing what they committed to do and discourage them from making changes as circumstances warrant. At a large defense contractor, for instance, people got low marks for not delivering exactly what they had promised, even if they delivered something better—which led people to underpromise, eventually reducing employees' aspirations and driving out innovation.

In the early 1990s, Bank of Boston (now part of Bank of America) set up an innovative unit called First Community Bank (FCB), the first comprehensive banking initiative to focus on inner-city markets. FCB struggled to convince mainstream managers in Bank of Boston's retail-banking group that the usual performance metrics, such as transaction time and profitability per customer, were not appropriate for this market—which required customer education, among other things—or for a new venture that still needed investment. Mainstream managers argued that "underperforming" branches should be closed. In order to save the innovation, FCB leaders had to invent their own metrics, based on customer satisfaction and loyalty, and find creative ways to show results by clusters of branches. The venture later proved both profitable and important to the parent bank as it embarked on a series of acquisitions.

Structure Mistakes: Connections Too Loose, Separations Too Sharp

While holding fledgling enterprises to the same processes as established businesses is dangerous, companies must be careful how they structure the two entities to avoid a clash of cultures or conflicting agendas.

The more dramatic approach is to create a unit apart from the mainstream business, which must still serve its embedded base. This was the logic behind the launch of Saturn as an autonomous subsidiary of General Motors. GM's rules were suspended, and the Saturn team was encouraged to innovate in every aspect of vehicle design, production, marketing, sales, and customer service. The hope was that the best ideas would be incorporated back at the parent company, but instead, after a successful launch, Saturn was reintegrated into GM, and many of its innovations disappeared.

In the time it took for Saturn to hit its stride, Toyota—which favored continuous improvement over blockbusters or greenfield initiatives like Saturn—was still ahead of GM in quality, customer satisfaction, and market share growth. Similarly, U.S. charter schools were freed from the rules of public school systems so they could innovate and thus serve as models for improved education. They've employed many innovative practices, including longer school days and focused curricula, but there is little evidence that charter schools have influenced changes in the rest of their school districts.

The problem in both cases can be attributed to poor connections between the greenfield and the mainstream. Indeed, when people operate in silos, companies may miss innovation opportunities altogether. Game-changing innovations often cut across established channels or combine elements of existing capacity in new ways. CBS was once the world's largest broadcaster and owned the world's largest record company, yet it failed to invent music video, losing this opportunity to MTV. In the late 1990s, Gillette had a toothbrush unit (Oral B), an appliance unit (Braun), and a battery unit (Duracell), but lagged in introducing a battery-powered toothbrush.

The likelihood that companies will miss or stifle innovations increases when the potential innovations involve expertise from different industries or knowledge of different technologies. Managers at established organizations may both fail to understand the nature of a new idea and feel threatened by it.

AT&T Worldnet, the Internet access venture of the venerable long-distance telephone company, faced this lethal mix in the mid-1990s. Managers in the traditional consumer services and business services units participated in a series of debates over whether to manage Worldnet as a distinct business unit, with its own P&L, or to include it in the existing business units focused primarily on the consumer sector. While consumer services managers were reluctant to let go of anything, they eventually agreed to a carve-out intended to protect the embryonic venture from being crushed by the bureaucracy and to keep it from being measured against more-mature businesses that were generating significant cash flow rather than requiring investment. They weren't all that concerned, because they believed an Internet service provider would never generate significant revenue and profitability.

But as Worldnet gained momentum, it attracted more attention. The people in consumer services began to view the innovation's possible expansion to provide voice over Internet protocol (VoIP) services as a threat that could cannibalize existing business. Consumer services managers grabbed control of Worldnet and proceeded to starve it. They used it as a platform to sell core land-based long-distance services and started applying the same metrics to the Internet business that were used for consumer long-distance. Pricing was an immediate problem. Worldnet's services had been priced low to fuel growth, to get the scale and network effects of a large group of subscribers, but the mainstream unit did not want to incur losses on any line of business. So it raised prices, and Worldnet's growth stalled. Consumer services managers could then treat Worldnet as a trivial, slow-growing business, not worthy of large investment. They did not allocate sufficient resources to develop Internet access and VoIP technology, restraining important telecom innovations in which AT&T could have been the pioneer.

Cultural clashes exacerbated tensions at AT&T. Mainstream managers had long tenures in the Bell system. The Internet group, however, hired external tech professionals who spoke the language of computers, not telephony.

Even when a new venture is launched within an existing business, culture clashes become class warfare if there are two classes of corporate citizens—those who have all the fun and those who make all the money. The designated innovators, whether an R&D group or a new-venture unit, are identified as creators of the future. They are free of rules or revenue demands and are allowed to play with ideas that don't yet work. Their colleagues are expected to follow rules, meet demands, and make money while feeling like grinds and sometimes being told they are dinosaurs whose business models will soon be obsolete.

In the early 2000s, Arrow Electronics' attempt at an Internet venture, Arrow.com, was given space in the same facility as the traditional sales force. The similarities stopped there. The Internet group was composed of new hires, often young, from a different background, who dressed in a completely different style. It spent money on cushy furniture, including a big expenditure on a new kitchen—justified, it was said, because the Arrow.com team worked 24/7. The traditional sales force, already anxious about the threat

Internet-enabled sales posed to its commissions and now aware of its dingier offices, became overtly angry. Relations between the groups grew so acrimonious that a brick wall was erected to separate the two sides of the building. Both teams wasted time battling, endangering customer relationships when the two groups fought over the same customers—after all, Arrow.com was just another distribution channel. The CEO had to intervene and find structures to connect them.

Skills Mistakes: Leadership Too Weak, Communication Too Poor

Undervaluing and underinvesting in the human side of innovation is another common mistake. Top managers frequently put the best technical people in charge, not the best leaders. These technically oriented managers, in turn, mistakenly assume that ideas will speak for themselves if they are any good, so they neglect external communication. Or they emphasize tasks over relationships, missing opportunities to enhance the team chemistry necessary to turn undeveloped concepts into useful innovations.

Groups that are convened without attention to interpersonal skills find it difficult to embrace collective goals, take advantage of the different strengths various members bring, or communicate well enough to share the tacit knowledge that is still unformed and hard to document while an innovation is under development. It takes time to build the trust and interplay among team members that will spark great ideas. MIT researchers have found that for R&D team members to be truly productive, they have to have been on board for at least two years. At one point, Pillsbury realized that the average length of time the company took to go from new product idea to successful commercialization was 24 to 26 months, but the average length of time people spent on product teams was 18 months. No wonder the company was falling behind in innovation.

Changes in team composition that result from companies' preferences for the frequency with which individuals make career moves can make it hard for new ventures to deal with difficult challenges, prompting them to settle for quick, easy, conventional solutions.

At Honeywell in the 1980s, leaders of new-venture teams were often promoted out of them before the work had been completed. Because promotions were take-it-or-leave-it offers and pay was tied to size of assets controlled (small by definition in new ventures) rather than difficulty of task, even dedicated innovators saw the virtues of leaving their projects midstream. Honeywell was undermining its own innovation efforts. An executive review of why new ventures failed uncovered this problem, but a technology bias made it hard for old-school managers of that era to increase their appreciation for the value of team bonding and continuity.

Innovation efforts also bog down when communication and relationship building outside the team are neglected. When Gap Incorporated was struggling in the late 1990s, the company mounted several cross-unit projects to find innovations in products, retail concepts, and operations. Some of the project teams quickly became closed environments, and members cut themselves off from their former peers. By failing to tap others' ideas, they produced lackluster recommendations; and by failing to keep peers informed, they missed getting buy-in for even their weak proposals.

Innovators cannot work in isolation if they want their concepts to catch on. They must build coalitions of supporters who will provide air cover for the project, speak up for them in meetings they don't attend, or sponsor the embryonic innovation as it moves into the next stages of diffusion and use. To establish the foundation for successful reception of an innovation, groups must be able to present the radical so it can be understood in familiar terms and to cushion disruptive innovations with assurances that the disruption will be manageable. When technical experts mystify their audiences rather than enlighten them, they lose support—and "no" is always an easier answer than "yes." Groups that work in secret and then present their ideas full-blown at the end face unexpected objections that sometimes kill the project.

Such inattention to relationships and communication with mainstream business managers doomed the launch of Timberland's promising TravelGear line. Developed by an R&D group called the Invention Factory, which was independent of the company's mainstream businesses, TravelGear allowed a user to travel with a single pair of shoes, adding or subtracting components suitable for a range of outdoor activities. The concept won a design award from *BusinessWeek* in 2005. But some existing business teams had not been included in the Invention Factory's developments, and the traditional sales force refused to sell TravelGear products.

By contrast, Dr. Craig Feied's success in developing a state-of-the-art digital network for Washington Hospital Center and its parent, MedStar Health, was a testimony to investment in the human dimension. A small group of programmers designed a user-friendly information system in the emergency department, not the IT department, so they were already close to users. Dr. Feied and his partner, Dr. Mark Smith, made a point of sitting on numerous hospital committees so they would have a wide base of relationships. Their investment in people and their contributions toward shared hospital goals had a positive effect: Feied and Smith's actions helped create good word of mouth and support among other departments for their information system (now called Azyxxi), which resulted in saved time and lives.

The climate for relationships within an innovation group is shaped by the climate outside it. Having a negative instead of a positive culture can cost a company real money. During Seagate Technology's troubled period in the mid-to-late 1990s, the company, a large manufacturer of disk drives for personal computers, had seven different design centers working on innovation, yet it had the lowest R&D productivity in the industry because the centers competed rather than cooperated. Attempts to bring them together merely led people to advocate for their own groups rather than find common ground. Not only did Seagate's engineers and managers lack positive norms for group interaction, but they had the opposite in place: People who yelled in executive meetings received "Dog's Head" awards for the worst conduct. Lack of product and process innovation was reflected in loss of market share, disgruntled customers, and declining sales. Seagate, with its dwindling PC sales and fading customer base, was threatening to become a commodity producer in a changing technology environment.

Under a new CEO and COO, Steve Luczo and Bill Watkins, who operated as partners, Seagate developed new norms for how people should treat one another, starting with the executive group. Their raised consciousness led to a systemic process for forming and running "core teams" (cross-functional innovation groups), and Seagate employees were trained in common methodologies for team building, both in conventional training programs and through participation in difficult outdoor activities in New Zealand and other remote locations. To lead core teams, Seagate promoted people who were known for strong relationship skills above others with greater technical skills. Unlike the antagonistic committees convened during the years of decline, the core teams created dramatic process and product innovations that brought the company back to market leadership. The new Seagate was able to create innovations embedded in a wide range of new electronic devices, such as iPods and cell phones.

Innovation Remedies

The quest for breakthrough ideas, products, and services can get derailed in any or all of the ways described earlier. Fortunately, however, history also shows how innovation succeeds. "Corporate entrepreneurship" need not be an oxymoron. Here are four ways to win.

Strategy remedy: widen the search, broaden the scope

Companies can develop an innovation strategy that works at the three levels of what I call the "innovation pyramid": a few big bets at the top that represent clear directions for the future and receive the lion's share of investment; a portfolio of promising midrange ideas pursued by designated teams that develop and test them; and a broad base of early-stage ideas or incremental innovations permitting continuous improvement. Influence flows down the pyramid, as the big bets encourage small wins heading in the same direction, but it also can flow up, because big innovations sometimes begin life as small bits of tinkering—as in the famously accidental development of 3M's Post-it Notes.

Thinking of innovation in terms of this pyramid gives senior managers a tool for assessing current efforts, making adjustments as ideas prove their value and require further support, and ensuring that there is activity at all levels. A culture of innovation grows because everyone can play. While dedicated groups pursue the big projects and temporary teams develop midrange ideas, everyone else in the company can be invited to contribute ideas. Every employee can be a potential idea scout and project initiator, as IBM is demonstrating. This past July, the company held a three-day InnovationJam on the Web, during which about 140,000 employees and clients—representing 104 countries—contributed about 37,000 ideas and ranked them, giving the company an enormous pool of raw ideas, some of them big, most of them small. Indeed, an organization is more likely to get bigger ideas if it has a wide funnel into which numerous small ideas can be poured. One of the secrets of success for companies that demonstrate high rates of innovation is that they simply try more things.

Gillette adopted the pyramid model as part of its push to accelerate innovation in 2003 and 2004. The result was a stream of innovations in every function and business unit that raised revenues and profits. They included new products such as a battery-powered toothbrush; new concepts in the R&D pipeline, such as the 2006 five-blade, battery-powered Fusion shaving system; innovative marketing campaigns that neutralized the competition, such as the campaign for the Mach3Turbo, which outshone Schick's introduction of its Quattro razor; and new technology in HR. At the first Gillette innovation fair in March 2004, every unit showcased its best ideas of the year in a creative way. The legal department promoted its novel online ethics course with a joke: distributing "get out of jail free" cards like those in *Monopoly*. Having the legal department embrace innovation was a plus for a company in which innovators needed speedy service to file patent applications or help to clear regulatory hurdles.

An innovation strategy that includes incremental innovations and continuous improvement can help to liberate minds throughout the company, making people more receptive to change when big breakthroughs occur.

Process remedy: add flexibility to planning and control systems

One way to encourage innovation to flourish outside the normal planning cycles is to reserve pools of special funds for unexpected opportunities. That way, promising ideas do not have to wait for the next budget cycle, and innovators do not have to beg for funds from mainstream managers who are measured on current revenues and profits. In the mid-to-late 1990s, autocratic management and rigid controls caused the BBC to slip in program innovation and, consequently, audience share. Budgets were tight, and, once they were set, expenditures were confined to predetermined categories. In 2000, a new CEO and his CFO relaxed the rules and began setting aside funds in a corporate account to support proposals for innovation, making it clear that bureaucratic rules should not stand in the way of creative ideas. The BBC's biggest hit comedy in decades, *The Office,* was an accident, made possible when a new recruit took the initiative to use money originally allocated for a BBC training film to make the pilot.

IBM is building such flexibility directly into its infrastructure. The company established a $100 million innovation fund to support the best ideas arising from its InnovationJam, independent of the normal planning and budgeting processes, to allow bottom-up ideas to flourish. "No one has ever before brought together such a global and diverse set of business thought leaders on this scale to discuss the most pressing issues and opportunities of our age," says Nick Donofrio, IBM's executive vice president of innovation and technology. "We have companies literally knocking at the door and saying, 'Give us your best and brightest ideas, and let's work together to make them a reality.' It's a golden opportunity to create entirely new markets and partnerships."

Besides needing different funding models and development partnerships, the innovation process requires exemption from some corporate requirements; after all, there are numerous differences between established businesses and new ventures. For example, the knowledge that innovations could move forward through rapid prototyping—learning from a series of fast trials—might mean that certain milestones triggering review and additional funding would occur faster than they would for established businesses, following the rhythm of the project rather than a fixed quarterly or annual calendar. For other kinds of projects, greater patience might be required—for instance, when an innovation group encounters unexpected obstacles and needs to rethink its model. The key is flexible, customized treatment.

Structure remedy: facilitate close connections between innovators and mainstream businesses

While loosening the formal controls that would otherwise stifle innovations, companies should tighten the human connections between those pursuing innovation efforts and others throughout the rest of the business. Productive conversations should take place regularly between innovators and mainstream business managers. Innovation teams should be charged with external communication as part of their responsibility, but senior leaders should also convene discussions to encourage mutual respect rather than tensions and antagonism. Such conversations should be aimed at mutual learning, to minimize cannibalization and to maximize effective reintegration of innovations that become new businesses. In addition to formal meetings, companies can facilitate informal conversations—as Steelcase did by building a design center that would force people to bump into one another—or identify the people who lead informal cross-unit networks and encourage their efforts at making connections.

Innovation groups can be told at the outset that they have a responsibility to serve the mainstream while also seeking bigger innovations to start new businesses. This can be built into their charters and reinforced by overlapping relationships—whether it involves representatives from mainstream businesses rotating through innovation groups or advisory boards overseeing innovation efforts. After its first great idea flopped, Timberland's Invention Factory learned to work closely with mainstream teams to meet their needs for immediate innovations, such as recreational shoes lined with SmartWool, and to seek game-changing breakthroughs. Turner Broadcasting's new-products group mixes project types: stand-alone developments, enhancements for current channels, external partnerships, and venture capital investments. PNC Financial Services Group recently established a new-products group to oversee mainstream developments, such as pricing and product enhancements, as well as growth engines in new capabilities, such as technology-enabled services and back-office services for investment funds. The company's sales of emerging products were up 21% in 2005, accounting for 46% of all sales.

Flexible organizational structures, in which teams across functions or disciplines organize around solutions, can facilitate good connections. Media conglomerate Publicis has "holistic communication" teams, which combine people across its ad agencies (Saatchi & Saatchi, Leo Burnett, Publicis Worldwide, and so on) and technology groups to focus on customers and brands. Novartis has organized around diseases, with R&D more closely connected to markets and customers; this has helped the company introduce pathbreaking innovations faster, such as its cancer drug Gleevec. The success of Seagate's companywide Factory of the Future team at introducing seemingly miraculous process innovations led to widespread use of its core-teams model.

Would-be innovators at AlliedSignal discovered that tackling promising opportunities required outreach across silos. For example, the aerospace division was organized into groups that were dedicated to large commercial airlines, small commercial airlines, and general aviation (private and charter planes), but the best new idea involved differentiating customers by whether they performed their own maintenance or contracted it to others. The division needed to create new connections across previously divided territories in order to begin the innovation process.

The success of Williams-Sonoma as a multichannel retailer innovating in e-commerce can be attributed to the ways its Web pioneers connected their developments to the rest of the company. From the very beginning, CEO Howard Lester refused to consider Internet ventures that were independent of other company operations. The first main Web development was a bridal registry to create new functionality for the mainstream business. When this pilot project proved its value, an e-commerce department was launched and housed in its own building. But rather than standing apart and pursuing its own direction, that department sought to enhance existing channels, not compete with them. It measured its success not only according to e-commerce sales but also according to incremental sales through other channels that the Web had facilitated. To further its close connections with the mainstream business, the department offered free training to the rest of the company.

Skills remedy: select for leadership and interpersonal skills, and surround innovators with a supportive culture of collaboration
Companies that cultivate leadership skills are more likely to net successful innovations. One reason Williams-Sonoma could succeed in e-commerce quickly and profitably was its careful attention to the human dimension. Shelley Nandkeolyar, the first manager of Williams-Sonoma's e-commerce group, was not the most knowledgeable about the technology, but he was a leader who could assemble the right team. He valued relationships, so he chose a mixture of current employees from other units, who could be ambassadors to their former groups, and new hires that brought new skills. He added cross-company teams to advise and link to the e-commerce team. He invented an integrator role to better connect operations groups and chose Patricia Skerritt, known for being relationship oriented, to fill it.

Similarly, Gail Snowden was able to steer Bank of Boston's First Community Bank through the minefields of middle-manager antagonism toward a successful innovation that produced other innovations (new products and services) because of her leadership skills, not her banking skills. She built a close-knit team of talented people who bonded with one another and felt passion for the mission. Soon her group became one of the parent bank's most desirable places to work. She developed strong relationships with senior executives who helped her deal with tensions in the middle, and she communicated well and often about why her unit needed to be different. Her creativity, vision, teamwork, and persistence helped this group succeed and become a national role model, while other banks' efforts faltered.

IBM's big innovations, such as demonstrating grid computing through World Community Grid, are possible only because the company's culture encourages people to collaborate. CEO Sam Palmisano has engaged hundreds of thousands of IBMers in a Web-based discussion of company values, and Nick Donofrio, IBM's executive vice president for innovation and technology, works to make 90,000 technical people around the world feel part of one innovation-seeking community. The corporate champion of World Community Grid, IBM vice president Stanley Litow, sought out partners in its business units and geographies to move the innovation forward.

Established companies can avoid falling into the classic traps that stifle innovation by widening the search for new ideas, loosening overly tight controls and rigid structures, forging better connections between innovators and mainstream operations, and cultivating communication and collaboration skills.

Innovation involves ideas that create the future. But the quest for innovation is doomed unless the managers who seek it take time to learn from the past. Getting the balance right between exploiting (getting the highest returns from current activities) and exploring (seeking the new) requires organizational flexibility and a great deal of attention to relationships. It always has, and it always will.

Originally published in November 2006. Reprint R0611C

Leading Change

Why Transformation Efforts Fail. *by John P. Kotter*

OVER THE PAST DECADE, I have watched more than 100 companies try to remake themselves into significantly better competitors. They have included large organizations (Ford) and small ones (Landmark Communications), companies based in the United States (General Motors) and elsewhere (British Airways), corporations that were on their knees (Eastern Airlines), and companies that were earning good money (Bristol-Myers Squibb). These efforts have gone under many banners: total quality management, reengineering, rightsizing, restructuring, cultural change, and turnaround. But, in almost every case, the basic goal has been the same: to make fundamental changes in how business is conducted in order to help cope with a new, more challenging market environment.

A few of these corporate change efforts have been very successful. A few have been utter failures. Most fall somewhere in between, with a distinct tilt toward the lower end of the scale. The lessons that can be drawn are interesting and will probably be relevant to even more organizations in the increasingly competitive business environment of the coming decade.

The most general lesson to be learned from the more successful cases is that the change process goes through a series of phases that, in total, usually require a considerable length of time. Skipping steps creates only the illusion of speed and never produces a satisfying result. A second very general lesson is that critical mistakes in any of the phases can have a devastating impact, slowing momentum and

Eight steps to transforming your organization

1 Establishing a sense of urgency
- Examining market and competitive realities
- Identifying and discussing crises, potential crises, or major opportunities

2 Forming a powerful guiding coalition
- Assembling a group with enough power to lead the change effort
- Encouraging the group to work together as a team

3 Creating a vision
- Creating a vision to help direct the change effort
- Developing strategies for achieving that vision

4 Communicating the vision
- Using every vehicle possible to communicate the new vision and strategies
- Teaching new behaviors by the example of the guiding coalition

5 Empowering others to act on the vision
- Getting rid of obstacles to change
- Changing systems or structures that seriously undermine the vision
- Encouraging risk taking and nontraditional ideas, activities, and actions

6 Planning for and creating short-term wins
- Planning for visible performance improvements
- Creating those improvements
- Recognizing and rewarding employees involved in the improvements

7 Consolidating improvements and producing still more change
- Using increased credibility to change systems, structures, and policies that don't fit the vision
- Hiring, promoting, and developing employees who can implement the vision
- Reinvigorating the process with new projects, themes, and change agents

8 Institutionalizing new approaches
- Articulating the connections between the new behaviors and corporate success
- Developing the means to ensure leadership development and succession

Idea in Brief

Most major change initiatives—whether intended to boost quality, improve culture, or reverse a corporate death spiral—generate only lukewarm results. Many fail miserably.

Why? Kotter maintains that too many managers don't realize transformation is a *process*, not an event. It advances through stages that build on each other. And it takes years. Pressured to accelerate the process, managers skip stages. But shortcuts never work.

Equally troubling, even highly capable managers make critical mistakes—such as declaring victory too soon. Result? Loss of momentum, reversal of hard-won gains, and devastation of the entire transformation effort.

By understanding the stages of change—and the pitfalls unique to each stage—you boost your chances of a successful transformation. The payoff? Your organization flexes with tectonic shifts in competitors, markets, and technologies—leaving rivals far behind.

negating hard-won gains. Perhaps because we have relatively little experience in renewing organizations, even very capable people often make at least one big error.

Error 1: Not Establishing a Great Enough Sense of Urgency

Most successful change efforts begin when some individuals or some groups start to look hard at a company's competitive situation, market position, technological trends, and financial performance. They focus on the potential revenue drop when an important patent expires, the five-year trend in declining margins in a core business, or an emerging market that everyone seems to be ignoring. They then find ways to communicate this information broadly and dramatically, especially with respect to crises, potential crises, or great opportunities that are very timely. This first step is essential because just getting a transformation program started requires the aggressive cooperation of many individuals. Without motivation, people won't help, and the effort goes nowhere.

Compared with other steps in the change process, phase one can sound easy. It is not. Well over 50% of the companies I have watched

Idea in Practice

To give your transformation effort the best chance of succeeding, take the right actions at each stage—and avoid common pitfalls

Stage	Actions needed	Pitfalls
Establish a sense of urgency	• Examine market and competitive realities for potential crises and untapped opportunities. • Convince at least 75% of your managers that the status quo is more dangerous than the unknown.	• Underestimating the difficulty of driving people from their comfort zones • Becoming paralyzed by risks
Form a powerful guiding coalition	• Assemble a group with shared commitment and enough power to lead the change effort. • Encourage them to work as a team outside the normal hierarchy.	• No prior experience in teamwork at the top • Relegating team leadership to an HR, quality, or strategic-planning executive rather than a senior line manager
Create a vision	• Create a vision to direct the change effort. • Develop strategies for realizing that vision.	• Presenting a vision that's too complicated or vague to be communicated in five minutes
Communicate the vision	• Use every vehicle possible to communicate the new vision and strategies for achieving it. • Teach new behaviors by the example of the guiding coalition.	• Undercommunicating the vision • Behaving in ways antithetical to the vision

fail in this first phase. What are the reasons for that failure? Sometimes executives underestimate how hard it can be to drive people out of their comfort zones. Sometimes they grossly overestimate how successful they have already been in increasing urgency. Sometimes they lack patience: "Enough with the preliminaries; let's get on

Empower others to act on the vision	• Remove or alter systems or structures undermining the vision. • Encourage risk taking and nontraditional ideas, activities, and actions.	• Failing to remove powerful individuals who resist the change effort
Plan for and create short term wins	• Define and engineer visible performance improvements. • Recognize and reward employees contributing to those improvements.	• Leaving short-term successes up to chance • Failing to score successes early enough (12–24 months into the change effort)
Consolidate improvements and produce more change	• Use increased credibility from early wins to change systems, structures, and policies undermining the vision. • Hire, promote, and develop employees who can implement the vision. • Reinvigorate the change process with new projects and change agents.	• Declaring victory too soon—with the first performance improvement • Allowing resistors to convince "troops" that the war has been won
Institutionalize new approaches	• Articulate connections between new behaviors and corporate success. • Create leadership development and succession plans consistent with the new approach.	• Not creating new social norms and shared values consistent with changes • Promoting people into leadership positions who don't personify the new approach

with it." In many cases, executives become paralyzed by the down-side possibilities. They worry that employees with seniority will become defensive, that morale will drop, that events will spin out of control, that short-term business results will be jeopardized, that the stock will sink, and that they will be blamed for creating a crisis.

A paralyzed senior management often comes from having too many managers and not enough leaders. Management's mandate is to minimize risk and to keep the current system operating. Change, by definition, requires creating a new system, which in turn always demands leadership. Phase one in a renewal process typically goes nowhere until enough real leaders are promoted or hired into senior-level jobs.

Transformations often begin, and begin well, when an organization has a new head who is a good leader and who sees the need for a major change. If the renewal target is the entire company, the CEO is key. If change is needed in a division, the division general manager is key. When these individuals are not new leaders, great leaders, or change champions, phase one can be a huge challenge.

Bad business results are both a blessing and a curse in the first phase. On the positive side, losing money does catch people's attention. But it also gives less maneuvering room. With good business results, the opposite is true: Convincing people of the need for change is much harder, but you have more resources to help make changes.

But whether the starting point is good performance or bad, in the more successful cases I have witnessed, an individual or a group always facilitates a frank discussion of potentially unpleasant facts about new competition, shrinking margins, decreasing market share, flat earnings, a lack of revenue growth, or other relevant indices of a declining competitive position. Because there seems to be an almost universal human tendency to shoot the bearer of bad news, especially if the head of the organization is not a change champion, executives in these companies often rely on outsiders to bring unwanted information. Wall Street analysts, customers, and consultants can all be helpful in this regard. The purpose of all this activity, in the words of one former CEO of a large European company, is "to make the status quo seem more dangerous than launching into the unknown."

In a few of the most successful cases, a group has manufactured a crisis. One CEO deliberately engineered the largest accounting loss in the company's history, creating huge pressures from Wall Street in the process. One division president commissioned first-ever customer satisfaction surveys, knowing full well that the results would be terrible. He then made these findings public. On the surface, such moves can look unduly risky. But there is also risk in playing it too safe: When the urgency rate is not pumped up enough, the transformation process cannot succeed, and the long-term future of the organization is put in jeopardy.

When is the urgency rate high enough? From what I have seen, the answer is when about 75% of a company's management is honestly convinced that business as usual is totally unacceptable. Anything less can produce very serious problems later on in the process.

Error 2: Not Creating a Powerful Enough Guiding Coalition

Major renewal programs often start with just one or two people. In cases of successful transformation efforts, the leadership coalition grows and grows over time. But whenever some minimum mass is not achieved early in the effort, nothing much worthwhile happens.

It is often said that major change is impossible unless the head of the organization is an active supporter. What I am talking about goes far beyond that. In successful transformations, the chairman or president or division general manager, plus another five or 15 or 50 people, come together and develop a shared commitment to excellent performance through renewal. In my experience, this group never includes all of the company's most senior executives because some people just won't buy in, at least not at first. But in the most successful cases, the coalition is always pretty powerful—in terms of titles, information and expertise, reputations, and relationships.

In both small and large organizations, a successful guiding team may consist of only three to five people during the first year of a renewal effort. But in big companies, the coalition needs to grow to the 20 to 50 range before much progress can be made in phase three and beyond. Senior managers always form the core of the group. But sometimes you find board members, a representative from a key customer, or even a powerful union leader.

Because the guiding coalition includes members who are not part of senior management, it tends to operate outside of the normal hierarchy by definition. This can be awkward, but it is clearly neces-sary. If the existing hierarchy were working well, there would be no need for a major transformation. But since the current system is not working, reform generally demands activity outside of formal boundaries, expectations, and protocol.

A high sense of urgency within the managerial ranks helps enor-mously in putting a guiding coalition together. But more is usually required. Someone needs to get these people together, help them develop a shared assessment of their company's problems and op-portunities, and create a minimum level of trust and communica-tion. Off-site retreats, for two or three days, are one popular vehicle for accomplishing this task. I have seen many groups of five to 35 ex-ecutives attend a series of these retreats over a period of months.

Companies that fail in phase two usually underestimate the diffi-culties of producing change and thus the importance of a powerful guiding coalition. Sometimes they have no history of teamwork at the top and therefore undervalue the importance of this type of coalition. Sometimes they expect the team to be led by a staff exec-utive from human resources, quality, or strategic planning instead of a key line manager. No matter how capable or dedicated the staff head, groups without strong line leadership never achieve the power that is required.

Efforts that don't have a powerful enough guiding coalition can make apparent progress for a while. But, sooner or later, the opposi-tion gathers itself together and stops the change.

Error 3: Lacking a Vision

In every successful transformation effort that I have seen, the guid-ing coalition develops a picture of the future that is relatively easy to communicate and appeals to customers, stockholders, and employ-ees. A vision always goes beyond the numbers that are typically found in five-year plans. A vision says something that helps clarify the direction in which an organization needs to move. Sometimes the first draft comes mostly from a single individual. It is usually a bit blurry, at least initially. But after the coalition works at it for three or five or even 12 months, something much better emerges through their tough analytical thinking and a little dreaming. Eventually, a strategy for achieving that vision is also developed.

In one midsize European company, the first pass at a vision contained two-thirds of the basic ideas that were in the final product. The concept of global reach was in the initial version from the beginning. So was the idea of becoming preeminent in certain businesses. But one central idea in the final version—getting out of low value-added activities—came only after a series of discussions over a period of several months.

Without a sensible vision, a transformation effort can easily dissolve into a list of confusing and incompatible projects that can take the organization in the wrong direction or nowhere at all. Without a sound vision, the reengineering project in the accounting department, the new 360-degree performance appraisal from the human resources department, the plant's quality program, the cultural change project in the sales force will not add up in a meaningful way.

In failed transformations, you often find plenty of plans, directives, and programs but no vision. In one case, a company gave out four-inch-thick notebooks describing its change effort. In mind-numbing detail, the books spelled out procedures, goals, methods, and deadlines. But nowhere was there a clear and compelling statement of where all this was leading. Not surprisingly, most of the employees with whom I talked were either confused or alienated. The big, thick books did not rally them together or inspire change. In fact, they probably had just the opposite effect.

In a few of the less successful cases that I have seen, management had a sense of direction, but it was too complicated or blurry to be useful. Recently, I asked an executive in a midsize company to describe his vision and received in return a barely comprehensible 30-minute lecture. Buried in his answer were the basic elements of a sound vision. But they were buried—deeply.

A useful rule of thumb: If you can't communicate the vision to someone in five minutes or less and get a reaction that signifies both understanding and interest, you are not yet done with this phase of the transformation process.

Error 4: Undercommunicating the Vision by a Factor of Ten

I've seen three patterns with respect to communication, all very common. In the first, a group actually does develop a pretty good transformation vision and then proceeds to communicate it by holding a single meeting or sending out a single communication. Having used about 0.0001% of the yearly intracompany communication, the group is startled when few people seem to understand the new approach. In the second pattern, the head of the organization spends a considerable amount of time making speeches to employee groups, but most people still don't get it (not surprising, since vision captures only 0.0005% of the total yearly communication). In the third pattern, much more effort goes into newsletters and speeches, but some very visible senior executives still behave in ways that are antithetical to the vision. The net result is that cynicism among the troops goes up, while belief in the communication goes down.

Transformation is impossible unless hundreds or thousands of people are willing to help, often to the point of making short-term sacrifices. Employees will not make sacrifices, even if they are unhappy with the status quo, unless they believe that useful change is possible. Without credible communication, and a lot of it, the hearts and minds of the troops are never captured.

This fourth phase is particularly challenging if the short-term sacrifices include job losses. Gaining understanding and support is tough when downsizing is a part of the vision. For this reason, successful visions usually include new growth possibilities and the commitment to treat fairly anyone who is laid off.

Executives who communicate well incorporate messages into their hour-by-hour activities. In a routine discussion about a business problem, they talk about how proposed solutions fit (or don't fit) into the bigger picture. In a regular performance appraisal, they talk about how the employee's behavior helps or undermines the vision. In a review of a division's quarterly performance, they talk not only about the numbers but also about how the division's executives are contributing to the transformation. In a routine Q&A with employees at a company facility, they tie their answers back to renewal goals.

In more successful transformation efforts, executives use all existing communication channels to broadcast the vision. They turn boring, unread company newsletters into lively articles about the vision. They take ritualistic, tedious quarterly management meetings and turn them into exciting discussions of the transformation. They throw out much of the company's generic management education and replace it with courses that focus on business problems and the new vision. The guiding principle is simple: Use every possible channel, especially those that are being wasted on nonessential information.

Perhaps even more important, most of the executives I have known in successful cases of major change learn to "walk the talk." They consciously attempt to become a living symbol of the new corporate culture. This is often not easy. A 60-year-old plant manager who has spent precious little time over 40 years thinking about customers will not suddenly behave in a customer-oriented way. But I have witnessed just such a person change, and change a great deal. In that case, a high level of urgency helped. The fact that the man was a part of the guiding coalition and the vision-creation team also helped. So did all the communication, which kept reminding him of the desired behavior, and all the feedback from his peers and subordinates, which helped him see when he was not engaging in that behavior.

Communication comes in both words and deeds, and the latter are often the most powerful form. Nothing undermines change more than behavior by important individuals that is inconsistent with their words.

Error 5: Not Removing Obstacles to the New Vision

Successful transformations begin to involve large numbers of people as the process progresses. Employees are emboldened to try new approaches, to develop new ideas, and to provide leadership. The only constraint is that the actions fit within the broad parameters of the overall vision. The more people involved, the better the outcome.

To some degree, a guiding coalition empowers others to take action simply by successfully communicating the new direction. But communication is never sufficient by itself. Renewal also requires the removal of obstacles. Too often, an employee understands the new vision and wants to help make it happen, but an elephant appears to be blocking the path. In some cases, the elephant is in the person's head, and the challenge is to convince the individual that no external obstacle exists. But in most cases, the blockers are very real.

Sometimes the obstacle is the organizational structure: Narrow job categories can seriously undermine efforts to increase productivity or make it very difficult even to think about customers. Sometimes compensation or performance-appraisal systems make people choose between the new vision and their own self-interest. Perhaps worst of all are bosses who refuse to change and who make demands that are inconsistent with the overall effort.

One company began its transformation process with much publicity and actually made good progress through the fourth phase. Then the change effort ground to a halt because the officer in charge of the company's largest division was allowed to undermine most of the new initiatives. He paid lip service to the process but did not change his behavior or encourage his managers to change. He did not reward the unconventional ideas called for in the vision. He allowed human resource systems to remain intact even when they were clearly inconsistent with the new ideals. I think the officer's motives were complex. To some degree, he did not believe the company needed major change. To some degree, he felt personally threatened by all the change. To some degree, he was afraid that he could not produce both change and the expected operating profit. But despite the fact that they backed the renewal effort, the other officers did virtually nothing to stop the one blocker. Again, the reasons were complex. The company had no history of confronting problems like this. Some people were afraid of the officer. The CEO was concerned that he might lose a talented executive. The net result was disastrous. Lower-level managers concluded that senior management had lied to them about their commitment to renewal, cynicism grew, and the whole effort collapsed.

In the first half of a transformation, no organization has the momentum, power, or time to get rid of all obstacles. But the big ones must be confronted and removed. If the blocker is a person, it is important that he or she be treated fairly and in a way that is consistent with the new vision. Action is essential, both to empower others and to maintain the credibility of the change effort as a whole.

Error 6: Not Systematically Planning for, and Creating, Short-Term Wins

Real transformation takes time, and a renewal effort risks losing momentum if there are no short-term goals to meet and celebrate. Most people won't go on the long march unless they see compelling evidence in 12 to 24 months that the journey is producing expected results. Without short-term wins, too many people give up or actively join the ranks of those people who have been resisting change.

One to two years into a successful transformation effort, you find quality beginning to go up on certain indices or the decline in net income stopping. You find some successful new product introductions or an upward shift in market share. You find an impressive productivity improvement or a statistically higher customer satisfaction rating. But whatever the case, the win is unambiguous. The result is not just a judgment call that can be discounted by those opposing change.

Creating short-term wins is different from hoping for short-term wins. The latter is passive, the former active. In a successful transformation, managers actively look for ways to obtain clear performance improvements, establish goals in the yearly planning system, achieve the objectives, and reward the people involved with recognition, promotions, and even money. For example, the guiding coalition at a U.S. manufacturing company produced a highly visible and successful new product introduction about 20 months after the start of its renewal effort. The new product was selected about six months into the effort because it met multiple criteria: It could be designed and launched in a relatively short period, it could be handled by a small team of people who were devoted to the new vision, it had upside potential, and the new product-development team could operate outside the established departmental structure without practical problems. Little was left to chance, and the win boosted the credibility of the renewal process.

Managers often complain about being forced to produce short-term wins, but I've found that pressure can be a useful element in a change effort. When it becomes clear to people that major change will take a long time, urgency levels can drop. Commitments to produce short-term wins help keep the urgency level up and force detailed analytical thinking that can clarify or revise visions.

Error 7: Declaring Victory Too Soon

After a few years of hard work, managers may be tempted to declare victory with the first clear performance improvement. While celebrating a win is fine, declaring the war won can be catastrophic. Until changes sink deeply into a company's culture, a process that can take five to ten years, new approaches are fragile and subject to regression.

In the recent past, I have watched a dozen change efforts operate under the reengineering theme. In all but two cases, victory was declared and the expensive consultants were paid and thanked when the first major project was completed after two to three years. Within two more years, the useful changes that had been introduced slowly disappeared. In two of the ten cases, it's hard to find any trace of the reengineering work today.

Over the past 20 years, I've seen the same sort of thing happen to huge quality projects, organizational development efforts, and more. Typically, the problems start early in the process: The urgency level is not intense enough, the guiding coalition is not powerful enough, and the vision is not clear enough. But it is the premature victory celebration that kills momentum. And then the powerful forces associated with tradition take over.

Ironically, it is often a combination of change initiators and change resistors that creates the premature victory celebration. In their enthusiasm over a clear sign of progress, the initiators go overboard. They are then joined by resistors, who are quick to spot any opportunity to stop change. After the celebration is over, the resistors point to the victory as a sign that the war has been won and the troops should be sent home. Weary troops allow themselves to be convinced that they won. Once home, the foot soldiers are reluctant to climb back on the ships. Soon thereafter, change comes to a halt, and tradition creeps back in.

Instead of declaring victory, leaders of successful efforts use the credibility afforded by short-term wins to tackle even bigger problems. They go after systems and structures that are not consistent with the transformation vision and have not been confronted before. They pay great attention to who is promoted, who is hired, and how people are developed. They include new reengineering projects that are even bigger in scope than the initial ones. They understand that renewal efforts take not months but years. In fact, in one of the most successful transformations that I have ever seen, we quantified the amount of change that occurred each year over a seven-year period. On a scale of one (low) to ten (high), year one received a two, year two a four, year three a three, year four a seven, year five an eight, year six a four, and year seven a two. The peak came in year five, fully 36 months after the first set of visible wins.

Error 8: Not Anchoring Changes in the Corporation's Culture

In the final analysis, change sticks when it becomes "the way we do things around here," when it seeps into the bloodstream of the corporate body. Until new behaviors are rooted in social norms and shared values, they are subject to degradation as soon as the pressure for change is removed.

Two factors are particularly important in institutionalizing change in corporate culture. The first is a conscious attempt to show people how the new approaches, behaviors, and attitudes have helped improve performance. When people are left on their own to make the connections, they sometimes create very inaccurate links. For example, because results improved while charismatic Harry was boss, the troops link his mostly idiosyncratic style with those results instead of seeing how their own improved customer service and productivity were instrumental. Helping people see the right connections requires communication. Indeed, one company was relentless, and it paid off enormously. Time was spent at every major management meeting to discuss why performance was increasing. The company newspaper ran article after article showing how changes had boosted earnings.

The second factor is taking sufficient time to make sure that the next generation of top management really does personify the new approach. If the requirements for promotion don't change, renewal rarely lasts. One bad succession decision at the top of an organization can undermine a decade of hard work. Poor succession decisions are possible when boards of directors are not an integral part of the renewal effort. In at least three instances I have seen, the champion for change was the retiring executive, and although his successor was not a resistor, he was not a change champion. Because the boards did not understand the transformations in any detail, they could not see that their choices were not good fits. The retiring executive in one case tried unsuccessfully to talk his board into a less seasoned candidate who better personified the transformation. In the other two cases, the CEOs did not resist the boards' choices, because they felt the transformation could not be undone by their successors. They were wrong. Within two years, signs of renewal began to disappear at both companies.

————————

There are still more mistakes that people make, but these eight are the big ones. I realize that in a short article everything is made to sound a bit too simplistic. In reality, even successful change efforts are messy and full of surprises. But just as a relatively simple vision is needed to guide people through a major change, so a vision of the change process can reduce the error rate. And fewer errors can spell the difference between success and failure.

Originally published March 1995. Reprint R0701J

Marketing Myopia

by Theodore Levitt

EVERY MAJOR INDUSTRY WAS once a growth industry. But some that are now riding a wave of growth enthusiasm are very much in the shadow of decline. Others that are thought of as seasoned growth industries have actually stopped growing. In every case, the reason growth is threatened, slowed, or stopped is *not* because the market is saturated. It is because there has been a failure of management.

Fateful Purposes

The failure is at the top. The executives responsible for it, in the last analysis, are those who deal with broad aims and policies. Thus:

- The railroads did not stop growing because the need for passenger and freight transportation declined. That grew. The railroads are in trouble today not because that need was filled by others (cars, trucks, airplanes, and even telephones) but because it was *not* filled by the railroads themselves. They let others take customers away from them because they assumed themselves to be in the railroad business rather than in the transportation business. The reason they defined their industry incorrectly was that they were railroad oriented instead of transportation oriented; they were product oriented instead of customer oriented.

- Hollywood barely escaped being totally ravished by television. Actually, all the established film companies went through drastic reorganizations. Some simply disappeared. All of them got into trouble not because of TV's inroads but because of their own myopia. As with the railroads, Hollywood defined its business incorrectly. It thought it was in the movie business when it was actually in the entertainment business. "Movies" implied a specific, limited product. This produced a fatuous contentment that from the beginning led producers to view TV as a threat. Hollywood scorned and rejected TV when it should have welcomed it as an opportunity—an opportunity to expand the entertainment business.

Today, TV is a bigger business than the old narrowly defined movie business ever was. Had Hollywood been customer oriented (providing entertainment) rather than product oriented (making movies), would it have gone through the fiscal purgatory that it did? I doubt it. What ultimately saved Hollywood and accounted for its resurgence was the wave of new young writers, producers, and directors whose previous successes in television had decimated the old movie companies and toppled the big movie moguls.

There are other, less obvious examples of industries that have been and are now endangering their futures by improperly defining their purposes. I shall discuss some of them in detail later and analyze the kind of policies that lead to trouble. Right now, it may help to show what a thoroughly customer-oriented management can do to keep a growth industry growing, even after the obvious opportunities have been exhausted, and here there are two examples that have been around for a long time. They are nylon and glass—specifically, E.I. du Pont de Nemours and Company and Corning Glass Works.

Both companies have great technical competence. Their product orientation is unquestioned. But this alone does not explain their success. After all, who was more pridefully product oriented and product conscious than the erstwhile New England textile companies that have been so thoroughly massacred? The DuPonts and the Cornings have succeeded not primarily because of their product or research

Idea in Brief

What business are you *really* in? A seemingly obvious question—but one we should all ask *before* demand for our companies' products or services dwindles.

The railroads failed to ask this same question—and stopped growing. Why? Not because people no longer needed transportation. And not because other innovations (cars, airplanes) filled transportation needs. Rather, railroads stopped growing because *railroads* didn't move to fill those needs. Their executives incorrectly thought that they were in the railroad business, not the transportation business. They viewed themselves as providing a product instead of serving customers. Too many other industries make the same mistake—putting themselves at risk of obsolescence.

How to ensure continued growth for your company? Concentrate on meeting customers' needs rather than selling products. Chemical powerhouse DuPont kept a close eye on its customers' most pressing concerns—and deployed its technical know-how to create an ever-expanding array of products that appealed to customers and continuously enlarged its market. If DuPont had merely found more uses for its flagship invention, nylon, it might not be around today.

orientation but because they have been thoroughly customer oriented also. It is constant watchfulness for opportunities to apply their technical know-how to the creation of customer-satisfying uses that accounts for their prodigious output of successful new products. Without a very sophisticated eye on the customer, most of their new products might have been wrong, their sales methods useless.

Aluminum has also continued to be a growth industry, thanks to the efforts of two wartime-created companies that deliberately set about inventing new customer-satisfying uses. Without Kaiser Aluminum & Chemical Corporation and Reynolds Metals Company, the total demand for aluminum today would be vastly less.

Error of analysis

Some may argue that it is foolish to set the railroads off against aluminum or the movies off against glass. Are not aluminum and glass naturally so versatile that the industries are bound to have more growth opportunities than the railroads and the movies? This view

Idea in Practice

We put our businesses at risk of obsolescence when we accept any of the following myths:

Myth 1: An ever-expanding and more affluent population will ensure our growth. When markets are expanding, we often assume we don't have to think imaginatively about our businesses. Instead, we seek to outdo rivals simply by improving on what we're already doing. The consequence: We increase the efficiency of *making* our products, rather than boosting the value those products deliver to customers.

Myth 2: There is no competitive substitute for our industry's major product. Believing that our products have no rivals makes our companies vulnerable to dramatic innovations from outside our

industries—often by smaller, newer companies that are focusing on customer needs rather than the products themselves.

Myth 3: We can protect ourselves through mass production. Few of us can resist the prospect of the increased profits that come with steeply declining unit costs. But focusing on mass production emphasizes our *company's* needs— when we should be emphasizing our *customers'.*

Myth 4: Technical research and development will ensure our growth. When R&D produces breakthrough products, we may be tempted to organize our companies around the technology rather than the consumer. Instead, we should remain focused on satisfying customer needs.

commits precisely the error I have been talking about. It defines an industry or a product or a cluster of know-how so narrowly as to guarantee its premature senescence. When we mention "railroads," we should make sure we mean "transportation." As transporters, the railroads still have a good chance for very considerable growth. They are not limited to the railroad business as such (though in my opinion, rail transportation is potentially a much stronger transportation medium than is generally believed).

What the railroads lack is not opportunity but some of the managerial imaginativeness and audacity that made them great. Even an amateur like Jacques Barzun can see what is lacking when he says, "I grieve to see the most advanced physical and social organization of the last century go down in shabby disgrace for lack of the same comprehensive imagination that built it up. [What is lacking is] the will of the companies to survive and to satisfy the public by inventiveness and skill."[1]

Shadow of Obsolescence

It is impossible to mention a single major industry that did not at one time qualify for the magic appellation of "growth industry." In each case, the industry's assumed strength lay in the apparently unchallenged superiority of its product. There appeared to be no effective substitute for it. It was itself a runaway substitute for the product it so triumphantly replaced. Yet one after another of these celebrated industries has come under a shadow. Let us look briefly at a few more of them, this time taking examples that have so far received a little less attention.

Dry cleaning

This was once a growth industry with lavish prospects. In an age of wool garments, imagine being finally able to get them clean safely and easily. The boom was on. Yet here we are 30 years after the boom started, and the industry is in trouble. Where has the competition come from? From a better way of cleaning? No. It has come from synthetic fibers and chemical additives that have cut the need for dry cleaning. But this is only the beginning. Lurking in the wings and ready to make chemical dry cleaning totally obsolete is that powerful magician, ultrasonics.

Electric utilities

This is another one of those supposedly "no substitute" products that has been enthroned on a pedestal of invincible growth. When the incandescent lamp came along, kerosene lights were finished. Later, the waterwheel and the steam engine were cut to ribbons by the flexibility, reliability, simplicity, and just plain easy availability of electric motors. The prosperity of electric utilities continues to wax extravagant as the home is converted into a museum of electric gadgetry. How can anybody miss by investing in utilities, with no competition, nothing but growth ahead?

But a second look is not quite so comforting. A score of nonutility companies are well advanced toward developing a powerful chemical fuel cell, which could sit in some hidden closet of every home silently ticking off electric power. The electric lines that vulgarize so many neighborhoods would be eliminated. So would the endless demolition of streets and service interruptions during storms. Also on the horizon is solar energy, again pioneered by nonutility companies.

Who says that the utilities have no competition? They may be natural monopolies now, but tomorrow they may be natural deaths. To avoid this prospect, they too will have to develop fuel cells, solar energy, and other power sources. To survive, they themselves will have to plot the obsolescence of what now produces their livelihood.

Grocery stores

Many people find it hard to realize that there ever was a thriving establishment known as the "corner store." The supermarket took over with a powerful effectiveness. Yet the big food chains of the 1930s narrowly escaped being completely wiped out by the aggressive expansion of independent supermarkets. The first genuine supermarket was opened in 1930, in Jamaica, Long Island. By 1933, supermarkets were thriving in California, Ohio, Pennsylvania, and elsewhere. Yet the established chains pompously ignored them. When they chose to notice them, it was with such derisive descriptions as "cheapy," "horse-and-buggy," "cracker-barrel storekeeping," and "unethical opportunists."

The executive of one big chain announced at the time that he found it "hard to believe that people will drive for miles to shop for foods and sacrifice the personal service chains have perfected and to which [the consumer] is accustomed."[2] As late as 1936, the National Wholesale Grocers convention and the New Jersey Retail Grocers Association said there was nothing to fear. They said that the supers' narrow appeal to the price buyer limited the size of their market. They had to draw from miles around. When imitators came, there would be wholesale liquidations as volume fell. The high sales of the supers were said to be partly due to their novelty. People wanted convenient neighborhood grocers. If the neighborhood stores would "cooperate with their suppliers, pay attention to their costs, and improve their service," they would be able to weather the competition until it blew over.[3]

It never blew over. The chains discovered that survival required going into the supermarket business. This meant the wholesale destruction of their huge investments in corner store sites and in established distribution and merchandising methods. The companies with "the courage of their convictions" resolutely stuck to the corner store philosophy. They kept their pride but lost their shirts.

A self-deceiving cycle

But memories are short. For example, it is hard for people who today confidently hail the twin messiahs of electronics and chemicals to see how things could possibly go wrong with these galloping industries. They probably also cannot see how a reasonably sensible businessperson could have been as myopic as the famous Boston millionaire who early in the twentieth century unintentionally sentenced his heirs to poverty by stipulating that his entire estate be forever invested exclusively in electric streetcar securities. His posthumous declaration, "There will always be a big demand for efficient urban transportation," is no consolation to his heirs, who sustain life by pumping gasoline at automobile filling stations.

Yet, in a casual survey I took among a group of intelligent business executives, nearly half agreed that it would be hard to hurt their heirs by tying their estates forever to the electronics industry. When I then confronted them with the Boston streetcar example, they chorused unanimously, "That's different!" But is it? Is not the basic situation identical?

In truth, *there is no such thing as a growth industry,* I believe. There are only companies organized and operated to create and capitalize on growth opportunities. Industries that assume themselves to be riding some automatic growth escalator invariably descend into stagnation. The history of every dead and dying "growth" industry shows a self-deceiving cycle of bountiful expansion and undetected decay. There are four conditions that usually guarantee this cycle:

1. The belief that growth is assured by an expanding and more affluent population;

2. The belief that there is no competitive substitute for the industry's major product;

3. Too much faith in mass production and in the advantages of rapidly declining unit costs as output rises;

4. Preoccupation with a product that lends itself to carefully controlled scientific experimentation, improvement, and manufacturing cost reduction.

I should like now to examine each of these conditions in some detail. To build my case as boldly as possible, I shall illustrate the points with reference to three industries: petroleum, automobiles, and electronics. I'll focus on petroleum in particular, because it spans more years and more vicissitudes. Not only do these three industries have excellent reputations with the general public and also enjoy the confidence of sophisticated investors, but their managements have become known for progressive thinking in areas like financial control, product research, and management training. If obsolescence can cripple even these industries, it can happen anywhere.

Population Myth

The belief that profits are assured by an expanding and more affluent population is dear to the heart of every industry. It takes the edge off the apprehensions everybody understandably feels about the future. If consumers are multiplying and also buying more of your product or service, you can face the future with considerably more comfort than if the market were shrinking. An expanding market keeps the manufacturer from having to think very hard or imaginatively. If thinking is an intellectual response to a problem, then the absence of a problem leads to the absence of thinking. If your product has an automatically expanding market, then you will not give much thought to how to expand it.

One of the most interesting examples of this is provided by the petroleum industry. Probably our oldest growth industry, it has an enviable record. While there are some current concerns about its growth rate, the industry itself tends to be optimistic.

But I believe it can be demonstrated that it is undergoing a fundamental yet typical change. It is not only ceasing to be a growth industry but may actually be a declining one, relative to other businesses. Although there is widespread unawareness of this fact, it is conceivable that in time, the oil industry may find itself in much the same position of retrospective glory that the railroads are now in. Despite its pioneering work in developing and applying the present-value method of investment evaluation, in employee relations, and in working with developing countries, the petroleum business is a distressing example of how complacency and wrongheadedness can stubbornly convert opportunity into near disaster.

One of the characteristics of this and other industries that have believed very strongly in the beneficial consequences of an expanding population, while at the same time having a generic product for which there has appeared to be no competitive substitute, is that the individual companies have sought to outdo their competitors by improving on what they are already doing. This makes sense, of course, if one assumes that sales are tied to the country's population strings, because the customer can compare products only on a feature-by-feature basis. I believe it is significant, for example, that not since John D. Rockefeller sent free kerosene lamps to China has the oil industry done anything really outstanding to create a demand for its product. Not even in product improvement has it showered itself with eminence. The greatest single improvement—the development of tetraethyl lead—came from outside the industry, specifically from General Motors and DuPont. The big contributions made by the industry itself are confined to the technology of oil exploration, oil production, and oil refining.

Asking for trouble

In other words, the petroleum industry's efforts have focused on improving the *efficiency* of getting and making its product, not really on improving the generic product or its marketing. Moreover, its chief product has continually been defined in the narrowest possible terms—namely, gasoline, not energy, fuel, or transportation. This attitude has helped assure that:

- Major improvements in gasoline quality tend not to originate in the oil industry. The development of superior alternative fuels also comes from outside the oil industry, as will be shown later.

- Major innovations in automobile fuel marketing come from small, new oil companies that are not primarily preoccupied with production or refining. These are the companies that have been responsible for the rapidly expanding multipump gasoline stations, with their successful emphasis on large and clean layouts, rapid and efficient driveway service, and quality gasoline at low prices.

Thus, the oil industry is asking for trouble from outsiders. Sooner or later, in this land of hungry investors and entrepreneurs, a threat is sure to come. The possibility of this will become more apparent when we turn to the next dangerous belief of many managements. For the sake of continuity, because this second belief is tied closely to the first, I shall continue with the same example.

The idea of indispensability

The petroleum industry is pretty much convinced that there is no competitive substitute for its major product, gasoline—or, if there is, that it will continue to be a derivative of crude oil, such as diesel fuel or kerosene jet fuel.

There is a lot of automatic wishful thinking in this assumption. The trouble is that most refining companies own huge amounts of crude oil reserves. These have value only if there is a market for products into which oil can be converted. Hence the tenacious belief in the continuing competitive superiority of automobile fuels made from crude oil.

This idea persists despite all historic evidence against it. The evidence not only shows that oil has never been a superior product for any purpose for very long but also that the oil industry has never really been a growth industry. Rather, it has been a succession of different businesses that have gone through the usual historic cycles of growth, maturity, and decay. The industry's overall survival is owed to a series of miraculous escapes from total obsolescence, of last-minute and unexpected reprieves from total disaster reminiscent of the perils of Pauline.

The perils of petroleum

To illustrate, I shall sketch in only the main episodes. First, crude oil was largely a patent medicine. But even before that fad ran out, demand was greatly expanded by the use of oil in kerosene lamps. The prospect of lighting the world's lamps gave rise to an extravagant promise of growth. The prospects were similar to those the industry now holds for gasoline in other parts of the world. It can hardly wait for the underdeveloped nations to get a car in every garage.

In the days of the kerosene lamp, the oil companies competed with each other and against gaslight by trying to improve the illuminating characteristics of kerosene. Then suddenly the impossible happened. Edison invented a light that was totally nondependent on crude oil. Had it not been for the growing use of kerosene in space heaters, the incandescent lamp would have completely finished oil as a growth industry at that time. Oil would have been good for little else than axle grease.

Then disaster and reprieve struck again. Two great innovations occurred, neither originating in the oil industry. First, the successful development of coal-burning domestic central-heating systems made the space heater obsolete. While the industry reeled, along came its most magnificent boost yet: the internal combustion engine, also invented by outsiders. Then, when the prodigious expansion for gasoline finally began to level off in the 1920s, along came the miraculous escape of the central oil heater. Once again, the escape was provided by an outsider's invention and development. And when that market weakened, wartime demand for aviation fuel came to the rescue. After the war, the expansion of civilian aviation, the dieselization of railroads, and the explosive demand for cars and trucks kept the industry's growth in high gear.

Meanwhile, centralized oil heating—whose boom potential had only recently been proclaimed—ran into severe competition from natural gas. While the oil companies themselves owned the gas that now competed with their oil, the industry did not originate the natural gas revolution, nor has it to this day greatly profited from its gas ownership. The gas revolution was made by newly formed transmission companies that marketed the product with an aggressive ardor. They started a magnificent new industry, first against the advice and then against the resistance of the oil companies.

By all the logic of the situation, the oil companies themselves should have made the gas revolution. They not only owned the gas, they also were the only people experienced in handling, scrubbing, and using it and the only people experienced in pipeline technology and transmission. They also understood heating problems. But, partly because they knew that natural gas would compete with their own sale of heating oil, the oil companies pooh-poohed the potential of gas. The revolution was finally started by oil pipeline executives who, unable to persuade their own companies to go into gas, quit and organized the spectacularly successful gas transmission companies. Even after their success became painfully evident to the oil companies, the latter did not go into gas transmission. The multibillion-dollar business that should have been theirs went to others. As in the past, the industry was blinded by its narrow preoccupation with a specific product and the value of its reserves. It paid little or no attention to its customers' basic needs and preferences.

The postwar years have not witnessed any change. Immediately after World War II, the oil industry was greatly encouraged about its future by the rapid increase in demand for its traditional line of products. In 1950, most companies projected annual rates of domestic expansion of around 6% through at least 1975. Though the ratio of crude oil reserves to demand in the free world was about 20 to 1, with 10 to 1 being usually considered a reasonable working ratio in the United States, booming demand sent oil explorers searching for more without sufficient regard to what the future really promised. In 1952, they "hit" in the Middle East; the ratio skyrocketed to 42 to 1. If gross additions to reserves continue at the average rate of the past five years (37 billion barrels annually), then by 1970, the reserve ratio will be up to 45 to 1. This abundance of oil has weakened crude and product prices all over the world.

An uncertain future

Management cannot find much consolation today in the rapidly expanding petrochemical industry, another oil-using idea that did not originate in the leading firms. The total U.S. production of petrochemicals is equivalent to about 2% (by volume) of the demand for all petroleum products. Although the petrochemical industry is now expected to grow by about 10% per year, this will not offset other drains on the growth of crude oil consumption. Furthermore, while petrochemical products are many and growing, it is important to remember that there are nonpetroleum sources of the basic raw material, such as coal. Besides, a lot of plastics can be produced with relatively little oil. A 50,000-barrel-per-day oil refinery is now considered the absolute minimum size for efficiency. But a 5,000-barrel-per-day chemical plant is a giant operation.

Oil has never been a continuously strong growth industry. It has grown by fits and starts, always miraculously saved by innovations and developments not of its own making. The reason it has not grown in a smooth progression is that each time it thought it had a superior product safe from the possibility of competitive substitutes, the product turned out to be inferior and notoriously subject to obsolescence. Until now, gasoline (for motor fuel, anyhow) has escaped this fate. But, as we shall see later, it too may be on its last legs.

The point of all this is that there is no guarantee against product obsolescence. If a company's own research does not make a product obsolete, another's will. Unless an industry is especially lucky, as oil has been until now, it can easily go down in a sea of red figures—just as the railroads have, as the buggy whip manufacturers have, as the corner grocery chains have, as most of the big movie companies have, and, indeed, as many other industries have.

The best way for a firm to be lucky is to make its own luck. That requires knowing what makes a business successful. One of the greatest enemies of this knowledge is mass production.

Production Pressures

Mass production industries are impelled by a great drive to produce all they can. The prospect of steeply declining unit costs as output rises is more than most companies can usually resist. The profit possibilities look spectacular. All effort focuses on production. The result is that marketing gets neglected.

John Kenneth Galbraith contends that just the opposite occurs.[4] Output is so prodigious that all effort concentrates on trying to get rid of it. He says this accounts for singing commercials, the desecration of the countryside with advertising signs, and other wasteful and vulgar practices. Galbraith has a finger on something real, but he misses the strategic point. Mass production does indeed generate great pressure to "move" the product. But what usually gets emphasized is selling, not marketing. Marketing, a more sophisticated and complex process, gets ignored.

The difference between marketing and selling is more than semantic. Selling focuses on the needs of the seller, marketing on the needs of the buyer. Selling is preoccupied with the seller's need to convert the product into cash, marketing with the idea of satisfying the needs of the customer by means of the product and the whole cluster of things associated with creating, delivering, and, finally, consuming it.

In some industries, the enticements of full mass production have been so powerful that top management in effect has told the sales department, "You get rid of it; we'll worry about profits." By contrast, a truly marketing-minded firm tries to create value-satisfying goods and services that consumers will want to buy. What it offers for sale includes not only the generic product or service but also how it is made available to the customer, in what form, when, under what conditions, and at what terms of trade. Most important, what it offers for sale is determined not by the seller but by the buyer. The seller takes cues from the buyer in such a way that the product becomes a consequence of the marketing effort, not vice versa.

A lag in Detroit
This may sound like an elementary rule of business, but that does not keep it from being violated wholesale. It is certainly more violated than honored. Take the automobile industry.

Here mass production is most famous, most honored, and has the greatest impact on the entire society. The industry has hitched its fortune to the relentless requirements of the annual model change, a policy that makes customer orientation an especially urgent necessity. Consequently, the auto companies annually spend millions of dollars on consumer research. But the fact that the new compact cars are selling so well in their first year indicates that Detroit's vast researches have for a long time failed to reveal what customers really wanted. Detroit was not convinced that people wanted anything different from what they had been getting until it lost millions of customers to other small-car manufacturers.

How could this unbelievable lag behind consumer wants have been perpetuated for so long? Why did not research reveal consumer preferences before consumers' buying decisions themselves revealed the facts? Is that not what consumer research is for—to find out before the fact what is going to happen? The answer is that Detroit never really researched customers' wants. It only researched their preferences between the kinds of things it had already decided to offer them. For Detroit is mainly product oriented, not customer oriented. To the extent that the customer is recognized as having needs that the manufacturer should try to satisfy, Detroit usually acts as if the job can be done entirely by product changes. Occasionally, attention gets paid to financing, too, but that is done more in order to sell than to enable the customer to buy.

As for taking care of other customer needs, there is not enough being done to write about. The areas of the greatest unsatisfied needs are ignored or, at best, get stepchild attention. These are at the point of sale and on the matter of automotive repair and maintenance. Detroit views these problem areas as being of secondary importance. That is underscored by the fact that the retailing and servicing ends of this industry are neither owned and operated nor controlled by the manufacturers. Once the car is produced, things are pretty much in the dealer's inadequate hands. Illustrative of Detroit's arms-length attitude is the fact that, while servicing holds enormous sales-stimulating, profit-building opportunities, only 57 of Chevrolet's 7,000 dealers provide night maintenance service.

Motorists repeatedly express their dissatisfaction with servicing and their apprehensions about buying cars under the present selling setup. The anxieties and problems they encounter during the auto buying and maintenance processes are probably more intense and widespread today than many years ago. Yet the automobile companies do not seem to listen to or take their cues from the anguished consumer. If they do listen, it must be through the filter of their own preoccupation with production. The marketing effort is still viewed as a necessary consequence of the product—not vice versa, as it should be. That is the legacy of mass production, with its parochial view that profit resides essentially in low-cost full production.

What Ford put first
The profit lure of mass production obviously has a place in the plans and strategy of business management, but it must always *follow* hard thinking about the customer. This is one of the most important lessons we can learn from the contradictory behavior of Henry Ford. In a sense, Ford was both the most brilliant and the most senseless marketer in American history. He was senseless because he refused to give the customer anything but a black car. He was brilliant because he fashioned a production system designed to fit market needs. We habitually celebrate him for the wrong reason: for his production genius. His real genius was marketing. We think he was able to cut his selling price and therefore sell millions of $500 cars because his invention of the assembly line had reduced the costs. Actually, he invented the assembly line because he had concluded

that at $500 he could sell millions of cars. Mass production was the *result,* not the cause, of his low prices.

Ford emphasized this point repeatedly, but a nation of production-oriented business managers refuses to hear the great lesson he taught. Here is his operating philosophy as he expressed it succinctly:

> Our policy is to reduce the price, extend the operations, and improve the article. You will notice that the reduction of price comes first. We have never considered any costs as fixed. Therefore we first reduce the price to the point where we believe more sales will result. Then we go ahead and try to make the prices. We do not bother about the costs. The new price forces the costs down. The more usual way is to take the costs and then determine the price; and although that method may be scientific in the narrow sense, it is not scientific in the broad sense, because what earthly use is it to know the cost if it tells you that you cannot manufacture at a price at which the article can be sold? But more to the point is the fact that, although one may calculate what a cost is, and of course all of our costs are carefully calculated, no one knows what a cost ought to be. One of the ways of discovering . . . is to name a price so low as to force everybody in the place to the highest point of efficiency. The low price makes everybody dig for profits. We make more discoveries concerning manufacturing and selling under this forced method than by any method of leisurely investigation.[5]

Product provincialism

The tantalizing profit possibilities of low unit production costs may be the most seriously self-deceiving attitude that can afflict a company, particularly a "growth" company, where an apparently assured expansion of demand already tends to undermine a proper concern for the importance of marketing and the customer.

The usual result of this narrow preoccupation with so-called concrete matters is that instead of growing, the industry declines. It usually means that the product fails to adapt to the constantly changing patterns of consumer needs and tastes, to new and modified marketing institutions and practices, or to product developments in competing or complementary industries. The industry has its eyes so firmly on its own specific product that it does not see how it is being made obsolete.

The classic example of this is the buggy whip industry. No amount of product improvement could stave off its death sentence. But had the industry defined itself as being in the transportation business rather than in the buggy whip business, it might have survived. It would have done what survival always entails—that is, change. Even if it had only defined its business as providing a stimulant or catalyst to an energy source, it might have survived by becoming a manufacturer of, say, fan belts or air cleaners.

What may someday be a still more classic example is, again, the oil industry. Having let others steal marvelous opportunities from it (including natural gas, as already mentioned; missile fuels; and jet engine lubricants), one would expect it to have taken steps never to let that happen again. But this is not the case. We are now seeing extraordinary new developments in fuel systems specifically designed to power automobiles. Not only are these developments concentrated in firms outside the petroleum industry, but petroleum is almost systematically ignoring them, securely content in its wedded bliss to oil. It is the story of the kerosene lamp versus the incandescent lamp all over again. Oil is trying to improve hydrocarbon fuels rather than develop *any* fuels best suited to the needs of their users, whether or not made in different ways and with different raw materials from oil.

Here are some things that nonpetroleum companies are working on. More than a dozen such firms now have advanced working models of energy systems which, when perfected, will replace the internal combustion engine and eliminate the demand for gasoline. The superior merit of each of these systems is their elimination of frequent, time-consuming, and irritating refueling stops. Most of these systems are fuel cells designed to create electrical energy directly from chemicals without combustion. Most of them use chemicals that are not derived from oil—generally, hydrogen and oxygen.

Several other companies have advanced models of electric storage batteries designed to power automobiles. One of these is an aircraft producer that is working jointly with several electric utility companies. The latter hope to use off-peak generating capacity to supply overnight plug-in battery regeneration. Another company, also using the battery approach, is a medium-sized electronics firm with extensive small-battery experience that it developed in connection with its work on hearing aids. It is collaborating with an automobile manufacturer. Recent improvements arising from the need for high-powered miniature power storage plants in rockets have put us within reach of a relatively small battery capable of withstanding great overloads or surges of power. Germanium diode applications and batteries using sintered plate and nickel cadmium techniques promise to make a revolution in our energy sources.

Solar energy conversion systems are also getting increasing attention. One usually cautious Detroit auto executive recently ventured that solar-powered cars might be common by 1980.

As for the oil companies, they are more or less "watching developments," as one research director put it to me. A few are doing a bit of research on fuel cells, but this research is almost always confined to developing cells powered by hydrocarbon chemicals. None of them is enthusiastically researching fuel cells, batteries, or solar power plants. None of them is spending a fraction as much on research in these profoundly important areas as it is on the usual run-of-the-mill things like reducing combustion chamber deposits in gasoline engines. One major integrated petroleum company recently took a tentative look at the fuel cell and concluded that although "the companies actively working on it indicate a belief in ultimate success . . . the timing and magnitude of its impact are too remote to warrant recognition in our forecasts."

One might, of course, ask, Why should the oil companies do anything different? Would not chemical fuel cells, batteries, or solar energy kill the present product lines? The answer is that they would indeed, and that is precisely the reason for the oil firms' having to develop these power units before their competitors do, so they will not be companies without an industry.

Management might be more likely to do what is needed for its own preservation if it thought of itself as being in the energy business. But even that will not be enough if it persists in imprisoning itself in the narrow grip of its tight product orientation. It has to think of itself as taking care of customer needs, not finding, refining, or even selling oil. Once it genuinely thinks of its business as taking care of people's transportation needs, nothing can stop it from creating its own extravagantly profitable growth.

Creative destruction

Since words are cheap and deeds are dear, it may be appropriate to indicate what this kind of thinking involves and leads to. Let us start at the beginning: the customer. It can be shown that motorists strongly dislike the bother, delay, and experience of buying gasoline. People actually do not buy gasoline. They cannot see it, taste it, feel it, appreciate it, or really test it. What they buy is the right to continue driving their cars. The gas station is like a tax collector to whom people are compelled to pay a periodic toll as the price of using their cars. This makes the gas station a basically unpopular institution. It can never be made popular or pleasant, only less unpopular, less unpleasant.

Reducing its unpopularity completely means eliminating it. Nobody likes a tax collector, not even a pleasantly cheerful one. Nobody likes to interrupt a trip to buy a phantom product, not even from a handsome Adonis or a seductive Venus. Hence, companies that are working on exotic fuel substitutes that will eliminate the need for frequent refueling are heading directly into the outstretched arms of the irritated motorist. They are riding a wave of inevitability, not because they are creating something that is technologically superior or more sophisticated but because they are satisfying a powerful customer need. They are also eliminating noxious odors and air pollution.

Once the petroleum companies recognize the customer-satisfying logic of what another power system can do, they will see that they have no more choice about working on an efficient, long-lasting fuel (or some way of delivering present fuels without bothering the motorist) than the big food chains had a choice about going into the supermarket business or the vacuum tube companies had a choice about making semiconductors. For their own good, the oil firms will have to destroy their own highly profitable assets. No amount of wishful thinking can save them from the necessity of engaging in this form of "creative destruction."

I phrase the need as strongly as this because I think management must make quite an effort to break itself loose from conventional ways. It is all too easy in this day and age for a company or industry to let its sense of purpose become dominated by the economies of full production and to develop a dangerously lopsided product orientation. In short, if management lets itself drift, it invariably drifts in the direction of thinking of itself as producing goods and services, not customer satisfactions. While it probably will not descend to the depths of telling its salespeople, "You get rid of it; we'll worry about profits," it can, without knowing it, be practicing precisely that formula for withering decay. The historic fate of one growth industry after another has been its suicidal product provincialism.

Dangers of R&D

Another big danger to a firm's continued growth arises when top management is wholly transfixed by the profit possibilities of technical research and development. To illustrate, I shall turn first to a new industry—electronics—and then return once more to the oil companies. By comparing a fresh example with a familiar one, I hope to emphasize the prevalence and insidiousness of a hazardous way of thinking.

Marketing shortchanged
In the case of electronics, the greatest danger that faces the glamorous new companies in this field is not that they do not pay enough attention to research and development but that they pay too much attention to it. And the fact that the fastest-growing electronics firms owe their eminence to their heavy emphasis on technical research is completely beside the point. They have vaulted to affluence on

a sudden crest of unusually strong general receptiveness to new technical ideas. Also, their success has been shaped in the virtually guaranteed market of military subsidies and by military orders that in many cases actually preceded the existence of facilities to make the products. Their expansion has, in other words, been almost totally devoid of marketing effort.

Thus, they are growing up under conditions that come dangerously close to creating the illusion that a superior product will sell itself. It is not surprising that, having created a successful company by making a superior product, management continues to be oriented toward the product rather than the people who consume it. It develops the philosophy that continued growth is a matter of continued product innovation and improvement.

A number of other factors tend to strengthen and sustain this belief:

1. Because electronic products are highly complex and sophisticated, managements become top-heavy with engineers and scientists. This creates a selective bias in favor of research and production at the expense of marketing. The organization tends to view itself as making things rather than as satisfying customer needs. Marketing gets treated as a residual activity, "something else" that must be done once the vital job of product creation and production is completed.

2. To this bias in favor of product research, development, and production is added the bias in favor of dealing with controllable variables. Engineers and scientists are at home in the world of concrete things like machines, test tubes, production lines, and even balance sheets. The abstractions to which they feel kindly are those that are testable or manipulatable in the laboratory or, if not testable, then functional, such as Euclid's axioms. In short, the managements of the new glamour-growth companies tend to favor business activities that lend themselves to careful study, experimentation, and control—the hard, practical realities of the lab, the shop, and the books.

What gets shortchanged are the realities of the *market*. Consumers are unpredictable, varied, fickle, stupid, shortsighted, stubborn, and generally bothersome. This is not what the engineer managers say, but deep down in their consciousness, it is what they believe. And this accounts for their concentration on what they know and what they can control—namely, product research, engineering, and production. The emphasis on production becomes particularly attractive when the product can be made at declining unit costs. There is no more inviting way of making money than by running the plant full blast.

The top-heavy science-engineering-production orientation of so many electronics companies works reasonably well today because they are pushing into new frontiers in which the armed services have pioneered virtually assured markets. The companies are in the felicitous position of having to fill, not find, markets, of not having to discover what the customer needs and wants but of having the customer voluntarily come forward with specific new product demands. If a team of consultants had been assigned specifically to design a business situation calculated to prevent the emergence and development of a customer-oriented marketing viewpoint, it could not have produced anything better than the conditions just described.

Stepchild treatment

The oil industry is a stunning example of how science, technology, and mass production can divert an entire group of companies from their main task. To the extent the consumer is studied at all (which is not much), the focus is forever on getting information that is designed to help the oil companies improve what they are now doing. They try to discover more convincing advertising themes, more effective sales promotional drives, what the market shares of the various companies are, what people like or dislike about service station dealers and oil companies, and so forth. Nobody seems as interested in probing deeply into the basic human needs that the industry might be trying to satisfy as in probing into the basic properties of the raw material that the companies work with in trying to deliver customer satisfactions.

Basic questions about customers and markets seldom get asked. The latter occupy a stepchild status. They are recognized as existing, as having to be taken care of, but not worth very much real thought or dedicated attention. No oil company gets as excited about the customers in its own backyard as about the oil in the Sahara Desert. Nothing illustrates better the neglect of marketing than its treatment in the industry press.

The centennial issue of the *American Petroleum Institute Quarterly,* published in 1959 to celebrate the discovery of oil in Titusville, Pennsylvania, contained 21 feature articles proclaiming the industry's greatness. Only one of these talked about its achievements in marketing, and that was only a pictorial record of how service station architecture has changed. The issue also contained a special section on "New Horizons," which was devoted to showing the magnificent role oil would play in America's future. Every reference was ebulliently optimistic, never implying once that oil might have some hard competition. Even the reference to atomic energy was a cheerful catalog of how oil would help make atomic energy a success. There was not a single apprehension that the oil industry's affluence might be threatened or a suggestion that one "new horizon" might include new and better ways of serving oil's present customers.

But the most revealing example of the stepchild treatment that marketing gets is still another special series of short articles on "The Revolutionary Potential of Electronics." Under that heading, this list of articles appeared in the table of contents:

- "In the Search for Oil"
- "In Production Operations"
- "In Refinery Processes"
- "In Pipeline Operations"

Significantly, every one of the industry's major functional areas is listed, *except* marketing. Why? Either it is believed that electronics holds no revolutionary potential for petroleum marketing (which is palpably wrong), or the editors forgot to discuss marketing (which is more likely and illustrates its stepchild status).

The order in which the four functional areas are listed also betrays the alienation of the oil industry from the consumer. The industry is implicitly defined as beginning with the search for oil and ending with its distribution from the refinery. But the truth is, it seems to me, that the industry begins with the needs of the customer for its products. From that primal position its definition moves steadily back stream to areas of progressively lesser importance until it finally comes to rest at the search for oil.

The beginning and end

The view that an industry is a customer-satisfying process, not a goods-producing process, is vital for all businesspeople to understand. An industry begins with the customer and his or her needs, not with a patent, a raw material, or a selling skill. Given the customer's needs, the industry develops backwards, first concerning itself with the physical *delivery* of customer satisfactions. Then it moves back further to *creating* the things by which these satisfactions are in part achieved. How these materials are created is a matter of indifference to the customer, hence the particular form of manufacturing, processing, or what have you cannot be considered as a vital aspect of the industry. Finally, the industry moves back still further to *finding* the raw materials necessary for making its products.

The irony of some industries oriented toward technical research and development is that the scientists who occupy the high executive positions are totally unscientific when it comes to defining their companies' overall needs and purposes. They violate the first two rules of the scientific method: being aware of and defining their companies' problems and then developing testable hypotheses about solving them. They are scientific only about the convenient things, such as laboratory and product experiments.

The customer (and the satisfaction of his or her deepest needs) is not considered to be "the problem"—not because there is any certain belief that no such problem exists but because an organizational lifetime has conditioned management to look in the opposite direction. Marketing is a stepchild.

I do not mean that selling is ignored. Far from it. But selling, again, is not marketing. As already pointed out, selling concerns itself with the tricks and techniques of getting people to exchange their cash for your product. It is not concerned with the values that the exchange is all about. And it does not, as marketing invariably does, view the entire business process as consisting of a tightly integrated effort to discover, create, arouse, and satisfy customer needs. The customer is somebody "out there" who, with proper cunning, can be separated from his or her loose change.

Actually, not even selling gets much attention in some technologically minded firms. Because there is a virtually guaranteed market for the abundant flow of their new products, they do not actually know what a real market is. It is as if they lived in a planned economy, moving their products routinely from factory to retail outlet. Their successful concentration on products tends to convince them of the soundness of what they have been doing, and they fail to see the gathering clouds over the market.

Less than 75 years ago, American railroads enjoyed a fierce loyalty among astute Wall Streeters. European monarchs invested in them heavily. Eternal wealth was thought to be the benediction for anybody who could scrape together a few thousand dollars to put into rail stocks. No other form of transportation could compete with the railroads in speed, flexibility, durability, economy, and growth potentials.

As Jacques Barzun put it, "By the turn of the century it was an institution, an image of man, a tradition, a code of honor, a source of poetry, a nursery of boyhood desires, a sublimest of toys, and the most solemn machine—next to the funeral hearse—that marks the epochs in man's life."[6]

Even after the advent of automobiles, trucks, and airplanes, the railroad tycoons remained imperturbably self-confident. If you had told them 60 years ago that in 30 years they would be flat on their backs, broke, and pleading for government subsidies, they would have thought you totally demented. Such a future was simply not considered possible. It was not even a discussable subject, or an askable question, or a matter that any sane person would consider worth speculating about. Yet a lot of "insane" notions now have matter-of-fact acceptance—for example, the idea of 100-ton tubes of metal moving smoothly through the air 20,000 feet above the earth, loaded with 100 sane and solid citizens casually drinking martinis—and they have dealt cruel blows to the railroads.

What specifically must other companies do to avoid this fate? What does customer orientation involve? These questions have in part been answered by the preceding examples and analysis. It would take another article to show in detail what is required for specific industries. In any case, it should be obvious that building an effective customer-oriented company involves far more than good intentions or promotional tricks; it involves profound matters of human organization and leadership. For the present, let me merely suggest what appear to be some general requirements.

The visceral feel of greatness

Obviously, the company has to do what survival demands. It has to adapt to the requirements of the market, and it has to do it sooner rather than later. But mere survival is a so-so aspiration. Anybody can survive in some way or other, even the skid row bum. The trick is to survive gallantly, to feel the surging impulse of commercial mastery: not just to experience the sweet smell of success but to have the visceral feel of entrepreneurial greatness.

No organization can achieve greatness without a vigorous leader who is driven onward by a pulsating *will to succeed.* A leader has to have a vision of grandeur, a vision that can produce eager followers in vast numbers. In business, the followers are the customers.

In order to produce these customers, the entire corporation must be viewed as a customer-creating and customer-satisfying organism. Management must think of itself not as producing products but as providing customer-creating value satisfactions. It must push this idea (and everything it means and requires) into every nook and cranny of the organization. It has to do this continuously and with the kind of flair that excites and stimulates the people in it. Otherwise, the company will be merely a series of pigeonholed parts, with no consolidating sense of purpose or direction.

In short, the organization must learn to think of itself not as producing goods or services but as *buying customers,* as doing the things that will make people *want* to do business with it. And the chief executive has the inescapable responsibility for creating this environment, this viewpoint, this attitude, this aspiration. The chief executive must set the company's style, its direction, and its goals. This means knowing precisely where he or she wants to go and making sure the whole organization is enthusiastically aware of where that is. This is a first requisite of leadership, for *unless a leader knows where he is going, any road will take him there.*

If any road is okay, the chief executive might as well pack his 179 attaché case and go fishing. If an organization does not know or care where it is going, it does not need to advertise that fact with a ceremonial figurehead. Everybody will notice it soon enough.

Originally published in 1960. Reprint R0407L

Notes

1. Jacques Barzun, "Trains and the Mind of Man," *Holiday,* February 1960.
2. For more details, see M.M. Zimmerman, *The Super Market: A Revolution in Distribution* (McGraw-Hill, 1955).
3. Ibid., pp. 45–47.
4. John Kenneth Galbraith, *The Affluent Society* (Houghton Mifflin, 1958).
5. Henry Ford, *My Life and Work* (Doubleday, 1923).
6. Barzun, "Trains and the Mind of Man."

What Is Strategy?

by Michael E. Porter

I. Operational Effectiveness Is Not Strategy

For almost two decades, managers have been learning to play by a new set of rules. Companies must be flexible to respond rapidly to competitive and market changes. They must benchmark continuously to achieve best practice. They must outsource aggressively to gain efficiencies. And they must nurture a few core competencies in race to stay ahead of rivals.

Positioning—once the heart of strategy—is rejected as too static for today's dynamic markets and changing technologies. According to the new dogma, rivals can quickly copy any market position, and competitive advantage is, at best, temporary.

But those beliefs are dangerous half-truths, and they are leading more and more companies down the path of mutually destructive competition. True, some barriers to competition are falling as regulation eases and markets become global. True, companies have properly invested energy in becoming leaner and more nimble. In many industries, however, what some call *hypercompetition* is a self-inflicted wound, not the inevitable outcome of a changing paradigm of competition.

The root of the problem is the failure to distinguish between operational effectiveness and strategy. The quest for productivity, quality, and speed has spawned a remarkable number of management tools and techniques: total quality management, benchmarking, time-based competition, outsourcing, partnering, reengineering, change management. Although the resulting operational improvements have often been dramatic, many companies have been frustrated by their inability to translate those gains into sustainable profitability. And bit by bit, almost imperceptibly, management tools have taken the place of strategy. As managers push to improve on all fronts, they move farther away from viable competitive positions.

Operational effectiveness: necessary but not sufficient

Operational effectiveness and strategy are both essential to superior performance, which, after all, is the primary goal of any enterprise. But they work in very different ways.

A company can outperform rivals only if it can establish a difference that it can preserve. It must deliver greater value to customers or create comparable value at a lower cost, or do both. The arithmetic of superior profitability then follows: delivering greater value allows a company to charge higher average unit prices; greater efficiency results in lower average unit costs.

Ultimately, all differences between companies in cost or price derive from the hundreds of activities required to create, produce, sell, and deliver their products or services, such as calling on customers, assembling final products, and training employees. Cost is generated by performing activities, and cost advantage arises from performing particular activities more efficiently than competitors. Similarly, differentiation arises from both the choice of activities and how they are performed. Activities, then, are the basic units of competitive advantage. Overall advantage or disadvantage results from all a company's activities, not only a few.[1]

Operational effectiveness (OE) means performing similar activities *better* than rivals perform them. Operational effectiveness includes but is not limited to efficiency. It refers to any number of practices that allow a company to better utilize its inputs by, for example, reducing defects in products or developing better products faster. In contrast, strategic positioning means performing *different* activities from rivals' or performing similar activities in *different* ways.

Differences in operational effectiveness among companies are pervasive. Some companies are able to get more out of their inputs

Idea in Brief

The myriad activities that go into creating, producing, selling, and delivering a product or service are the basic units of competitive advantage. **Operational effectiveness** means performing these activities better—that is, faster, or with fewer inputs and defects—than rivals. Companies can reap enormous advantages from operational effectiveness, as Japanese firms demonstrated in the 1970s and 1980s with such practices as total quality management and continuous improvement. But from a competitive standpoint, the problem with operational effectiveness is that best practices are easily emulated. As all competitors in an industry adopt them, the **productivity frontier**—the maximum value a company can deliver at a given cost, given the best available technology, skills, and management techniques—shifts outward, lowering costs and improving value at the same time. Such competition produces absolute improvement in operational effectiveness, but relative improvement for no one. And the more benchmarking that companies do, the more **competitive convergence** you have—that is, the more indistinguishable companies are from one another.

Strategic positioning attempts to achieve sustainable competitive advantage by preserving what is distinctive about a company. It means performing *different* activities from rivals, or performing *similar* activities in different ways.

than others because they eliminate wasted effort, employ more advanced technology, motivate employees better, or have greater insight into managing particular activities or sets of activities. Such differences in operational effectiveness are an important source of differences in profitability among competitors because they directly affect relative cost positions and levels of differentiation.

Differences in operational effectiveness were at the heart of the Japanese challenge to Western companies in the 1980s. The Japanese were so far ahead of rivals in operational effectiveness that they could offer lower cost and superior quality at the same time. It is worth dwelling on this point, because so much recent thinking about competition depends on it. Imagine for a moment a *productivity frontier* that constitutes the sum of all existing best practices at any given time. Think of it as the maximum value that a

Idea in Practice

Three key principles underlie strategic positioning.

1. **Strategy is the creation of a unique and valuable position, involving a different set of activities.** Strategic position emerges from three distinct sources:

   - serving few needs of many customers (Jiffy Lube provides only auto lubricants)

   - serving broad needs of few customers (Bessemer Trust targets only very high-wealth clients)

   - serving broad needs of many customers in a narrow market (Carmike Cinemas operates only in cities with a population under 200,000)

2. **Strategy requires you to make trade-offs in competing—to choose what *not* to do.** Some competitive activities are incompatible; thus, gains in one area can be achieved only at the expense of another area. For example, Neutrogena soap is positioned more as a medicinal product than as a cleansing agent. The company says "no" to sales based on deodorizing, gives up large volume, and sacrifices manufacturing efficiencies. By contrast, Maytag's decision to extend its product line and acquire other brands

represented a failure to make difficult trade-offs: the boost in revenues came at the expense of return on sales.

3. **Strategy involves creating "fit" among a company's activities.** Fit has to do with the ways a company's activities interact and reinforce one another. For example, Vanguard Group aligns all of its activities with a low-cost strategy; it distributes funds directly to consumers and minimizes portfolio turnover. Fit drives both competitive advantage and sustainability: when activities mutually reinforce each other, competitors can't easily imitate them. When Continental Lite tried to match a few of Southwest Airlines' activities, but not the whole interlocking system, the results were disastrous.

Employees need guidance about how to deepen a strategic position rather than broaden or compromise it. About how to extend the company's uniqueness while strengthening the fit among its activities. This work of deciding which target group of customers and needs to serve requires discipline, the ability to set limits, and forthright communication. Clearly, strategy and leadership are inextricably linked.

company delivering a particular product or service can create at a given cost, using the best available technologies, skills, management techniques, and purchased inputs. The productivity frontier can apply to individual activities, to groups of linked activities such as order processing and manufacturing, and to an entire company's activities. When a company improves its operational effectiveness, it moves toward the frontier. Doing so may require capital investment, different personnel, or simply new ways of managing.

The productivity frontier is constantly shifting outward as new technologies and management approaches are developed and as new inputs become available. Laptop computers, mobile communications, the Internet, and software such as Lotus Notes, for example, have redefined the productivity frontier for sales-force operations and created rich possibilities for linking sales with such activities as order processing and after-sales support. Similarly, lean production, which involves a family of activities, has allowed substantial improvements in manufacturing productivity and asset utilization.

Operational effectiveness versus strategic positioning

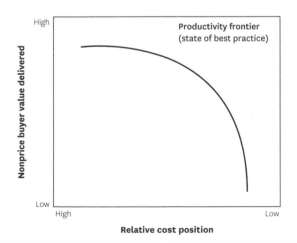

For at least the past decade, managers have been preoccupied with improving operational effectiveness. Through programs such as TQM, time-based competition, and benchmarking, they have changed how they perform activities in order to eliminate inefficiencies, improve customer satisfaction, and achieve best practice. Hoping to keep up with shifts in the productivity frontier, managers have embraced continuous improvement, empowerment, change management, and the so-called learning organization. The popularity of outsourcing and the virtual corporation reflect the growing recognition that it is difficult to perform all activities as productively as specialists.

As companies move to the frontier, they can often improve on multiple dimensions of performance at the same time. For example, manufacturers that adopted the Japanese practice of rapid changeovers in the 1980s were able to lower cost and improve differentiation simultaneously. What were once believed to be real trade-offs—between defects and costs, for example—turned out to be illusions created by poor operational effectiveness. Managers have learned to reject such false trade-offs.

Constant improvement in operational effectiveness is necessary to achieve superior profitability. However, it is not usually sufficient. Few companies have competed successfully on the basis of operational effectiveness over an extended period, and staying ahead of rivals gets harder every day. The most obvious reason for that is the rapid diffusion of best practices. Competitors can quickly imitate management techniques, new technologies, input improvements, and superior ways of meeting customers' needs. The most generic solutions—those that can be used in multiple settings—diffuse the fastest. Witness the proliferation of OE techniques accelerated by support from consultants.

OE competition shifts the productivity frontier outward, effectively raising the bar for everyone. But although such competition produces absolute improvement in operational effectiveness, it leads to relative improvement for no one. Consider the $5 billion-plus U.S. commercial-printing industry. The major players—R.R. Donnelley & Sons Company, Quebecor, World Color Press, and

Big Flower Press—are competing head to head, serving all types of customers, offering the same array of printing technologies (gravure and web offset), investing heavily in the same new equipment, running their presses faster, and reducing crew sizes. But the resulting major productivity gains are being captured by customers and equipment suppliers, not retained in superior profitability. Even industry-leader Donnelley's profit margin, consistently higher than 7% in the 1980s, fell to less than 4.6% in 1995. This pattern is playing itself out in industry after industry. Even the Japanese, pioneers of the new competition, suffer from persistently low profits. (See the sidebar "Japanese Companies Rarely Have Strategies.")

The second reason that improved operational effectiveness is insufficient—competitive convergence—is more subtle and insidious. The more benchmarking companies do, the more they look alike. The more that rivals outsource activities to efficient third parties, often the same ones, the more generic those activities become. As rivals imitate one another's improvements in quality, cycle times, or supplier partnerships, strategies converge and competition becomes a series of races down identical paths that no one can win. Competition based on operational effectiveness alone is mutually destructive, leading to wars of attrition that can be arrested only by limiting competition.

The recent wave of industry consolidation through mergers makes sense in the context of OE competition. Driven by performance pressures but lacking strategic vision, company after company has had no better idea than to buy up its rivals. The competitors left standing are often those that outlasted others, not companies with real advantage.

After a decade of impressive gains in operational effectiveness, many companies are facing diminishing returns. Continuous improvement has been etched on managers' brains. But its tools unwittingly draw companies toward imitation and homogeneity. Gradually, managers have let operational effectiveness supplant strategy. The result is zero-sum competition, static or declining prices, and pressures on costs that compromise companies' ability to invest in the business for the long term.

Japanese Companies Rarely Have Strategies

The Japanese triggered a global revolution in operational effectiveness in the 1970s and 1980s, pioneering practices such as total quality management and continuous improvement. As a result, Japanese manufacturers enjoyed substantial cost and quality advantages for many years.

But Japanese companies rarely developed distinct strategic positions of the kind discussed in this article. Those that did—Sony, Canon, and Sega, for example—were the exception rather than the rule. Most Japanese companies imitate and emulate one another. All rivals offer most if not all product varieties, features, and services; they employ all channels and match one anothers' plant configurations.

The dangers of Japanese-style competition are now becoming easier to recognize. In the 1980s, with rivals operating far from the productivity frontier, it seemed possible to win on both cost and quality indefinitely. Japanese companies were all able to grow in an expanding domestic economy and by penetrating global markets. They appeared unstoppable. But as the gap in operational effectiveness narrows, Japanese companies are increasingly caught in a trap of their own making. If they are to escape the mutually destructive battles now ravaging their performance, Japanese companies will have to learn strategy.

To do so, they may have to overcome strong cultural barriers. Japan is notoriously consensus oriented, and companies have a strong tendency to mediate differences among individuals rather than accentuate them. Strategy, on the other hand, requires hard choices. The Japanese also have a deeply ingrained service tradition that predisposes them to go to great lengths to satisfy any need a customer expresses. Companies that compete in that way end up blurring their distinct positioning, becoming all things to all customers.

This discussion of Japan is drawn from the author's research with Hirotaka Takeuchi, with help from Mariko Sakakibara.

II. Strategy Rests on Unique Activities

Competitive strategy is about being different. It means deliberately choosing a different set of activities to deliver a unique mix of value.

Southwest Airlines Company, for example, offers short-haul, low-cost, point-to-point service between midsize cities and secondary airports in large cities. Southwest avoids large airports and does not fly great distances. Its customers include business travelers, families, and students. Southwest's frequent departures and low fares attract price-sensitive customers who otherwise would travel by bus or car, and convenience-oriented travelers who would choose a full-service airline on other routes.

Most managers describe strategic positioning in terms of their customers: "Southwest Airlines serves price- and convenience-sensitive travelers," for example. But the essence of strategy is in the activities—choosing to perform activities differently or to perform different activities than rivals. Otherwise, a strategy is nothing more than a marketing slogan that will not withstand competition.

A full-service airline is configured to get passengers from almost any point A to any point B. To reach a large number of destinations and serve passengers with connecting flights, full-service airlines employ a hub-and-spoke system centered on major airports. To attract passengers who desire more comfort, they offer first-class or business-class service. To accommodate passengers who must change planes, they coordinate schedules and check and transfer baggage. Because some passengers will be traveling for many hours, full service airlines serve meals.

Southwest, in contrast, tailors all its activities to deliver low-cost, convenient service on its particular type of route. Through fast turnarounds at the gate of only 15 minutes, Southwest is able to keep planes flying longer hours than rivals and provide frequent departures with fewer aircraft. Southwest does not offer meals, assigned seats, interline baggage checking, or premium classes of service. Automated ticketing at the gate encourages customers to bypass travel agents, allowing Southwest to avoid their commissions. A standardized fleet of 737 aircraft boosts the efficiency of maintenance.

Southwest has staked out a unique and valuable strategic position based on a tailored set of activities. On the routes served by Southwest, a full-service airline could never be as convenient or as low cost.

Ikea, the global furniture retailer based in Sweden, also has a clear strategic positioning. Ikea targets young furniture buyers who want style at low cost. What turns this marketing concept into a strategic

Finding New Positions: The Entrepreneurial Edge

Strategic competition can be thought of as the process of perceiving new positions that woo customers from established positions or draw new customers into the market. For example, superstores offering depth of merchandise in a single product category take market share from broad-line department stores offering a more limited selection in many categories. Mail-order catalogs pick off customers who crave convenience. In principle, incumbents and entrepreneurs face the same challenges in finding new strategic positions. In practice, new entrants often have the edge.

Strategic positionings are often not obvious, and finding them requires creativity and insight. New entrants often discover unique positions that have been available but simply overlooked by established competitors. Ikea, for example, recognized a customer group that had been ignored or served poorly. Circuit City Stores' entry into used cars, CarMax, is based on a new way of performing activities—extensive refurbishing of cars, product guarantees, no-haggle pricing, sophisticated use of in-house customer financing—that has long been open to incumbents.

New entrants can prosper by occupying a position that a competitor once held but has ceded through years of imitation and straddling. And entrants coming from other industries can create new positions because of distinctive activities drawn from their other businesses. CarMax borrows heavily from Circuit City's expertise in inventory management, credit, and other activities in consumer electronics retailing.

Most commonly, however, new positions open up because of change. New customer groups or purchase occasions arise; new needs emerge as societies evolve; new distribution channels appear; new technologies are developed; new machinery or information systems become available. When such changes happen, new entrants, unencumbered by a long history in the industry, can often more easily perceive the potential for a new way of competing. Unlike incumbents, newcomers can be more flexible because they face no trade-offs with their existing activities.

---

positioning is the tailored set of activities that make it work. Like Southwest, Ikea has chosen to perform activities differently from its rivals.

Consider the typical furniture store. Showrooms display samples of the merchandise. One area might contain 25 sofas; another will display five dining tables. But those items represent only a fraction of the choices available to customers. Dozens of books displaying fabric swatches or wood samples or alternate styles offer customers thousands of product varieties to choose from. Salespeople often escort customers through the store, answering questions and helping them navigate this maze of choices. Once a customer makes a selection, the order is relayed to a third-party manufacturer. With luck, the furniture will be delivered to the customer's home within six to eight weeks. This is a value chain that maximizes customization and service but does so at high cost.

In contrast, Ikea serves customers who are happy to trade off service for cost. Instead of having a sales associate trail customers around the store, Ikea uses a self-service model based on clear, in-store displays. Rather than rely solely on third-party manufacturers, Ikea designs its own low-cost, modular, ready-to-assemble furniture to fit its positioning. In huge stores, Ikea displays every product it sells in room-like settings, so customers don't need a decorator to help them imagine how to put the pieces together. Adjacent to the furnished showrooms is a warehouse section with the products in boxes on pallets. Customers are expected to do their own pickup and delivery, and Ikea will even sell you a roof rack for your car that you can return for a refund on your next visit.

Although much of its low-cost position comes from having customers "do it themselves," Ikea offers a number of extra services that its competitors do not. In-store child care is one. Extended hours are another. Those services are uniquely aligned with the needs of its customers, who are young, not wealthy, likely to have children (but no nanny), and, because they work for a living, have a need to shop at odd hours.

The origins of strategic positions
Strategic positions emerge from three distinct sources, which are not mutually exclusive and often overlap. First, positioning can be based on producing a subset of an industry's products or services. I call this *variety-based positioning* because it is based on the choice of product or service varieties rather than customer segments.

Variety-based positioning makes economic sense when a company can best produce particular products or services using distinctive sets of activities.

Jiffy Lube International, for instance, specializes in automotive lubricants and does not offer other car repair or maintenance services. Its value chain produces faster service at a lower cost than broader line repair shops, a combination so attractive that many customers subdivide their purchases, buying oil changes from the focused competitor, Jiffy Lube, and going to rivals for other services.

The Vanguard Group, a leader in the mutual fund industry, is another example of variety-based positioning. Vanguard provides an array of common stock, bond, and money market funds that offer predictable performance and rock-bottom expenses. The company's investment approach deliberately sacrifices the possibility of extraordinary performance in any one year for good relative performance in every year. Vanguard is known, for example, for its index funds. It avoids making bets on interest rates and steers clear of narrow stock groups. Fund managers keep trading levels low, which holds expenses down; in addition, the company discourages customers from rapid buying and selling because doing so drives up costs and can force a fund manager to trade in order to deploy new capital and raise cash for redemptions. Vanguard also takes a consistent low-cost approach to managing distribution, customer service, and marketing. Many investors include one or more Vanguard funds in their portfolio, while buying aggressively managed or specialized funds from competitors.

The people who use Vanguard or Jiffy Lube are responding to a superior value chain for a particular type of service. A variety-based positioning can serve a wide array of customers, but for most it will meet only a subset of their needs.

A second basis for positioning is that of serving most or all the needs of a particular group of customers. I call this *needs-based positioning,* which comes closer to traditional thinking about targeting a segment of customers. It arises when there are groups of customers with differing needs, and when a tailored set of activities can serve those needs best. Some groups of customers are more price sensitive

The Connection with Generic Strategies

In *Competitive Strategy* (The Free Press, 1985), I introduced the concept of generic strategies—cost leadership, differentiation, and focus—to represent the alternative strategic positions in an industry. The generic strategies remain useful to characterize strategic positions at the simplest and broadest level. Vanguard, for instance, is an example of a cost leadership strategy, whereas Ikea, with its narrow customer group, is an example of cost-based focus. Neutrogena is a focused differentiator. The bases for positioning—varieties, needs, and access—carry the understanding of those generic strategies to a greater level of specificity. Ikea and Southwest are both cost-based focusers, for example, but Ikea's focus is based on the needs of a customer group, and Southwest's is based on offering a particular service variety.

The generic strategies framework introduced the need to choose in order to avoid becoming caught between what I then described as the inherent contradictions of different strategies. Trade-offs between the activities of incompatible positions explain those contradictions. Witness Continental Lite, which tried and failed to compete in two ways at once.

---

than others, demand different product features, and need varying amounts of information, support, and services. Ikea's customers are a good example of such a group. Ikea seeks to meet all the home furnishing needs of its target customers, not just a subset of them.

A variant of needs-based positioning arises when the same customer has different needs on different occasions or for different types of transactions. The same person, for example, may have different needs when traveling on business than when traveling for pleasure with the family. Buyers of cans—beverage companies, for example—will likely have different needs from their primary supplier than from their secondary source.

It is intuitive for most managers to conceive of their business in terms of the customers' needs they are meeting. But a critical element of needs-based positioning is not at all intuitive and is often overlooked. Differences in needs will not translate into meaningful positions unless the best set of activities to satisfy them *also* differs. If that were not the case, every competitor could meet those same needs, and there would be nothing unique or valuable about the positioning.

In private banking, for example, Bessemer Trust Company targets families with a minimum of $5 million in investable assets who want capital preservation combined with wealth accumulation. By assigning one sophisticated account officer for every 14 families, Bessemer has configured its activities for personalized service. Meetings, for example, are more likely to be held at a client's ranch or yacht than in the office. Bessemer offers a wide array of customized services, including investment management and estate administration, oversight of oil and gas investments, and accounting for racehorses and aircraft. Loans, a staple of most private banks, are rarely needed by Bessemer's clients and make up a tiny fraction of its client balances and income. Despite the most generous compensation of account officers and the highest personnel cost as a percentage of operating expenses, Bessemer's differentiation with its target families produces a return on equity estimated to be the highest of any private banking competitor.

Citibank's private bank, on the other hand, serves clients with minimum assets of about $250,000 who, in contrast to Bessemer's clients, want convenient access to loans—from jumbo mortgages to deal financing. Citibank's account managers are primarily lenders. When clients need other services, their account manager refers them to other Citibank specialists, each of whom handles prepackaged products. Citibank's system is less customized than Bessemer's and allows it to have a lower manager-to-client ratio of 1:125. Biannual office meetings are offered only for the largest clients. Both Bessemer and Citibank have tailored their activities to meet the needs of a different group of private banking customers. The same value chain cannot profitably meet the needs of both groups.

The third basis for positioning is that of segmenting customers who are accessible in different ways. Although their needs are similar to those of other customers, the best configuration of activities to reach them is different. I call this *access-based positioning*. Access can be a function of customer geography or customer scale—or of anything that requires a different set of activities to reach customers in the best way.

Segmenting by access is less common and less well understood than the other two bases. Carmike Cinemas, for example, operates movie theaters exclusively in cities and towns with populations under 200,000. How does Carmike make money in markets that are not only small but also won't support big-city ticket prices? It does so through a set of activities that result in a lean cost structure. Carmike's small-town customers can be served through standardized, low-cost theater complexes requiring fewer screens and less sophisticated projection technology than big-city theaters. The company's proprietary information system and management process eliminate the need for local administrative staff beyond a single theater manager. Carmike also reaps advantages from centralized purchasing, lower rent and payroll costs (because of its locations), and rock-bottom corporate overhead of 2% (the industry average is 5%). Operating in small communities also allows Carmike to practice a highly personal form of marketing in which the theater manager knows patrons and promotes attendance through personal contacts. By being the dominant if not the only theater in its markets—the main competition is often the high school football team—Carmike is also able to get its pick of films and negotiate better terms with distributors.

Rural versus urban-based customers are one example of access driving differences in activities. Serving small rather than large customers or densely rather than sparsely situated customers are other examples in which the best way to configure marketing, order processing, logistics, and after-sale service activities to meet the similar needs of distinct groups will often differ.

Positioning is not only about carving out a niche. A position emerging from any of the sources can be broad or narrow. A focused competitor, such as Ikea, targets the special needs of a subset of customers and designs its activities accordingly. Focused competitors thrive on groups of customers who are overserved (and hence overpriced) by more broadly targeted competitors, or underserved (and hence underpriced). A broadly targeted competitor—for example, Vanguard or Delta Air Lines—serves a wide array of customers, performing a set of activities designed to meet their common needs. It ignores or meets only partially the more idiosyncratic needs of particular customer customer groups.

Whatever the basis—variety, needs, access, or some combination of the three—positioning requires a tailored set of activities because it is always a function of differences on the supply side; that is, of differences in activities. However, positioning is not always a function of differences on the demand, or customer, side. Variety and access positionings, in particular, do not rely on *any* customer differences. In practice, however, variety or access differences often accompany needs differences. The tastes—that is, the needs—of Carmike's small-town customers, for instance, run more toward comedies, Westerns, action films, and family entertainment. Carmike does not run any films rated NC-17.

Having defined positioning, we can now begin to answer the question, "What is strategy?" Strategy is the creation of a unique and valuable position, involving a different set of activities. If there were only one ideal position, there would be no need for strategy. Companies would face a simple imperative—win the race to discover and preempt it. The essence of strategic positioning is to choose activities that are different from rivals'. If the same set of activities were best to produce all varieties, meet all needs, and access all customers, companies could easily shift among them and operational effectiveness would determine performance.

III. A Sustainable Strategic Position Requires Trade-offs

Choosing a unique position, however, is not enough to guarantee a sustainable advantage. A valuable position will attract imitation by incumbents, who are likely to copy it in one of two ways.

First, a competitor can reposition itself to match the superior performer. J.C. Penney, for instance, has been repositioning itself from a Sears clone to a more upscale, fashion-oriented, soft-goods retailer. A second and far more common type of imitation is straddling. The straddler seeks to match the benefits of a successful position while maintaining its existing position. It grafts new features, services, or technologies onto the activities it already performs.

For those who argue that competitors can copy any market position, the airline industry is a perfect test case. It would seem that nearly any competitor could imitate any other airline's activities. Any airline can buy the same planes, lease the gates, and match the menus and ticketing and baggage handling services offered by other airlines.

Continental Airlines saw how well Southwest was doing and decided to straddle. While maintaining its position as a full-service airline, Continental also set out to match Southwest on a number of point-to-point routes. The airline dubbed the new service Continental Lite. It eliminated meals and first-class service, increased departure frequency, lowered fares, and shortened turnaround time at the gate. Because Continental remained a full-service airline on other routes, it continued to use travel agents and its mixed fleet of planes and to provide baggage checking and seat assignments.

But a strategic position is not sustainable unless there are trade-offs with other positions. Trade-offs occur when activities are incompatible. Simply put, a trade-off means that more of one thing necessitates less of another. An airline can choose to serve meals—adding cost and slowing turnaround time at the gate—or it can choose not to, but it cannot do both without bearing major inefficiencies.

Trade-offs create the need for choice and protect against repositioners and straddlers. Consider Neutrogena soap. Neutrogena Corporation's variety-based positioning is built on a "kind to the skin," residue-free soap formulated for pH balance. With a large detail force calling on dermatologists, Neutrogena's marketing strategy looks more like a drug company's than a soap maker's. It advertises in medical journals, sends direct mail to doctors, attends medical conferences, and performs research at its own Skincare Institute. To reinforce its positioning, Neutrogena originally focused its distribution on drugstores and avoided price promotions. Neutrogena uses a slow, more expensive manufacturing process to mold its fragile soap.

In choosing this position, Neutrogena said no to the deodorants and skin softeners that many customers desire in their soap. It gave up the large-volume potential of selling through supermarkets and using price promotions. It sacrificed manufacturing efficiencies to achieve the soap's desired attributes. In its original positioning, Neutrogena made a whole raft of trade-offs like those, trade-offs that protected the company from imitators.

Trade-offs arise for three reasons. The first is inconsistencies in image or reputation. A company known for delivering one kind of value may lack credibility and confuse customers—or even undermine its reputation—if it delivers another kind of value or attempts to deliver two inconsistent things at the same time. For example, Ivory soap, with its position as a basic, inexpensive everyday soap, would have a hard time reshaping its image to match Neutrogena's premium "medical" reputation. Efforts to create a new image typically cost tens or even hundreds of millions of dollars in a major industry—a powerful barrier to imitation.

Second, and more important, trade-offs arise from activities themselves. Different positions (with their tailored activities) require different product configurations, different equipment, different employee behavior, different skills, and different management systems. Many trade-offs reflect inflexibilities in machinery, people, or systems. The more Ikea has configured its activities to lower costs by having its customers do their own assembly and delivery, the less able it is to satisfy customers who require higher levels of service.

However, trade-offs can be even more basic. In general, value is destroyed if an activity is overdesigned or underdesigned for its use. For example, even if a given salesperson were capable of providing a high level of assistance to one customer and none to another, the salesperson's talent (and some of his or her cost) would be wasted on the second customer. Moreover, productivity can improve when variation of an activity is limited. By providing a high level of assistance all the time, the salesperson and the entire sales activity can often achieve efficiencies of learning and scale.

Finally, trade-offs arise from limits on internal coordination and control. By clearly choosing to compete in one way and not another, senior management makes organizational priorities clear. Companies that try to be all things to all customers, in contrast, risk confusion in the trenches as employees attempt to make day-to-day operating decisions without a clear framework.

Positioning trade-offs are pervasive in competition and essential to strategy. They create the need for choice and purposefully limit what a company offers. They deter straddling or repositioning, because competitors that engage in those approaches undermine their strategies and degrade the value of their existing activities.

Trade-offs ultimately grounded Continental Lite. The airline lost hundreds of millions of dollars, and the CEO lost his job. Its planes were delayed leaving congested hub cities or slowed at the gate by baggage transfers. Late flights and cancellations generated a thousand complaints a day. Continental Lite could not afford to compete on price and still pay standard travel-agent commissions, but neither could it do without agents for its full-service business. The airline compromised by cutting commissions for all Continental flights across the board. Similarly, it could not afford to offer the same frequent-flier benefits to travelers paying the much lower ticket prices for Lite service. It compromised again by lowering the rewards of Continental's entire frequent-flier program. The results: angry travel agents and full-service customers.

Continental tried to compete in two ways at once. In trying to be low cost on some routes and full service on others, Continental paid an enormous straddling penalty. If there were no trade-offs between the two positions, Continental could have succeeded. But the absence of trade-offs is a dangerous half-truth that managers must unlearn. Quality is not always free. Southwest's convenience, one kind of high quality, happens to be consistent with low costs because its frequent departures are facilitated by a number of low-cost practices—fast gate turnarounds and automated ticketing, for example. However, other dimensions of airline quality—an assigned seat, a meal, or baggage transfer—require costs to provide.

In general, false trade-offs between cost and quality occur primarily when there is redundant or wasted effort, poor control or accuracy, or weak coordination. Simultaneous improvement of cost and differentiation is possible only when a company begins far behind the productivity frontier or when the frontier shifts outward. At the frontier, where companies have achieved current best practice, the trade-off between cost and differentiation is very real indeed.

After a decade of enjoying productivity advantages, Honda Motor Company and Toyota Motor Corporation recently bumped up against the frontier. In 1995, faced with increasing customer resistance to higher automobile prices, Honda found that the only way to produce a less-expensive car was to skimp on features. In the United States, it replaced the rear disk brakes on the Civic with lower-cost drum brakes and used cheaper fabric for the back seat, hoping customers would not notice. Toyota tried to sell a version of its best-selling Corolla in Japan with unpainted bumpers and cheaper seats. In Toyota's case, customers rebelled, and the company quickly dropped the new model.

For the past decade, as managers have improved operational effectiveness greatly, they have internalized the idea that eliminating trade-offs is a good thing. But if there are no trade-offs companies will never achieve a sustainable advantage. They will have to run faster and faster just to stay in place.

As we return to the question, What is strategy? we see that trade-offs add a new dimension to the answer. Strategy is making trade-offs in competing. The essence of strategy is choosing what *not* to do. Without trade-offs, there would be no need for choice and thus no need for strategy. Any good idea could and would be quickly imitated. Again, performance would once again depend wholly on operational effectiveness.

IV. Fit Drives Both Competitive Advantage and Sustainability

Positioning choices determine not only which activities a company will perform and how it will configure individual activities but also how activities relate to one another. While operational effectiveness is about achieving excellence in individual activities, or functions, strategy is about *combining* activities.

Southwest's rapid gate turnaround, which allows frequent departures and greater use of aircraft, is essential to its high-convenience, low-cost positioning. But how does Southwest achieve it? Part of the answer lies in the company's well-paid gate and ground crews, whose productivity in turnarounds is enhanced by flexible union rules. But the bigger part of the answer lies in how Southwest performs other activities. With no meals, no seat assignment, and no interline baggage transfers, Southwest avoids having to perform activities that slow down other airlines. It selects airports and routes to avoid congestion that introduces delays. Southwest's strict limits on the type and length of routes make standardized aircraft possible: every aircraft Southwest turns is a Boeing 737.

What is Southwest's core competence? Its key success factors? The correct answer is that everything matters. Southwest's strategy involves a whole system of activities, not a collection of parts. Its competitive advantage comes from the way its activities fit and reinforce one another.

Fit locks out imitators by creating a chain that is as strong as its *strongest* link. As in most companies with good strategies, Southwest's activities complement one another in ways that create real economic value. One activity's cost, for example, is lowered because of the way other activities are performed. Similarly, one activity's value to customers can be enhanced by a company's other activities. That is the way strategic fit creates competitive advantage and superior profitability.

Types of fit
The importance of fit among functional policies is one of the oldest ideas in strategy. Gradually, however, it has been supplanted on the management agenda. Rather than seeing the company as a whole, managers have turned to "core" competencies, "critical" resources, and "key" success factors. In fact, fit is a far more central component of competitive advantage than most realize.

Fit is important because discrete activities often affect one another. A sophisticated sales force, for example, confers a greater advantage when the company's product embodies premium technology and its marketing approach emphasizes customer assistance and support. A production line with high levels of model variety is more valuable when combined with an inventory and order processing system that minimizes the need for stocking finished goods, a sales process equipped to explain and encourage customization, and an advertising theme that stresses the benefits of product variations that meet a customer's special needs. Such complementarities are pervasive in strategy. Although some fit among activities is generic and applies to many companies, the most valuable fit is strategy-specific because it enhances a position's uniqueness and amplifies trade-offs.[2]

There are three types of fit, although they are not mutually exclusive. First-order fit is *simple consistency* between each activity (function) and the overall strategy. Vanguard, for example, aligns all activities with its low-cost strategy. It minimizes portfolio turnover and does not need highly compensated money managers. The company distributes its funds directly, avoiding commissions to brokers. It also limits advertising, relying instead on public relations and word-of-mouth recommendations. Vanguard ties its employees' bonuses to cost savings.

Consistency ensures that the competitive advantages of activities cumulate and do not erode or cancel themselves out. It makes the strategy easier to communicate to customers, employees, and shareholders, and improves implementation through single-mindedness in the corporation.

Second-order fit occurs when *activities are reinforcing*. Neutrogena, for example, markets to upscale hotels eager to offer their guests a soap recommended by dermatologists. Hotels grant Neutrogena the privilege of using its customary packaging while requiring other soaps to feature the hotel's name. Once guests have tried Neutrogena in a luxury hotel, they are more likely to purchase it at the drugstore or ask their doctor about it. Thus Neutrogena's medical and hotel marketing activities reinforce one another, lowering total marketing costs.

In another example, Bic Corporation sells a narrow line of standard, low-priced pens to virtually all major customer markets (retail, commercial, promotional, and giveaway) through virtually all available channels. As with any variety-based positioning serving a broad group of customers, Bic emphasizes a common need (low price for an acceptable pen) and uses marketing approaches with a broad reach

Mapping activity systems

Activity-system maps, such as this one for Ikea, show how a company's strategic position is contained in a set of tailored activities designed to deliver it. In companies with a clear strategic position, a number of higher-order strategic themes (in dark grey) can be identified and implemented through clusters of tightly linked activities (in light grey).

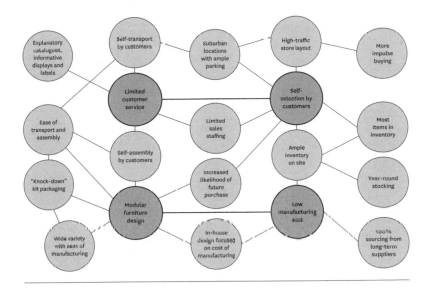

(a large sales force and heavy television advertising). Bic gains the benefits of consistency across nearly all activities, including product design that emphasizes ease of manufacturing, plants configured for low cost, aggressive purchasing to minimize material costs, and in-house parts production whenever the economics dictate.

Yet Bic goes beyond simple consistency because its activities are reinforcing. For example, the company uses point-of-sale displays and frequent packaging changes to stimulate impulse buying. To handle point-of-sale tasks, a company needs a large sales force. Bic's is the largest in its industry, and it handles point-of-sale activities better than its rivals do. Moreover, the combination of point-of-sale

Vanguard's activity system

Activity-system maps can be useful for examining and strengthening strategic fit. A set of basic questions should guide the process. First, is each activity consistent with the overall positioning—the varieties produced, the needs served, and the type of customers accessed? Ask those responsible for each activity to identify how other activities within the company improve or detract from their performance. Second, are there ways to strengthen how activities and groups of activities reinforce one another? Finally, could changes in one activity eliminate the need to perform others?

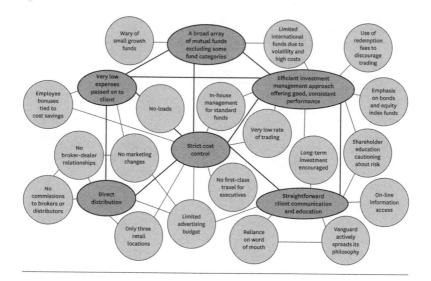

activity, heavy television advertising, and packaging changes yields far more impulse buying than any activity in isolation could.

Third-order fit goes beyond activity reinforcement to what I call *optimization of effort*. The Gap, a retailer of casual clothes, considers product availability in its stores a critical element of its strategy. The Gap could keep products either by holding store inventory or by re-stocking from warehouses. The Gap has optimized its effort across these activities by restocking its selection of basic clothing almost daily out of three warehouses, thereby minimizing the need to carry

Southwest Airlines' activity system

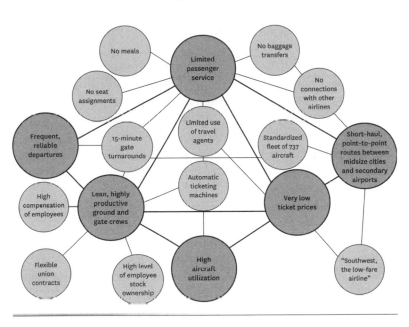

large in-store inventories. The emphasis is on restocking because the Gap's merchandising strategy sticks to basic items in relatively few colors. While comparable retailers achieve turns of three to four times per year, the Gap turns its inventory seven and a half times per year. Rapid restocking, moreover, reduces the cost of implementing the Gap's short model cycle, which is six to eight weeks long.[3]

Coordination and information exchange across activities to eliminate redundancy and minimize wasted effort are the most basic types of effort optimization. But there are higher levels as well. Product design choices, for example, can eliminate the need for after-sale service or make it possible for customers to perform service activities themselves. Similarly, coordination with suppliers or distribution channels can eliminate the need for some in-house activities, such as end-user training.

In all three types of fit, the whole matters more than any individual part. Competitive advantage grows out of the *entire system* of activities. The fit among activities substantially reduces cost or increases differentiation. Beyond that, the competitive value of individual activities—or the associated skills, competencies, or resources—cannot be decoupled from the system or the strategy. Thus in competitive companies it can be misleading to explain success by specifying individual strengths, core competencies, or critical resources. The list of strengths cuts across many functions, and one strength blends into others. It is more useful to think in terms of themes that pervade many activities, such as low cost, a particular notion of customer service, or a particular conception of the value delivered. These themes are embodied in nests of tightly linked activities.

Fit and sustainability

Strategic fit among many activities is fundamental not only to competitive advantage but also to the sustainability of that advantage. It is harder for a rival to match an array of interlocked activities than it is merely to imitate a particular sales-force approach, match a process technology, or replicate a set of product features. Positions built on systems of activities are far more sustainable than those built on individual activities.

Consider this simple exercise. The probability that competitors can match any activity is often less than one. The probabilities then quickly compound to make matching the entire system highly unlikely (.9 x .9 = .81; .9 x .9 x .9 x .9 = .66, and so on). Existing companies that try to reposition or straddle will be forced to reconfigure many activities. And even new entrants, though they do not confront the trade-offs facing established rivals, still face formidable barriers to imitation.

The more a company's positioning rests on activity systems with second- and third-order fit, the more sustainable its advantage will be. Such systems, by their very nature, are usually difficult to untangle from outside the company and therefore hard to imitate. And even if rivals can identify the relevant interconnections, they will have difficulty replicating them. Achieving fit is difficult because it requires the integration of decisions and actions across many independent subunits.

A competitor seeking to match an activity system gains little by imitating only some activities and not matching the whole. Performance does not improve; it can decline. Recall Continental Lite's disastrous attempt to imitate Southwest.

Finally, fit among a company's activities creates pressures and incentives to improve operational effectiveness, which makes imitation even harder. Fit means that poor performance in one activity will degrade the performance in others, so that weaknesses are exposed and more prone to get attention. Conversely, improvements in one activity will pay dividends in others. Companies with strong fit among their activities are rarely inviting targets. Their superiority in strategy and in execution only compounds their advantages and raises the hurdle for imitators.

When activities complement one another, rivals will get little benefit from imitation unless they successfully match the whole system. Such situations tend to promote winner-take-all competition. The company that builds the best activity system—Toys R Us, for instance—wins, while rivals with similar strategies—Child World and Lionel Leisure—fall behind. Thus finding a new strategic position is often preferable to being the second or third imitator of an occupied position.

The most viable positions are those whose activity systems are incompatible because of tradeoffs. Strategic positioning sets the trade-off rules that define how individual activities will be configured and integrated. Seeing strategy in terms of activity systems only makes it clearer why organizational structure, systems, and processes need to be strategy-specific. Tailoring organization to strategy, in turn, makes complementarities more achievable and contributes to sustainability.

One implication is that strategic positions should have a horizon of a decade or more, not of a single planning cycle. Continuity fosters improvements in individual activities and the fit across activities, allowing an organization to build unique capabilities and skills tailored to its strategy. Continuity also reinforces a company's identity.

Conversely, frequent shifts in positioning are costly. Not only must a company reconfigure individual activities, but it must also realign entire systems. Some activities may never catch up to the vacillating strategy. The inevitable result of frequent shifts in strategy, or of failure to choose a distinct position in the first place, is "me-too" or hedged activity configurations, inconsistencies across functions, and organizational dissonance.

What is strategy? We can now complete the answer to this question. Strategy is creating fit among a company's activities. The success of a strategy depends on doing many things well—not just a few—and integrating among them. If there is no fit among activities, there is no distinctive strategy and little sustainability. Management reverts to the simpler task of overseeing independent functions, and operational effectiveness determines an organization's relative performance.

V. Rediscovering Strategy

The failure to choose

Why do so many companies fail to have a strategy? Why do managers avoid making strategic choices? Or, having made them in the past, why do managers so often let strategies decay and blur?

Commonly, the threats to strategy are seen to emanate from outside a company because of changes in technology or the behavior of competitors. Although external changes can be the problem, the greater threat to strategy often comes from within. A sound strategy is undermined by a misguided view of competition, by organizational failures, and, especially, by the desire to grow.

Managers have become confused about the necessity of making choices. When many companies operate far from the productivity frontier, trade-offs appear unnecessary. It can seem that a well-run company should be able to beat its ineffective rivals on all dimensions simultaneously. Taught by popular management thinkers that they do not have to make trade-offs, managers have acquired a macho sense that to do so is a sign of weakness.

Unnerved by forecasts of hypercompetition, managers increase its likelihood by imitating everything about their competitors.

Alternative Views of Strategy

The Implicit Strategy Model of the Past Decade

- One ideal competitive position in the industry
- Benchmarking of all activities and achieving best practice
- Aggressive outsourcing and partnering to gain efficiencies
- Advantages rest on a few key success factors, critical resources, core competencies
- Flexibility and rapid responses to all competitive and market changes

Sustainable Competitive Advantage

- Unique competitive position for the company
- Activities tailored to strategy
- Clear trade-offs and choices vis-à-vis competitors
- Competitive advantage arises from fit across activities
- Sustainability comes from the activity system, not the parts
- Operational effectiveness a given

Exhorted to think in terms of revolution, managers chase every new technology for its own sake.

The pursuit of operational effectiveness is seductive because it is concrete and actionable. Over the past decade, managers have been under increasing pressure to deliver tangible, measurable performance improvements. Programs in operational effectiveness produce reassuring progress, although superior profitability may remain elusive. Business publications and consultants flood the market with information about what other companies are doing, reinforcing the best-practice mentality. Caught up in the race for operational effectiveness, many managers simply do not understand the need to have a strategy.

Companies avoid or blur strategic choices for other reasons as well. Conventional wisdom within an industry is often strong,

Reconnecting with Strategy

Most companies owe their initial success to a unique strategic position involving clear trade-offs. Activities once were aligned with that position. The passage of time and the pressures of growth, however, led to compromises that were, at first, almost imperceptible. Through a succession of incremental changes that each seemed sensible at the time, many established companies have compromised their way to homogeneity with their rivals.

The issue here is not with the companies whose historical position is no longer viable; their challenge is to start over, just as a new entrant would. At issue is a far more common phenomenon: the established company achieving mediocre returns and lacking a clear strategy. Through incremental additions of product varieties, incremental efforts to serve new customer groups, and emulation of rivals' activities, the existing company loses its clear competitive position. Typically, the company has matched many of its competitors' offerings and practices and attempts to sell to most customer groups.

A number of approaches can help a company reconnect with strategy. The first is a careful look at what it already does. Within most well-established companies is a core of uniqueness. It is identified by answering questions such as the following:

- Which of our product or service varieties are the most distinctive?
- Which of our product or service varieties are the most profitable?

homogenizing competition. Some managers mistake "customer focus" to mean they must serve all customer needs or respond to every request from distribution channels. Others cite the desire to preserve flexibility.

Organizational realities also work against strategy. Trade-offs are frightening, and making no choice is sometimes preferred to risking blame for a bad choice. Companies imitate one another in a type of herd behavior, each assuming rivals know something they do not. Newly empowered employees, who are urged to seek every possible source of improvement, often lack a vision of the whole and the perspective to recognize trade-offs. The failure to choose sometimes comes down to the reluctance to disappoint valued managers or employees.

- Which of our customers are the most satisfied?

- Which customers, channels, or purchase occasions are the most profitable?

- Which of the activities in our value chain are the most different and effective?

Around this core of uniqueness are encrustations added incrementally over time. Like barnacles, they must be removed to reveal the underlying strategic positioning. A small percentage of varieties or customers may well account for most of a company's sales and especially its profits. The challenge, then, is to refocus on the unique core and realign the company's activities with it. Customers and product varieties at the periphery can be sold or allowed through inattention or price increases to fade away.

A company's history can also be instructive. What was the vision of the founder? What were the products and customers that made the company? Looking backward, one can reexamine the original strategy to see if it is still valid. Can the historical positioning be implemented in a modern way, one consistent with today's technologies and practices? This sort of thinking may lead to a commitment to renew the strategy and may challenge the organization to recover its distinctiveness. Such a challenge can be galvanizing and can instill the confidence to make the needed trade-offs.

The growth trap

Among all other influences, the desire to grow has perhaps the most perverse effect on strategy. Trade-offs and limits appear to constrain growth. Serving one group of customers and excluding others, for instance, places a real or imagined limit on revenue growth. Broadly targeted strategies emphasizing low price result in lost sales with customers sensitive to features or service. Differentiators lose sales to price-sensitive customers.

Managers are constantly tempted to take incremental steps that surpass those limits but blur a company's strategic position. Eventually, pressures to grow or apparent saturation of the target market lead managers to broaden the position by extending product lines, adding new features, imitating competitors' popular services, matching processes, and even making acquisitions. For years, Maytag Corporation's success was based on its focus on reliable, durable washers and dryers, later extended to include dishwashers. However, conventional wisdom emerging within the industry supported the notion of selling a full line of products. Concerned with slow industry growth and competition from broad-line appliance makers, Maytag was pressured by dealers and encouraged by customers to extend its line. Maytag expanded into refrigerators and cooking products under the Maytag brand and acquired other brands—Jenn-Air, Hardwick Stove, Hoover, Admiral, and Magic Chef—with disparate positions. Maytag has grown substantially from $684 million in 1985 to a peak of $3.4 billion in 1994, but return on sales has declined from 8% to 12% in the 1970s and 1980s to an average of less than 1% between 1989 and 1995. Cost cutting will improve this performance, but laundry and dishwasher products still anchor Maytag's profitability.

Neutrogena may have fallen into the same trap. In the early 1990s, its U.S. distribution broadened to include mass merchandisers such as Wal-Mart Stores. Under the Neutrogena name, the company expanded into a wide variety of products—eye-makeup remover and shampoo, for example—in which it was not unique and which diluted its image, and it began turning to price promotions.

Compromises and inconsistencies in the pursuit of growth will erode the competitive advantage a company had with its original varieties or target customers. Attempts to compete in several ways at once create confusion and undermine organizational motivation and focus. Profits fall, but more revenue is seen as the answer. Managers are unable to make choices, so the company embarks on a new round of broadening and compromises. Often, rivals continue to match each other until desperation breaks the cycle, resulting in a merger or downsizing to the original positioning.

Profitable growth

Many companies, after a decade of restructuring and cost-cutting, are turning their attention to growth. Too often, efforts to grow blur uniqueness, create compromises, reduce fit, and ultimately

Emerging Industries and Technologies

Developing a strategy in a newly emerging industry or in a business undergoing revolutionary technological changes is a daunting proposition. In such cases, managers face a high level of uncertainty about the needs of customers, the products and services that will prove to be the most desired, and the best configuration of activities and technologies to deliver them. Because of all this uncertainty, imitation and hedging are rampant: unable to risk being wrong or left behind, companies match all features, offer all new services, and explore all technologies.

During such periods in an industry's development, its basic productivity frontier is being established or reestablished. Explosive growth can make such times profitable for many companies, but profits will be temporary because imitation and strategic convergence will ultimately destroy industry profitability. The companies that are enduringly successful will be those that begin as early as possible to define and embody in their activities a unique competitive position. A period of imitation may be inevitable in emerging industries, but that period reflects the level of uncertainty rather than a desired state of affairs.

In high-tech industries, this imitation phase often continues much longer than it should. Enraptured by technological change itself, companies pack more features—most of which are never used—into their products while slashing prices across the board. Rarely are trade-offs even considered. The drive for growth to satisfy market pressures leads companies into every product area. Although a few companies with fundamental advantages prosper, the majority are doomed to a rat race no one can win.

Ironically, the popular business press, focused on hot, emerging industries, is prone to presenting these special cases as proof that we have entered a new era of competition in which none of the old rules are valid. In fact, the opposite is true.

---

undermine competitive advantage. In fact, the growth imperative is hazardous to strategy.

What approaches to growth preserve and reinforce strategy? Broadly, the prescription is to concentrate on deepening a strategic position rather than broadening and compromising it. One approach is to look for extensions of the strategy that leverage the existing activity system by offering features or services that rivals would find impossible or costly to match on a stand-alone basis. In other words, managers can ask themselves which activities, features, or forms of competition are feasible or less costly to them because of complementary activities that their company performs.

Deepening a position involves making the company's activities more distinctive, strengthening fit, and communicating the strategy better to those customers who should value it. But many companies succumb to the temptation to chase "easy" growth by adding hot features, products, or services without screening them or adapting them to their strategy. Or they target new customers or markets in which the company has little special to offer. A company can often grow faster—and far more profitably—by better penetrating needs and varieties where it is distinctive than by slugging it out in potentially higher growth arenas in which the company lacks uniqueness. Carmike, now the largest theater chain in the United States, owes its rapid growth to its disciplined concentration on small markets. The company quickly sells any big-city theaters that come to it as part of an acquisition.

Globalization often allows growth that is consistent with strategy, opening up larger markets for a focused strategy. Unlike broadening domestically, expanding globally is likely to leverage and reinforce a company's unique position and identity.

Companies seeking growth through broadening within their industry can best contain the risks to strategy by creating stand-alone units, each with its own brand name and tailored activities. Maytag has clearly struggled with this issue. On the one hand, it has organized its premium and value brands into separate units with different strategic positions. On the other, it has created an umbrella appliance company for all its brands to gain critical mass. With shared design, manufacturing, distribution, and customer service, it will be hard to avoid homogenization. If a given business unit attempts to compete with different positions for different products or customers, avoiding compromise is nearly impossible.

The role of leadership
The challenge of developing or reestablishing a clear strategy is often primarily an organizational one and depends on leadership. With so many forces at work against making choices and tradeoffs in

organizations, a clear intellectual framework to guide strategy is a necessary counterweight. Moreover, strong leaders willing to make choices are essential.

In many companies, leadership has degenerated into orchestrating operational improvements and making deals. But the leader's role is broader and far more important. General management is more than the stewardship of individual functions. Its core is strategy: defining and communicating the company's unique position, making trade-offs, and forging fit among activities. The leader must provide the discipline to decide which industry changes and customer needs the company will respond to, while avoiding organizational distractions and maintaining the company's distinctiveness. Managers at lower levels lack the perspective and the confidence to maintain a strategy. There will be constant pressures to compromise, relax trade-offs, and emulate rivals. One of the leader's jobs is to teach others in the organization about strategy—and to say no.

Strategy renders choices about what not to do as important as choices about what to do. Indeed, setting limits is another function of leadership. Deciding which target group of customers, varieties, and needs the company should serve is fundamental to developing a strategy. But so is deciding not to serve other customers or needs and not to offer certain features or services. Thus strategy requires constant discipline and clear communication. Indeed, one of the most important functions of an explicit, communicated strategy is to guide employees in making choices that arise because of trade-offs in their individual activities and in day-to-day decisions.

Improving operational effectiveness is a necessary part of management, but it is *not* strategy. In confusing the two, managers have unintentionally backed into a way of thinking about competition that is driving many industries toward competitive convergence, which is in no one's best interest and is not inevitable.

Managers must clearly distinguish operational effectiveness from strategy. Both are essential, but the two agendas are different.

The operational agenda involves continual improvement everywhere there are no trade-offs. Failure to do this creates vulnerability even for companies with a good strategy. The operational agenda is the proper place for constant change, flexibility, and relentless efforts to achieve best practice. In contrast, the strategic agenda is the right place for defining a unique position, making clear trade-offs, and tightening fit. It involves the continual search for ways to reinforce and extend the company's position. The strategic agenda demands discipline and continuity; its enemies are distraction and compromise.

Strategic continuity does not imply a static view of competition. A company must continually improve its operational effectiveness and actively try to shift the productivity frontier; at the same time, there needs to be ongoing effort to extend its uniqueness while strengthening the fit among its activities. Strategic continuity, in fact, should make an organization's continual improvement more effective.

A company may have to change its strategy if there are major structural changes in its industry. In fact, new strategic positions often arise because of industry changes, and new entrants unencumbered by history often can exploit them more easily. However, a company's choice of a new position must be driven by the ability to find new trade-offs and leverage a new system of complementary activities into a sustainable advantage.

Originally published in November 1996. Reprint 96608

Notes

1. I first described the concept of activities and its use in understanding competitive advantage in *Competitive Advantage* (New York: The Free Press, 1985). The ideas in this article build on and extend that thinking.

2. Paul Milgrom and John Roberts have begun to explore the economics of systems of complementary functions, activities, and functions. Their focus is on the emergence of "modern manufacturing" as a new set of complementary activities, on the tendency of companies to react to external changes with coherent bundles of internal responses, and on the need for central coordination—a strategy—to align functional managers. In the latter case, they model what has long been a bedrock principle of strategy. See Paul Milgrom and John Roberts, "The Economics of Modern Manufacturing: Technology, Strategy, and Organization," *American Economic Review* 80 (1990): 511–528; Paul Milgrom, Yingyi Qian, and John Roberts, "Complementarities, Momentum, and Evolution of Modern Manufacturing," *American Economic Review* 81 (1991) 84–88; and Paul Milgrom and John Roberts,

"Complementarities and Fit: Strategy, Structure, and Organizational Changes in Manufacturing," *Journal of Accounting and Economics,* vol. 19 (March–May 1995): 179–208.

3. Material on retail strategies is drawn in part from Jan Rivkin, "The Rise of Retail Category Killers," unpublished working paper, January 1995. Nicolaj Siggelkow prepared the case study on the Gap.

The Core Competence of the Corporation

by C.K. Prahalad and Gary Hamel

THE MOST POWERFUL WAY to prevail in global competition is still invisible to many companies. During the 1980s, top executives were judged on their ability to restructure, declutter, and delayer their corporations. In the 1990s, they'll be judged on their ability to identify, cultivate, and exploit the core competencies that make growth possible—indeed, they'll have to rethink the concept of the corporation itself.

Consider the last ten years of GTE and NEC. In the early 1980s, GTE was well positioned to become a major player in the evolving information technology industry. It was active in telecommunications. Its operations spanned a variety of businesses including telephones, switching and transmission systems, digital PABX, semiconductors, packet switching, satellites, defense systems, and lighting products. And GTE's Entertainment Products Group, which produced Sylvania color TVs, had a position in related display technologies. In 1980, GTE's sales were $9.98 billion, and net cash flow was $1.73 billion. NEC, in contrast, was much smaller, at $3.8 billion in sales. It had a comparable technological base and computer businesses, but it had no experience as an operating telecommunications company.

Yet look at the positions of GTE and NEC in 1988. GTE's 1988 sales were $16.46 billion, and NEC's sales were considerably higher at $21.89 billion. GTE has, in effect, become a telephone operating company with a position in defense and lighting products. GTE's other businesses are small in global terms. GTE has divested Sylvania TV and Telenet, put switching, transmission, and digital PABX into joint ventures, and closed down semiconductors. As a result, the international position of GTE has eroded. Non-U.S. revenue as a percent of total revenue dropped from 20% to 15% between 1980 and 1988.

NEC has emerged as the world leader in semiconductors and as a first-tier player in telecommunications products and computers. It has consolidated its position in mainframe computers. It has moved beyond public switching and transmission to include such lifestyle products as mobile telephones, facsimile machines, and laptop computers—bridging the gap between telecommunications and office automation. NEC is the only company in the world to be in the top five in revenue in telecommunications, semiconductors, and mainframes. Why did these two companies, starting with comparable business portfolios, perform so differently? Largely because NEC conceived of itself in terms of "core competencies," and GTE did not.

Rethinking the Corporation

Once, the diversified corporation could simply point its business units at particular end product markets and admonish them to become world leaders. But with market boundaries changing ever more quickly, targets are elusive and capture is at best temporary. A few companies have proven themselves adept at inventing new markets, quickly entering emerging markets, and dramatically shifting patterns of customer choice in established markets. These are the ones to emulate. The critical task for management is to create an organization capable of infusing products with irresistible functionality or, better yet, creating products that customers need but have not yet even imagined.

This is a deceptively difficult task. Ultimately, it requires radical change in the management of major companies. It means, first of all,

Idea in Brief

Diversified giant NEC competed in seemingly disparate businesses—semiconductors, telecommunications, computing, and consumer electronics—*and* dominated them all.

How? It considered itself *not* a collection of strategic business units, but a portfolio of **core competencies**—the company's collective knowledge about how to coordinate diverse production skills and technologies.

NEC used its core competencies to achieve what most companies only attempt: invent new markets, exploit emerging ones, delight customers with products they hadn't even imagined—but definitely needed.

Think of a diversified company as a tree: the trunk and major limbs as core products, smaller branches as business units, leaves and fruit as end products. Nourishing and stabilizing everything is the root system: core competencies.

Focusing on core competencies creates unique, integrated systems that reinforce fit among your firm's diverse production and technology skills—a systemic advantage your competitors can't copy.

that top managements of Western companies must assume responsibility for competitive decline. Everyone knows about high interest rates, Japanese protectionism, outdated antitrust laws, obstreperous unions, and impatient investors. What is harder to see, or harder to acknowledge, is how little added momentum companies actually get from political or macroeconomic "relief." Both the theory and practice of Western management have created a drag on our forward motion. It is the principles of management that are in need of reform.

NEC versus GTE, again, is instructive and only one of many such comparative cases we analyzed to understand the changing basis for global leadership. Early in the 1970s, NEC articulated a strategic intent to exploit the convergence of computing and communications, what it called "C&C."[1] Success, top management reckoned, would hinge on acquiring *competencies,* particularly in semiconductors. Management adopted an appropriate "strategic architecture," summarized by C&C, and then communicated its intent to the whole organization and the outside world during the mid-1970s.

Idea in Practice

Clarify Core Competencies

When you clarify competencies, your entire organization knows how to support your competitive advantage—and readily allocates resources to build cross-unit technological and production links. Use these steps:

Articulate a strategic intent that defines your company and its markets (e.g., NEC's "exploit the convergence of computing and communications").

Identify core competencies that support that intent. Ask:

- How long could we dominate our business if we didn't control this competency?

- What future opportunities would we lose without it?

- Does it provide access to multiple markets? (Casio's core competence with display systems let it succeed in calculators, laptop monitors, *and* car dashboards.)

- Do customer benefits revolve around it? (Honda's competence with high-revving, lightweight engines offers multiple consumer benefits.)

Build Core Competencies

Once you've identified core competencies, enhance them:

Invest in needed technologies. Citicorp trumped rivals by adopting an operating system that leveraged its competencies—and let it participate in world markets 24 hours a day.

Infuse resources throughout business units to outpace rivals in new business development. 3M and Honda won races for

NEC constituted a "C&C Committee" of top managers to oversee the development of core products and core competencies. NEC put in place coordination groups and committees that cut across the interests of individual businesses. Consistent with its strategic architecture, NEC shifted enormous resources to strengthen its position in components and central processors. By using collaborative arrangements to multiply internal resources, NEC was able to accumulate a broad array of core competencies.

NEC carefully identified three interrelated streams of technological and market evolution. Top management determined that computing would evolve from large mainframes to distributed processing, components from simple ICs to VLSI, and communications global brand dominance by creating wide varieties of products from their core competencies. Results? They built image, customer loyalty, and access to distribution channels for all their businesses.

Forge strategic alliances. NEC's collaboration with partners like Honeywell gave it access to the mainframe and semiconductor technologies it needed to build core competencies.

Cultivate a Core-Competency Mind-Set

Competency-savvy managers work well across organizational boundaries, willingly share resources, and think long term. To encourage this mind-set:

Stop thinking of business units as sacrosanct. That imprisons resources in units and motivates managers to hide talent as the company pursues hot opportunities.

Identify projects and people who embody the firm's core competencies. This sends a message: Core competencies are corporate—not unit—resources, and those who embody them can be reallocated. (When Canon spotted opportunities in digital laser printers, it let managers raid other units to assemble talent.)

Gather managers to identify next-generation competencies. Decide how much investment each needs, and how much capital and staff each division should contribute.

---

from mechanical cross-bar exchange to complex digital systems we now call ISDN. As things evolved further, NEC reasoned, the computing, communications, and components businesses would so overlap that it would be very hard to distinguish among them, and that there would be enormous opportunities for any company that had built the competencies needed to serve all three markets.

NEC top management determined that semiconductors would be the company's most important "core product." It entered into myriad strategic alliances—over 100 as of 1987—aimed at building competencies rapidly and at low cost. In mainframe computers, its most noted relationship was with Honeywell and Bull. Almost all the collaborative arrangements in the semiconductor-component field were oriented toward technology access. As they entered collaborative arrangements, NEC's operating managers understood the rationale for these alliances and the goal of internalizing partner skills. NEC's director of research summed up its competence acquisition during the 1970s and 1980s this way: "From an investment standpoint, it was much quicker and cheaper to use foreign technology. There wasn't a need for us to develop new ideas."

No such clarity of strategic intent and strategic architecture appeared to exist at GTE. Although senior executives discussed the implications of the evolving information technology industry, no commonly accepted view of which competencies would be required to compete in that industry were communicated widely. While significant staff work was done to identify key technologies, senior line managers continued to act as if they were managing independent business units. Decentralization made it difficult to focus on core competencies. Instead, individual businesses became increasingly dependent on outsiders for critical skills, and collaboration became a route to staged exits. Today, with a new management team in place, GTE has repositioned itself to apply its competencies to emerging markets in telecommunications services.

The Roots of Competitive Advantage

The distinction we observed in the way NEC and GTE conceived of themselves—a portfolio of competencies versus a portfolio of businesses—was repeated across many industries. From 1980 to 1988, Canon grew by 264%, Honda by 200%. Compare that with Xerox and Chrysler. And if Western managers were once anxious about the low cost and high quality of Japanese imports, they are now overwhelmed by the pace at which Japanese rivals are inventing new markets, creating new products, and enhancing them. Canon has given us personal copiers; Honda has moved from motorcycles to four-wheel off-road buggies. Sony developed the 8mm camcorder, Yamaha, the digital piano. Komatsu developed an underwater remote-controlled bulldozer, while Casio's latest gambit is a small-screen color LCD television. Who would have anticipated the evolution of these vanguard markets?

In more established markets, the Japanese challenge has been just as disquieting. Japanese companies are generating a blizzard of features and functional enhancements that bring technological sophistication to everyday products. Japanese car producers have been pioneering four-wheel steering, four-valve-per-cylinder engines, in-car navigation systems, and sophisticated electronic engine-management systems. On the strength of its product features, Canon is now a player in facsimile transmission machines, desktop laser printers, even semi-conductor manufacturing equipment.

In the short run, a company's competitiveness derives from the price/performance attributes of current products. But the survivors of the first wave of global competition, Western and Japanese alike, are all converging on similar and formidable standards for product cost and quality—minimum hurdles for continued competition, but less and less important as sources of differential advantage. In the long run, competitiveness derives from an ability to build, at lower cost and more speedily than competitors, the core competencies that spawn unanticipated products. The real sources of advantage are to be found in management's ability to consolidate corporatewide technologies and production skills into competencies that empower individual businesses to adapt quickly to changing opportunities.

Senior executives who claim that they cannot build core competencies either because they feel the autonomy of business units is sacrosanct or because their feet are held to the quarterly budget fire should think again. The problem in many Western companies is not that their senior executives are any less capable than those in Japan nor that Japanese companies possess greater technical capabilities. Instead, it is their adherence to a concept of the corporation that unnecessarily limits the ability of individual businesses to fully exploit the deep reservoir of technological capability that many American and European companies possess.

The diversified corporation is a large tree. The trunk and major limbs are core products, the smaller branches are business units; the leaves, flowers, and fruit are end products. The root system that

Competencies: the roots of competitiveness

The corporation, like a tree, grows from its roots. Core products are nourished by competencies and engender business units, whose fruit are end products.

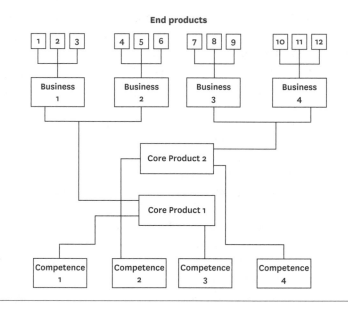

provides nourishment, sustenance, and stability is the core competence. You can miss the strength of competitors by looking only at their end products, in the same way you miss the strength of a tree if you look only at its leaves. (See the chart "Competencies: The Roots of Competitiveness.")

Core competencies are the collective learning in the organization, especially how to coordinate diverse production skills and integrate multiple streams of technologies. Consider Sony's capacity to miniaturize or Philips's optical-media expertise. The theoretical knowledge to put a radio on a chip does not in itself assure a company the skill to produce a miniature radio no bigger than a business card. To bring off this feat, Casio must harmonize know-how in miniaturization, microprocessor design, material science, and ultra-thin precision casing—the same skills it applies in its miniature card calculators, pocket TVs, and digital watches.

If core competence is about harmonizing streams of technology, it is also about the organization of work and the delivery of value. Among Sony's competencies is miniaturization. To bring miniaturization to its products, Sony must ensure that technologists, engineers, and marketers have a shared understanding of customer needs and of technological possibilities. The force of core competence is felt as decisively in services as in manufacturing. Citicorp was ahead of others investing in an operating system that allowed it to participate in world markets 24 hours a day. Its competence in systems has provided the company the means to differentiate itself from many financial service institutions.

Core competence is communication, involvement, and a deep commitment to working across organizational boundaries. It involves many levels of people and all functions. World-class research in, for example, lasers or ceramics can take place in corporate laboratories without having an impact on any of the businesses of the company. The skills that together constitute core competence must coalesce around individuals whose efforts are not so narrowly focused that they cannot recognize the opportunities for blending their functional expertise with those of others in new and interesting ways.

Core competence does not diminish with use. Unlike physical assets, which do deteriorate over time, competencies are enhanced as they are applied and shared. But competencies still need to be nurtured and protected; knowledge fades if it is not used. Competencies are the glue that binds existing businesses. They are also the engine for new business development. Patterns of diversification and market entry may be guided by them, not just by the attractiveness of markets.

Consider 3M's competence with sticky tape. In dreaming up businesses as diverse as "Post-it" notes, magnetic tape, photographic film, pressure-sensitive tapes, and coated abrasives, the company has brought to bear widely shared competencies in substrates, coatings, and adhesives and devised various ways to combine them.

Indeed, 3M has invested consistently in them. What seems to be an extremely diversified portfolio of businesses belies a few shared core competencies.

In contrast, there are major companies that have had the potential to build core competencies but failed to do so because top management was unable to conceive of the company as anything other than a collection of discrete businesses. GE sold much of its consumer electronics business to Thomson of France, arguing that it was becoming increasingly difficult to maintain its competitiveness in this sector. That was undoubtedly so, but it is ironic that it sold several key businesses to competitors who were already competence leaders—Black & Decker in small electrical motors, and Thomson, which was eager to build its competence in microelectronics and had learned from the Japanese that a position in consumer electronics was vital to this challenge.

Management trapped in the strategic business unit (SBU) mindset almost inevitably finds its individual businesses dependent on external sources for critical components, such as motors or compressors. But these are not just components. They are core products that contribute to the competitiveness of a wide range of end products. They are the physical embodiments of core competencies.

How Not to Think of Competence

Since companies are in a race to build the competencies that determine global leadership, successful companies have stopped imagining themselves as bundles of businesses making products. Canon, Honda, Casio, or NEC may seem to preside over portfolios of businesses unrelated in terms of customers, distribution channels, and merchandising strategy. Indeed, they have portfolios that may seem idiosyncratic at times: NEC is the only global company to be among leaders in computing, telecommunications, and semiconductors *and* to have a thriving consumer electronics business.

But looks are deceiving. In NEC, digital technology, especially VLSI and systems integration skills, is fundamental. In the core competencies underlying them, disparate businesses become coherent.

It is Honda's core competence in engines and power trains that gives it a distinctive advantage in car, motorcycle, lawn mower, and generator businesses. Canon's core competencies in optics, imaging, and microprocessor controls have enabled it to enter, even dominate, markets as seemingly diverse as copiers, laser printers, cameras, and image scanners. Philips worked for more than 15 years to perfect its optical-media (laser disc) competence, as did JVC in building a leading position in video recording. Other examples of core competencies might include mechantronics (the ability to marry mechanical and electronic engineering), video displays, bioengineering, and microelectronics. In the early stages of its competence building, Philips could not have imagined all the products that would be spawned by its optical-media competence, nor could JVC have anticipated miniature camcorders when it first began exploring videotape technologies.

Unlike the battle for global brand dominance, which is visible in the world's broadcast and print media and is aimed at building global "share of mind," the battle to build world-class competencies is invisible to people who aren't deliberately looking for it. Top management often tracks the cost and quality of competitors' products, yet how many managers untangle the web of alliances their Japanese competitors have constructed to acquire competencies at low cost? In how many Western boardrooms is there an explicit, shared understanding of the competencies the company must build for world leadership? Indeed, how many senior executives discuss the crucial distinction between competitive strategy at the level of a business and competitive strategy at the level of an entire company?

Let us be clear. Cultivating core competence does *not* mean outspending rivals on research and development. In 1983, when Canon surpassed Xerox in worldwide unit market share in the copier business, its R&D budget in reprographics was but a small fraction of Xerox's. Over the past 20 years, NEC has spent less on R&D as a percentage of sales than almost all of its American and European competitors.

Nor does core competence mean shared costs, as when two or more SBUs use a common facility—a plant, service facility, or sales force—or share a common component. The gains of sharing may be substantial, but the search for shared costs is typically a post hoc effort to rationalize production across existing businesses, not a premeditated effort to build the competencies out of which the businesses themselves grow.

Building core competencies is more ambitious and different than integrating vertically, moreover. Managers deciding whether to make or buy will start with end products and look upstream to the efficiencies of the supply chain and downstream toward distribution and customers. They do not take inventory of skills and look forward to applying them in nontraditional ways. (Of course, decisions about competencies *do* provide a logic for vertical integration. Canon is not particularly integrated in its copier business, except in those aspects of the vertical chain that support the competencies it regards as critical.)

Identifying Core Competencies—And Losing Them

At least three tests can be applied to identify core competencies in a company. First, a core competence provides potential access to a wide variety of markets. Competence in display systems, for example, enables a company to participate in such diverse businesses as calculators, miniature TV sets, monitors for laptop computers, and automotive dashboards—which is why Casio's entry into the handheld TV market was predictable. Second, a core competence should make a significant contribution to the perceived customer benefits of the end product. Clearly, Honda's engine expertise fills this bill.

Finally, a core competence should be difficult for competitors to imitate. And it *will* be difficult if it is a complex harmonization of individual technologies and production skills. A rival might acquire some of the technologies that comprise the core competence, but it will find it more difficult to duplicate the more or less comprehensive pattern of internal coordination and learning. JVC's decision in the early 1960s to pursue the development of a videotape competence passed the three tests outlined here. RCA's decision in the late 1970s to develop a stylus-based video turntable system did not.

Few companies are likely to build world leadership in more than five or six fundamental competencies. A company that compiles a list of 20 to 30 capabilities has probably not produced a list of core competencies. Still, it is probably a good discipline to generate a list of this sort and to see aggregate capabilities as building blocks. This tends to prompt the search for licensing deals and alliances through which the company may acquire, at low cost, missing pieces.

Most Western companies hardly think about competitiveness in these terms at all. It is time to take a tough-minded look at the risks they are running. Companies that judge competitiveness, their own and their competitors', primarily in terms of the price/performance of end products are courting the erosion of core competencies—or making too little effort to enhance them. The embedded skills that give rise to the next generation of competitive products cannot be "rented in" by outsourcing and OEM-supply relationships. In our view, too many companies have unwittingly surrendered core competencies when they cut internal investment in what they mistakenly thought were just "cost centers" in favor of outside suppliers.

Consider Chrysler. Unlike Honda, it has tended to view engines and power trains as simply one more component. Chrysler is becoming increasingly dependent on Mitsubishi and Hyundai: between 1985 and 1987, the number of outsourced engines went from 252,000 to 382,000. It is difficult to imagine Honda yielding manufacturing responsibility, much less design, of so critical a part of a car's function to an outside company—which is why Honda has made such an enormous commitment to Formula One auto racing. Honda has been able to pool its engine-related technologies; it has parlayed these into a corporatewide competency from which it develops world-beating products, despite R&D budgets smaller than those of GM and Toyota.

Of course, it is perfectly possible for a company to have a competitive product line-up but be a laggard in developing core competencies—at least for a while. If a company wanted to enter the copier business today, it would find a dozen Japanese companies more than willing to supply copiers on the basis of an OEM private label. But when fundamental technologies changed or if its supplier decided to enter the market directly and become a competitor, that company's product line, along with all of its investments in marketing and distribution, could be vulnerable. Outsourcing can provide a shortcut to a more competitive product, but it typically contributes little to building the people-embodied skills that are needed to sustain product leadership.

Nor is it possible for a company to have an intelligent alliance or sourcing strategy if it has not made a choice about where it will build competence leadership. Clearly, Japanese companies have benefited from alliances. They've used them to learn from Western partners who were not fully committed to preserving core competencies of their own. As we've argued in these pages before, learning within an alliance takes a positive commitment of resources—the travel, a pool of dedicated people, test-bed facilities, time to internalize and test what has been learned.[2] A company may not make this effort if it doesn't have clear goals for competence building.

Another way of losing is forgoing opportunities to establish competencies that are evolving in existing businesses. In the 1970s and 1980s, many American and European companies—like GE, Motorola, GTE, Thorn, and GEC—chose to exit the color television business, which they regarded as mature. If by "mature" they meant that they had run out of new product ideas at precisely the moment global rivals had targeted the TV business for entry, then yes, the industry was mature. But it certainly wasn't mature in the sense that all opportunities to enhance and apply video-based competencies had been exhausted.

In ridding themselves of their television businesses, these companies failed to distinguish between divesting the business and destroying their video media-based competencies. They not only got out of the TV business but they also closed the door on a whole stream of future opportunities reliant on video-based competencies. The television industry, considered by many U.S. companies in the 1970s to be unattractive, is today the focus of a fierce public policy debate about the inability of U.S. corporations to benefit from the $20-billion-a-year opportunity that HDTV will represent in the mid- to late 1990s. Ironically, the U.S. government is being asked to fund a massive research project—in effect, to compensate U.S. companies for their failure to preserve critical core competencies when they had the chance.

In contrast, one can see a company like Sony reducing its emphasis on VCRs (where it has not been very successful and where Korean companies now threaten) without reducing its commitment to video-related competencies. Sony's Betamax led to a debacle. But it emerged with its videotape recording competencies intact and is currently challenging Matsushita in the 8mm camcorder market.

There are two clear lessons here. First, the costs of losing a core competence can be only partly calculated in advance. The baby may be thrown out with the bathwater in divestment decisions. Second, since core competencies are built through a process of continuous improvement and enhancement that may span a decade or longer, a company that has failed to invest in core competence building will find it very difficult to enter an emerging market, unless, of course, it will be content simply to serve as a distribution channel.

American semiconductor companies like Motorola learned this painful lesson when they elected to forgo direct participation in the 256k generation of DRAM chips. Having skipped this round, Motorola, like most of its American competitors, needed a large infusion of technical help from Japanese partners to rejoin the battle in the 1-megabyte generation. When it comes to core competencies, it is difficult to get off the train, walk to the next station, and then reboard.

From Core Competencies to Core Products

The tangible link between identified core competencies and end products is what we call the core products—the physical embodiments of one or more core competencies. Honda's engines, for example, are core products, linchpins between design and development skills that ultimately lead to a proliferation of end products. Core products are the components or subassemblies that actually contribute to the value of the end products. Thinking in terms of core products forces a company to distinguish between the brand share it achieves in end product markets (for example, 40% of the U.S. refrigerator market) and the manufacturing share it achieves in any particular core product (for example, 5% of the world share of compressor output).

Canon is reputed to have an 84% world manufacturing share in desktop laser printer "engines," even though its brand share in the laser printer business is minuscule. Similarly, Matsushita has a world manufacturing share of about 45% in key VCR components, far in excess of its brand share (Panasonic, JVC, and others) of 20%. And Matsushita has a commanding core product share in compressors worldwide, estimated at 40%, even though its brand share in both the air-conditioning and refrigerator businesses is quite small.

It is essential to make this distinction between core competencies, core products, and end products because global competition is played out by different rules and for different stakes at each level. To build or defend leadership over the long term, a corporation will probably be a winner at each level. At the level of core competence, the goal is to build world leadership in the design and development of a particular class of product functionality—be it compact data storage and retrieval, as with Philips's optical-media competence, or compactness and ease of use, as with Sony's micromotors and microprocessor controls.

To sustain leadership in their chosen core competence areas, these companies *seek to maximize their world manufacturing share in core products*. The manufacture of core products for a wide variety of external (and internal) customers yields the revenue and market feedback that, at least partly, determines the pace at which core competencies can be enhanced and extended. This thinking was behind JVC's decision in the mid-1970s to establish VCR supply relationships with leading national consumer electronics companies in Europe and the United States. In supplying Thomson, Thorn, and Telefunken (all independent companies at that time) as well as U.S. partners, JVC was able to gain the cash and the diversity of market experience that ultimately enabled it to outpace Philips and Sony. (Philips developed videotape competencies in parallel with JVC, but it failed to build a worldwide network of OEM relationships that would have allowed it to accelerate the refinement of its videotape competence through the sale of core products.)

JVC's success has not been lost on Korean companies like Goldstar, Sam Sung, Kia, and Daewoo, who are building core product leadership in areas as diverse as displays, semiconductors, and automotive engines through their OEM-supply contracts with Western companies. Their avowed goal is to capture investment initiative away from potential competitors, often U.S. companies. In doing so, they accelerate their competence-building efforts while "hollowing out" their competitors. By focusing on competence and embedding it in core products, Asian competitors have built up advantages in component markets first and have then leveraged off their superior products to move downstream to build brand share. And they are not likely to remain the low-cost suppliers forever. As their reputation for brand leadership is consolidated, they may well gain price leadership. Honda has proven this with its Acura line, and other Japanese car makers are following suit.

Control over core products is critical for other reasons. A dominant position in core products allows a company to shape the evolution of applications and end markets. Such compact audio disc-related core products as data drives and lasers have enabled Sony and Philips to influence the evolution of the computer-peripheral business in optical-media storage. As a company multiplies the number of application arenas for its core products, it can consistently reduce the cost, time, and risk in new product development. In short, well-targeted core products can lead to economies of scale *and* scope.

The Tyranny of the SBU

The new terms of competitive engagement cannot be understood using analytical tools devised to manage the diversified corporation of 20 years ago, when competition was primarily domestic (GE versus Westinghouse, General Motors versus Ford) and all the key players were speaking the language of the same business schools and consultancies. Old prescriptions have potentially toxic side effects.

Two concepts of the corporation: SBU or core competence

	SBU	Core Competence
Basis for competition	Competitiveness of today's products	Interfirm competition to build competencies
Corporate structure	Portfolio of businesses related in product-market terms	Portfolio of competencies, core products, and businesses
Status of the business unit	Autonomy is sacrosanct; the SBU "owns" all resources other than cash	SBU is a potential reservoir of core competencies
Resource allocation	Discrete businesses are the unit of analysis; capital is allocated business by business	Businesses and competencies are the unit of analysis: top management allocates capital and talent
Value added of top management	Optimizing corporate returns through capital allocation trade-offs among businesses	Enunciating strategic architecture and building competencies to secure the future

---

The need for new principles is most obvious in companies organized exclusively according to the logic of SBUs. The implications of the two alternate concepts of the corporation are summarized in "Two Concepts of the Corporation: SBU or Core Competence."

Obviously, diversified corporations have a portfolio of products and a portfolio of businesses. But we believe in a view of the company as a portfolio of competencies as well. U.S. companies do not lack the technical resources to build competencies, but their top management often lacks the vision to build them and the administrative means for assembling resources spread across multiple businesses. A shift in commitment will inevitably influence patterns of diversification, skill deployment, resource allocation priorities, and approaches to alliances and outsourcing.

We have described the three different planes on which battles for global leadership are waged: core competence, core products, and end products. A corporation has to know whether it is winning or losing on each plane. By sheer weight of investment, a company might be able to beat its rivals to blue-sky technologies yet still lose the race to build core competence leadership. If a company is winning the race to build core competencies (as opposed to building leadership in a few technologies), it will almost certainly outpace rivals in new business development. If a company is winning the race to capture world manufacturing share in core products, it will probably outpace rivals in improving product features and the price/performance ratio.

Determining whether one is winning or losing end-product battles is more difficult because measures of product market share do not necessarily reflect various companies' underlying competitiveness. Indeed, companies that attempt to build market share by relying on the competitiveness of others, rather than investing in core competencies and world core-product leadership, may be treading on quicksand. In the race for global brand dominance, companies like 3M, Black & Decker, Canon, Honda, NEC, and Citicorp have built global brand umbrellas by proliferating products out of their core competencies. This has allowed their individual businesses to build image, customer loyalty, and access to distribution channels.

When you think about this reconceptualization of the corporation, the primacy of the SBU—an organizational dogma for a generation—is now clearly an anachronism. Where the SBU is an article of faith, resistance to the seductions of decentralization can seem heretical. In many companies, the SBU prism means that only one plane of the global competitive battle, the battle to put competitive products on the shelf *today,* is visible to top management. What are the costs of this distortion?

Underinvestment in Developing Core Competencies and Core Products. When the organization is conceived of as a multiplicity of SBUs, no single business may feel responsible for maintaining a viable position in core products nor be able to justify the investment required to build world leadership in some core competence. In the absence of a more comprehensive view imposed by corporate management, SBU managers will tend to underinvest. Recently, companies such as Kodak and Philips have recognized this as a potential problem and have begun searching for new organizational forms that will allow them to develop and manufacture core products for both internal and external customers.

SBU managers have traditionally conceived of competitors in the same way they've seen themselves. On the whole, they've failed to note the emphasis Asian competitors were placing on building leadership in core products or to understand the critical linkage between world manufacturing leadership and the ability to sustain development pace in core competence. They've failed to pursue OEM-supply opportunities or to look across their various product divisions in an attempt to identify opportunities for coordinated initiatives.

Imprisoned Resources. As an SBU evolves, it often develops unique competencies. Typically, the people who embody this competence are seen as the sole property of the business in which they grew up. The manager of another SBU who asks to borrow talented people is likely to get a cold rebuff. SBU managers are not only unwilling to lend their competence carriers but they may actually hide talent to prevent its redeployment in the pursuit of new opportunities. This may be compared to residents of an underdeveloped country hiding most of their cash under their mattresses. The benefits of competencies, like the benefits of the money supply, depend on the velocity of their circulation as well as on the size of the stock the company holds.

Western companies have traditionally had an advantage in the stock of skills they possess. But have they been able to reconfigure them quickly to respond to new opportunities? Canon, NEC, and Honda have had a lesser stock of the people and technologies that compose core competencies but could move them much quicker from one business unit to another. Corporate R&D spending at Canon is not fully indicative of the size of Canon's core competence stock and tells the casual observer nothing about the velocity with which Canon is able to move core competencies to exploit opportunities.

When competencies become imprisoned, the people who carry the competencies do not get assigned to the most exciting opportunities, and their skills begin to atrophy. Only by fully leveraging core competencies can small companies like Canon afford to compete with industry giants like Xerox. How strange that SBU managers, who are perfectly willing to compete for cash in the capital budgeting process,

THE CORE COMPETENCE OF THE CORPORATION

are unwilling to compete for people—the company's most precious asset. We find it ironic that top management devotes so much attention to the capital budgeting process yet typically has no comparable mechanism for allocating the human skills that embody core competencies. Top managers are seldom able to look four or five levels down into the organization, identify the people who embody critical competencies, and move them across organizational boundaries.

Bounded Innovation. If core competencies are not recognized, individual SBUs will pursue only those innovation opportunities that are close at hand—marginal product-line extensions or geographic expansions. Hybrid opportunities like fax machines, laptop computers, hand-held televisions, or portable music keyboards will emerge only when managers take off their SBU blinkers. Remember, Canon appeared to be in the camera business at the time it was preparing to become a world leader in copiers. Conceiving of the corporation in terms of core competencies widens the domain of innovation.

Developing Strategic Architecture

The fragmentation of core competencies becomes inevitable when a diversified company's information systems, patterns of communication, career paths, managerial rewards, and processes of strategy development do not transcend SBU lines. We believe that senior management should spend a significant amount of its time developing a corporatewide strategic architecture that establishes objectives for competence building. A strategic architecture is a road map of the future that identifies which core competencies to build and their constituent technologies.

By providing an impetus for learning from alliances and a focus for internal development efforts, a strategic architecture like NEC's C&C can dramatically reduce the investment needed to secure future market leadership. How can a company make partnerships intelligently without a clear understanding of the core competencies it is trying to build and those it is attempting to prevent from being unintentionally transferred?

Of course, all of this begs the question of what a strategic architecture should look like. The answer will be different for every company. But it is helpful to think again of that tree, of the corporation organized around core products and, ultimately, core competencies. To sink sufficiently strong roots, a company must answer some fundamental questions: How long could we preserve our competitiveness in this business if we did not control this particular core competence? How central is this core competence to perceived customer benefits? What future opportunities would be foreclosed if we were to lose this particular competence?

The architecture provides a logic for product and market diversification, moreover. An SBU manager would be asked: Does the new market opportunity add to the overall goal of becoming the best player in the world? Does it exploit or add to the core competence? At Vickers, for example, diversification options have been judged in the context of becoming the best power and motion control company in the world (see the sidebar "Vickers Learns the Value of Strategic Architecture").

The strategic architecture should make resource allocation priorities transparent to the entire organization. It provides a template for allocation decisions by top management. It helps lower-level managers understand the logic of allocation priorities and disciplines senior management to maintain consistency. In short, it yields a definition of the company and the markets it serves. 3M, Vickers, NEC, Canon, and Honda all qualify on this score. Honda *knew* it was exploiting what it had learned from motorcycles—how to make high-revving, smooth-running, lightweight engines—when it entered the car business. The task of creating a strategic architecture forces the organization to identify and commit to the technical and production linkages across SBUs that will provide a distinct competitive advantage.

It is consistency of resource allocation and the development of an administrative infrastructure appropriate to it that breathes life into a strategic architecture and creates a managerial culture, teamwork, a capacity to change, and a willingness to share resources, to protect proprietary skills, and to think long term. That is also the reason the specific architecture cannot be copied easily or overnight by competitors. Strategic architecture is a tool for communicating with customers

Vickers Learns the Value of Strategic Architecture

The idea that top management should develop a corporate strategy for acquiring and deploying core competencies is relatively new in most U.S. companies. There are a few exceptions. An early convert was Trinova (previously Libbey Owens Ford), a Toledo-based corporation, which enjoys a worldwide position in power and motion controls and engineered plastics. One of its major divisions is Vickers, a premier supplier of hydraulics components like valves, pumps, actuators, and filtration devices to aerospace, marine, defense, automotive, earth-moving, and industrial markets.

Vickers saw the potential for a transformation of its traditional business with the application of electronics disciplines in combination with its traditional technologies. The goal was "to ensure that change in technology does not displace Vickers from its customers." This, to be sure, was initially a defensive move: Vickers recognized that unless it acquired new skills, it could not protect existing markets or capitalize on new growth opportunities. Managers at Vickers attempted to conceptualize the likely evolution of (a) technologies relevant to the power and motion control business, (b) functionalities that would satisfy emerging customer needs, and (c) new competencies needed to creatively manage the marriage of technology and customer needs.

Despite pressure for short-term earnings, top management looked to a 10- to 15-year time horizon in developing a map of emerging customer needs, changing technologies, and the core competencies that would be necessary to bridge the gap between the two. Its slogan was "Into the 21st Century." (A simplified version of the overall architecture developed is shown here.) Vickers is currently in fluid-power components. The architecture identifies two additional competencies, electric-power components and electronic controls. A systems integration capability that would unite hardware, software, and service was also targeted for development.

The strategic architecture, as illustrated by the Vickers example, is not a forecast of specific products or specific technologies but a broad map of the evolving linkages between customer functionality requirements, potential technologies, and core competencies. It assumes that products and systems cannot be defined with certainty for the future but that preempting competitors in the development of new markets requires an early start to building core competencies. The strategic architecture developed by Vickers, while describing the future in competence terms, also provides the basis for making "here and now" decisions about product priorities, acquisitions, alliances, and recruitment.

(continued)

Vickers map of competencies

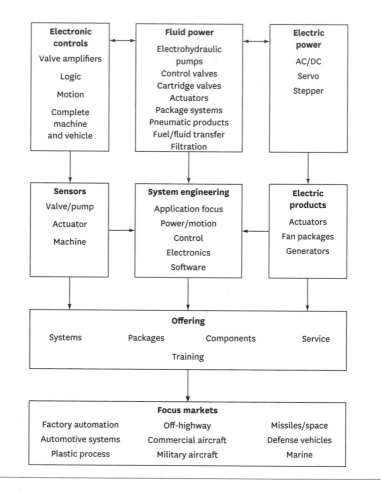

Since 1986, Vickers has made more than ten clearly targeted acquisitions, each one focused on a specific component or technology gap identified in the overall architecture. The architecture is also the basis for internal development of new competencies. Vickers has undertaken, in parallel, a reorganization to enable the integration of electronics and electrical capabilities with mechanical-based competencies. We believe that it will take another two to three years before Vickers reaps the total benefits from developing the strategic architecture, communicating it widely to all its employees, customers, and investors, and building administrative systems consistent with the architecture.

and other external constituents. It reveals the broad direction without giving away every step.

Redeploying to Exploit Competencies

If the company's core competencies are its critical resource and if top management must ensure that competence carriers are not held hostage by some particular business, then it follows that SBUs should bid for core competencies in the same way they bid for capital. We've made this point glancingly. It is important enough to consider more deeply.

Once top management (with the help of divisional and SBU managers) has identified overarching competencies, it must ask businesses to identify the projects and people closely connected with them. Corporate officers should direct an audit of the location, number, and quality of the people who embody competence.

This sends an important signal to middle managers: core competencies are *corporate* resources and may be reallocated by corporate management. An individual business doesn't own anybody. SBUs are entitled to the services of individual employees so long as SBU management can demonstrate that the opportunity it is pursuing yields the highest possible pay-off on the investment in their skills. This message is further underlined if each year in the strategic planning or budgeting process, unit managers must justify their hold on the people who carry the company's core competencies.

Core competencies at Canon

	Precision mechanics	Fine optics	Micro-electronics
Basic camera	■	□	
Compact fashion camera	■	□	
Electronic camera	■	□	
EOS autofocus camera	■	□	■
Video still camera	■	□	■
Laser beam printer	■	□	■
Color video printer	■		■
Bubble jet printer	■		■
Basic fax	■		■
Laser fax	■		■
Calculator			■
Plain paper copier	■	□	■
Battery PPC	■	□	■
Color copier	■	□	■
Laser copier	■	□	■
Color laser copier	■	□	■
NAVI	■	□	■
Still video system	■	□	■
Laser imager	■	□	■
Cell analyzer	■	□	■
Mask aligners	■		■
Stepper aligners	■		■
Excimer laser aligners	■	□	■

Every Canon product is the result of at least one core competency.

Elements of Canon's core competence in optics are spread across businesses as diverse as cameras, copiers, and semiconductor lithographic equipment and are shown in "Core Competencies at Canon." When Canon identified an opportunity in digital laser printers, it gave SBU managers the right to raid other SBUs to pull together the required pool of talent. When Canon's reprographics products division undertook to develop microprocessor-controlled copiers, it turned to the photo products group, which had developed the world's first microprocessor-controlled camera.

Also reward systems that focus only on product-line results and career paths that seldom cross SBU boundaries engender patterns of behavior among unit managers that are destructively competitive. At NEC, divisional managers come together to identify next-generation competencies. Together they decide how much investment needs to be made to build up each future competency and the contribution in capital and staff support that each division will need to make. There is also a sense of equitable exchange. One division may make a disproportionate contribution or may benefit less from the progress made, but such short-term inequalities will balance out over the long term.

Incidentally, the positive contribution of the SBU manager should be made visible across the company. An SBU manager is unlikely to surrender key people if only the other business (or the general manager of that business who may be a competitor for promotion) is going to benefit from the redeployment. Cooperative SBU managers should be celebrated as team players. Where priorities are clear, transfers are less likely to be seen as idiosyncratic and politically motivated.

Transfers for the sake of building core competence must be recorded and appreciated in the corporate memory. It is reasonable to expect a business that has surrendered core skills on behalf of corporate opportunities in other areas to lose, for a time, some of its competitiveness. If these losses in performance bring immediate censure, SBUs will be unlikely to assent to skills transfers next time.

Finally, there are ways to wean key employees off the idea that they belong in perpetuity to any particular business. Early in their careers, people may be exposed to a variety of businesses through a carefully planned rotation program. At Canon, critical people move regularly between the camera business and the copier business and between the copier business and the professional optical-products business. In mid-career, periodic assignments to cross-divisional project teams may be necessary, both for diffusing core competencies and for loosening the bonds that might tie an individual to one business even when brighter opportunities beckon elsewhere. Those who embody critical core competencies should know that their careers are tracked and guided by corporate human resource professionals. In the early 1980s at Canon, all engineers under 30 were invited to apply for membership on a seven-person committee that was to spend two years plotting Canon's future direction, including its strategic architecture.

Competence carriers should be regularly brought together from across the corporation to trade notes and ideas. The goal is to build a strong feeling of community among these people. To a great extent, their loyalty should be to the integrity of the core competence area they represent and not just to particular businesses. In traveling regularly, talking frequently to customers, and meeting with peers, competence carriers may be encouraged to discover new market opportunities.

Core competencies are the wellspring of new business development. They should constitute the focus for strategy at the corporate level. Managers have to win manufacturing leadership in core products and capture global share through brand-building programs aimed at exploiting economies of scope. Only if the company is conceived of as a hierarchy of core competencies, core products, and market-focused business units will it be fit to fight.

Nor can top management be just another layer of accounting consolidation, which it often is in a regime of radical decentralization. Top management must add value by enunciating the strategic architecture that guides the competence acquisition process. We believe an obsession with competence building will characterize the global winners of the 1990s. With the decade under way, the time for rethinking the concept of the corporation is already overdue.

Originally published in May 1990. Reprint 90311

Notes

1. For a fuller discussion, see our article, "Strategic Intent," *HBR,* May–June 1989, p. 63.

2. "Collaborate with Your Competitors and Win," *HBR,* January–February 1989, p. 133, with Yves L. Doz.

CLAYTON M. CHRISTENSEN is the Robert and Jane Cizik Professor of Business Administration at Harvard Business School.

THOMAS H. DAVENPORT is the President's Distinguished Professor of Information Technology and Management at Babson College.

PETER F. DRUCKER was a writer, teacher, and consultant. His thirty-four books have been published in more than seventy languages. He founded the Peter F. Drucker Foundation for Nonprofit Management.

DANIEL GOLEMAN is Codirector of the Consortium for Research on Emotional Intelligence in Organizations at Rutgers University.

GARY HAMEL is Visiting Professor of Strategic and International Management at the London Business School; cofounder of Strategos, an international consulting company; and director of the Management Innovation Lab.

ROSABETH MOSS KANTER is the Ernest L. Arbuckle Professor of Business Administration at Harvard Business School, specializing in strategy, innovation, and leadership for change

ROBERT S. KAPLAN is the Baker Foundation Professor at Harvard Business School.

JOHN P. KOTTER is the Konosuke Matsushita Professor of Leadership, Emeritus, at Harvard Business School.

THEODORE LEVITT is the Edward W. Carter Professor of Business Administration Emeritus at the Harvard Business School and former editor of the Harvard Business Review.

DAVID P. NORTON is the founder of The Balanced Scorecard Collaborative and a director of The Palladium Group.

MICHAEL OVERDORF is a Dean's research Fellow at Harvard Business School.

MICHAEL E. PORTER is the Bishop William Lawrence University Professor at Harvard Business School. He is the leader of the Institute for Strategy and Competitiveness at Harvard Business School.

C.K. PRAHALAD was the Paul and Ruth McCracken Distinguished University Professor of Corporate Strategy at the University of Michigan's Ross School of Business, until his death in April 2010.

Index

access-based positioning, 194–196
achieving beyond expectations, 76
acquisitions, 8
    capabilities through, 18–21
acting on knowledge, 50
activities
    access driving differences, 195
    affecting activities, 201–202
    combining, 200–208
    competitive advantage, 182, 206
    incompatible, 197
    performing better than competi-
      tors, 182–183
    positioning choices, 200
    productivity frontier, 185
    reinforcing, 202–204
    relationships, 200
    simple consistency, 202
    strategic fit, 206–208
    trade-offs arising from, 198
    unique, 188–196
activity-system maps, 203–205
Admiral, 212
advisers, 51
airline industry, 197
AlliedSignal, 115
    controls too tight on innovation,
      123
    flexible organizational structures,
      134
Allstate and analytics, 29
aluminum industry, growth of, 155
Amazon, 23, 34
    analytics and, 24
    business model, 36–37
    hiring right people, 36–37
    senior executive analytics
      advocates, 31
AMD (Advanced Micro Devices) and
    balanced scorecard, 97–98,
    101–103
American Airlines, 23, 114

American Hospital Supply, 23
*American Petroleum Institute
    Quarterly* (1959), 176
Analog Devices, 101
analysis-versus-instinct debate, 32
analysts, quantitative-analysis
    skills, 27
analytical competitors, 23–42
analytics
    common targets, 33–34
    culture of, 27
    European soccer and, 32
    pursuing strategies shaped by,
      39–42
    revenue management, 26–28
    senior executive advocates, 31–33
    sports and, 32
analytics competitors
    analytics culture, 27
    analytics-focused organizations,
      26
    anatomy of, 26–33
    centralized groups, 30
    employees, 24
    enterprise approach, 29–31
    focusing analytics effort, 26–27
    hiring right people, 27
    identifying characteristics, 25
    leaders in field, 39–42
    limits of knowable, 42
    modeling and optimization,
      28–29
    overall impact of intervention
      strategies, 28
    predictive modeling and opti-
      mization, 28–29
    processes, 24
    right culture, 35–36
    right focus, 33–35
    right people, 36–38
    right technology, 38–39
    senior executive advocates, 31–33

249

defining major product, 162
greatest improvement outside
industry, 161
growth rate, 161
improvements by, 161
indispensability idea, 162–163
internal combustion engine, 163
natural gas revolution, 164
perils of, 163–165
product orientation, 172
product provincialism, 170
stepchild treatment, 175–177
uncertain future of, 165–166
Philips
core competencies, 226, 229
core products, 235
underinvesting in core competencies and core products, 237–238
Pillsbury, 120–121, 127
Pinchot, Gifford, 118
planning flexibility, 132–133
PNC Financial Services Group, 134
population myth and risk of obsolescence, 156, 160–166
powerful guiding coalition, 140,
143–144
predictive modeling, 28–29
price
differences in, 182
statistics and modeling, 34
prioritization decisions, 6
processes
analytics competitors, 24
capabilities and concurrent disabilities, 5
capabilities shifting toward, 8–9
changes in, 31–33
failure to develop, 8–9
fitting well or poorly with innovation, 4
formal, 5
forming, 9

founder's impact on, 9
getting value from, 25
industry leaders, 12
inflexibility, 13
informal, 5
innovation and, 5
organizational boundaries, 14
organizational capabilities in, 14
organizations, 3
transformation, 139
value of, 20
process measures versus output
measures, 107–108
process mistakes, 116, 123–124
process remedy, 132–133
process-strangling innovation, 115
Procter & Gamble
analysts, 30–31
analytics initiative, 26
ideas hardly innovative, 120
Joint Value Creation, 35
product innovations, 122
Swiffer, 116
time required to master quantitative approaches, 41–42
product-centric company, 122–123
production pressures and risk of obsolescence, 166–173
productivity frontier, 183, 185–186
product provincialism and automobile industry, 169–172
products
diversification, 240
no competition to, 156
no guarantee against obsolescence, 165–166
quality statistics and modeling,
34
profitable growth, 212–214
Progressive, 34
modeling and optimization, 28–29
process and product changes, 36

You don't want to miss these...

We've combed through hundreds of *Harvard Business Review* articles on key management topics and selected *the* most important ones to help you maximize your own and your organization's performance.